W9-CEK-576

trail**dreams**

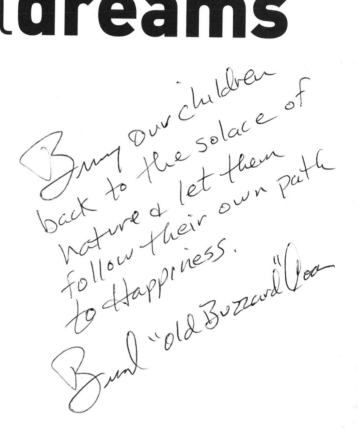

Bring our children back to the solace of nature & let them follow their own path to Happiness.

Bud "old Buzzard" Dea

trail**dreams**

Discover Your True Source of Happiness

BRAD COOK

Copyright © 2017 by Brad Cook

LCCN#
2017907073

10% of the sale profits of this book will be donated
to The Randolph Mountain Club of Randolph, NH.

Cover design and interior design: Samantha Cuozzo

ISBN#
978-0-692-87647-3

To Karen, my "Sugar Babes," who made all my dreams possible...

Table of Contents

Preface

O
n February 1, 1976, I ran out into the world to pursue a dream and everything changed. Forty years later, after much soul searching, I have also completed the dream of writing my story. I believe it is a story worthy to be read by others given the important discoveries I have made through my journey in life. In particular, I believe my story will be beneficial to our confused, angry, depressed youth as well as to the parents who raise them. The number of troubled kids seems to be growing. Too many kids today are miserably lost in a world that does not seem to make much sense to them as they struggle to find happiness. Hopefully, this book will be enlightening and have meaning for many audiences, but most especially for these young people, their parents, and the other adults in their lives.

There are two main themes I touch upon as I relate my story. First is the power of a dream, and how a single encounter can alter and change the direction of a life, thereby saving it. The other will explore the therapeutic value and power of nature and how its spirituality can reach into your soul and heal. It will also describe how this vital connection with nature and all it has to offer has been taken from our children by our society's misplaced priorities for money and power and by the over dependency on entertainment and communication technology.

Children are the future of America, and I will fight for them. By fighting for these children, who have no rights and no vote, I am fighting for America and what is left of it. I have hope.

Everything in life comes down to your mental state and how you choose to interpret each life experience you encounter. Your mental self will control and dictate the physical you. The mind is a most powerful thing. By having a purpose in life, combined with positive thoughts and focus, you can overcome what life throws your way and do just about anything you set out to do.

I was once a caterpillar, a worm. Please follow me through my cocoon stage in life, and finally my emergence as a butterfly with wings. Fulfillment and happiness can be found in each and every one of us. Finding these things need not be a complex process, but in this fast paced, technologically advanced, competitive society life's simplicity has become lost for too many.

I am so lucky to be alive and able to write this at all. My hopes and dreams are many, but the biggest among them is to help others by telling my story.

Chapter 1
The Flow of Life

"Life is not linear; you have ups and downs. It's how you deal with the troughs that defines you" – *Michael Lee-Chin*

I was banging off mile after mile in my attempt to reach the northern end of the Shenandoahs. "Sugar Babes" was coming down to her cousin's, who lived near Manassas, the scene of the Battle of Bull Run during the Civil War. It was the longest absence of our 35-year marriage, and I had miscalculated my progress north from Georgia. I didn't want to put her out, requiring her to drive farther south to pick me up for some much needed R&R. I was looking forward to our reunion and was eating up turf hiking mega miles day after day. I needed a day off, a zero, but kept blowing through the little hamlets running along the corridor of the "Trail" to resupply and occasionally shower. I had had it! I was wasted, and then after a day over rugged terrain for 22 miles, I came upon "Dragon's Tooth", an extremely dangerous decline down a cliff with sections of rebar to hold.

" No! Take it slow, don't slip and fall, or this dream of yours will be over," I muttered to myself. "Please get me down this treacherous section in one piece, and I'll call it a day, pitch my tent, and rest."

I was alone. "Don't look down, watch your footing, concentrate, and focus on each cautious step; relax, and you'll make it."

As soon as I hit flat ground, I set up camp and climbed into my inner bag. Due to a bicycle accident damaging my cervical spine, some 15 years ago, I had cut base pack weight to a mere 9 pounds and was carrying no sleeping bag.

I popped a few more Vitamin I (ibuprofen) into my shattered 59-year-old aching body, and then the clap of thunder and the rain came. It poured on my little tent all night long, and at what seemed dawn, I crawled out of my 24 ounce tent, packed up quickly in the rain, and moved on down the Trail northward, cold, wet, and tired.

I couldn't sleep all night due to the screaming of my aching feet, ankles, knees, and back. I had sent my rain gear home to cut more weight over 300 miles ago and was staying relatively dry thanks to my trusty hiking umbrella.

I hadn't seen anyone since late yesterday afternoon, when suddenly I heard the sound of footsteps coming toward me from the north. He introduced himself as "Southern Boy" from Maryland.

Both of us standing in the forest rain, I inquired in desperation, "I need to crash. Do you know of any place to get food or lodging coming up soon?"

"Ya, in about 4 miles, you'll hit VA311," he returned.

To save pack weight, instead of carrying the Thru-Hiker's Handbook, I had my wife rip pages out of the paperback and mail them to me. But I had run out of pages. So, I asked where the paved road led. The little town of Catawba, Virginia (pop. 300) was just a mile down. A post office, 2 gas pumps, and a general store was it, but that store had food and drink to replenish my old beaten body.

"Start writing down everything I consume because I'm going to eat the store," I relayed to the elderly woman behind the counter.

Twelve dollars later, I stepped back outside to retrieve a piece of plastic hidden in my pack. I felt the cold damp air, my teeth chattering, and the beginnings of hypothermia enveloping my exhausted body.

"I can't take it anymore. I have been pounding out miles for the past couple of weeks and have to rest. My wife is coming down to her cousin's place and ...," I babbled along as she stood listening. "Is there any place I can lie down in this little town?" I asked almost in delirium with tears in my eyes.

"Well, dear, it isn't much, but you are welcome to stay in the shed out back," she returned.

"God bless you! Thanks, I'll take it!" I replied.

At this moment, the shed sounded like the Hilton. I hunkered down for a much needed rest. The recharging of my hiking body and mind was only interrupted by visits back and forth to the little store to EAT.

The rainy weather continued into the morning and finally broke around 11 AM. I thanked the members of the family-owned store in the beautiful, tiny hamlet and headed back down the road to get back on the Trail.

Immediately after a storm has passed, hiking above tree line can be an extraordinary experience. The air is crystal clear, and with little humidity in the air the views are spectacular. I'll never forget the view from the summit of Mt. Washington on August 19, one day, probably in 1984, after a violent snow squall with hurricane force winds. After the snow ended, I battled 70 mile per hour winds from "Lake of the Clouds Hut" to the summit and found no fellow hikers or tourists around.

A long-time head of the NH State Park on the summit, Mike Pelchat, took the time to come outside with me. Now with clear blue skies and sunshine, we soaked up the 360 degree 120 mile view. Mike scanned the horizon pointing out a mountain to the north in Canada, a mountain to the west in New York, and showed me the Atlantic Ocean to the east. He told me out of 365 days you might have 5 days with this type of clarity and view. He explained that within hours the humidity would begin to build and the sights would diminish.

As I took the climb out of Catawba, the birds had come back to life, chirping and singing their soothing songs. I climbed higher into the wilds with renewed energy. Finally breaking out of the forest above tree line, I felt my heart pounding in my chest and my breathing temporarily cease. I stood in awe. I had seen pictures in books of this place.

Because of the missing handbook pages, I had no idea I would be walking into this amazing place. I stood motionless taking it all in, realizing this was the most spectacular scenic view I had ever witnessed. I was standing on McAfee Knob and viewed Tinker Cliffs in the distance. I began snapping pictures and cautiously ventured out on the famous ledge. I stared back into the valley of Catawba thousands of feet below.

I lounged around the cliffs and couldn't bring myself to move on. I soaked it all into my being and eventually slowly ventured along the 2 miles of ledges over to Tinker Cliffs. More than six hours had past; still I sat alone not able to bring myself to leave. I finally realized darkness was approaching and took in one last long look promising myself that some day I would return with "Hankshwa", my son, or one of my grandkids.

Now descending on a relatively smooth stretch of trail at a brisk pace, I was in search of a campsite for the evening. It was the latest I had ever hiked since leaving Springer. I thought about stopping to take off my pack to dig out my headlamp. I wondered if I would see some wildlife during my hike at dusk.

Our eyes caught for an instant, with me almost jumping out of my shoes! It was the biggest black bear I had ever set eyes on just 50 feet in front of me. As I stood frozen in the moment, the monster took off like a shot, charging up the open ridge. They say you can't out run a bear. I discovered that early evening that no Olympic sprinter could out run a bear, moving up hill at lightning speed. Thankfully, he ran away from me, not at me.

Life has its ups and downs. You have good days and bad days in these mountains. We have to go with the flow and when things get tough, hold on to hope, and believe there will be a better day.

My life hadn't always been this way, focusing on the positive, full of adventure, mentally strong, and living life to the fullest. It was just the opposite. I was a miserably depressed and rebellious young man, who had lost his way, struggling to hold on. I was trapped in a body with destructive anger and sadness pumping through my veins while searching for something my mind simply could not comprehend. There is so much to say, and I must start at the beginning to make sense of it all.

Chapter 2
My Back Story: The Early Years

"The very winds whispered in soothing accents, and Maternal Nature bade me weep no more." – *Mary Shelley*

I grew up in a once rural middle class town 20 miles from Boston. It was a different world and time. Mine was a wonderful world during an era in America with no leash laws for dogs and no leash laws for kids. We could run free, leaving home in the morning and returning that evening for dinner. The time in between was ours. It was a world with little adult supervision for much of the time. As children, my generation had something young people have little or no conception of today, personal freedom.

By the time I was 9 years old, I would get up on a Saturday morning, eat breakfast, pack a lunch, and head out to explore my world, which covered many miles from home. "Don't be late for dinner!" Mom would yell out. I did not have to ask for a more specific time because we always sat down together to eat in the tiny dining area right off the kitchen at exactly 6:00 PM.

I would spend my days in nearby Kovar's Woods, Baker's Pond, the Martha Jones Conservation Area, or the Swamp. The greatest adventure was when I hopped on my balloon-tired bicycle, passed down from my older brother, and either alone or with my friends, I would ride 4 miles out of town to explore the 420-acre woodland known as Rocky Woods. It was a time to hunt for snakes, frogs, turtles, salamanders, and trees to climb. In the summer, we would swim and fish in the lakes and ponds, and we skated and played hockey on them in the winter. There was a three-story lookout tower located on the highest place in Rocky Woods that we routinely climbed as we hiked the trails.

We had a nice hill to slide on too. With a good fast start, you would make it all the way down and onto a lake and continue your sledding escapade flying across the ice. These ponds were filled with large mouthed bass, pickerel and "sunnies." I will never forget that beautiful summer day when Bobby Fitch caught the biggest monster of a fish I had ever seen. It was a time in America when a child could run free and be imaginative and adventurous. This is all but a dream for many kids in today's world. The whole idea is inconceivable. Today, too many young people have no idea what they are missing.

When I was a kid, we had no umpire or referee to make calls during our pickup games, and the adults did not choose who was on which team. We determined the rosters of our teams, usually by "bucking up sides." Our "Sand Lot" generation somehow resolved the close calls without a mom, dad or an umpire taking over the decision-making process. We did it all, and no one got hurt over it. At the same time we learned great negotiating skills and the ability to survive in a world that was not always kind or fair. We learned to thrive and cope with life's realities at a young age.

Kids today have everything decided for them. Their curiosity, creativity, spontaneity and sense of adventure are inhibited by interfering adults. Well meaning adults do the planning and supervision of their every move. Many parents believe this is best for their little ones. But all too often the fear of failure and of disappointing the adults in their lives overwhelms children as they are smothered by regulated play and the rigors of their structured childhoods.

My early childhood was wonderful. Until the age of 10, I lived in a utopia. It was a loving perfect world as depicted in "Father Knows Best," "Leave It to Beaver," "Ozzie and Harriet," and so many of the other family TV shows so popular at the time. Then when I was 10 years old, it all changed. What happened? Was it a sexual assault by a stranger or by someone known and trusted? Were there suddenly bouts of heavy drinking and beatings at home? Did screaming and constant belittlement become routine? Did one of my parents have an extramarital affair? Did someone in the family suddenly die?

Well, something did happen, but the specific trauma that I endured is not what makes my story so compelling. The cold reality is that millions of innocent kids experience devastating childhood traumas, and they are left to deal with the horrific circumstances each and every day. The trauma

I experienced was the beginning of the hidden damage done to me as a young boy, and I had no idea of how to cope with it all. So began my struggle. I would bang my head on my pillow every night as sleep eluded me; many such sleepless nights would follow through the years.

As children who experience trauma, we feel helpless because we have no say, no rights, and no way to "fix" what we never asked for in the first place. This is the tragedy of it all, and children certainly deserve better. Such children are just victims of circumstances over which they have no control, and the collateral damage will be with them forever. Many of us are survivors who become functional and productive citizens in society, but the emotional shrapnel remains deep within us.

Certain horrific incidents in a person's life can not be totally erased from the soul. "Get over it" many will tell you, but this is impossible because it is now part of your being. You tell yourself: "I'm fine. It's no big deal. I'm over it. I have moved on." You do move on, as there is no other choice, but the effects of childhood trauma remain with you. Post Traumatic Stress Disorder (PTSD), which was referred to as "shell shock" a hundred years ago, lasts forever in some capacity. Just like those soldiers in battle, those who were at ground zero on 9/11, or those at the Boston Marathon's finish line area on April 15, 2013, many kids experience emotional childhood trauma. A young child helplessly caught up in a horrific emotional battle at a tender stage of development is likely to suffer its effects in some way forever. While it may seem an extreme comparison, many children are left to suffer from their own all too private wars in much the same way.

What many of my generation witnessed in the jungles of Vietnam cannot be erased. The "Vietnam Conflict" was never a declared war, yet the damage it caused is still carried today by those "Nam Vets" who have never been given the help they need to heal their emotional wounds. I had friends who were in battle in Vietnam. Some came home emotionally dead at 26 years old even though they did not get put in the ground until their 50's. Others are almost 70, but are still in anger management programs at the Veterans Administration. My heart goes out to these veterans who were never recognized for their sacrifices. Many came home and could not find jobs. After being drafted to fight in an extremely unpopular "war," many were vilified instead of receiving the heroes' welcome home they deserved.

To complicate my own situation, I am of English descent, more commonly referred to in New England as Yankee. My last name is Cook, and on my Mother's side the name Adams figures prominently on my family tree. As an American, you cannot get much more English than that background. Janet Butler, my cousin, checked it all out. She discovered that my Mom's side goes back to the Mayflower and that we are related to John Quincy Adams. I was raised in a stoic Yankee home, and I have suffered because of it. In a traditional English-American home, problems of emotional upheaval are often not dealt with adequately, if at all. Good Englishmen do not cry at funerals.

Our culture instructed us to keep a stiff upper lip, never show fear and never let people know what you are feeling. The home in which I was raised viewed being emotional as having lost control. We internalized everything. We did not talk about our feelings within the home and most certainly did not speak of them to anyone outside the home. Emotions were to be held private. It was driven into me not to reach out, express emotion, or talk about problems to anyone. To do so was considered a sign of weakness, especially for a boy or man. It is a proud and ridiculous tradition, but our traditions and culture run deeply within us and are difficult to overcome.

Therefore, by writing this book I am committing heresy. That, in and of itself, is troubling to me. It goes strongly against my family's culture. But I am silent no more. This book tells my story from misery to happiness, and hopefully it will benefit those who are struggling to find a way out of their private darkness and to break their long-held silence. If writing my story is disturbing to anyone, so be it. But that is not my intent. My wish is to let those who struggle know that they are not alone.

After the age of 10, I was living with the trauma and the chaos in silence and left to deal with it on my own terms. The age and stage of childhood development during which the trauma takes place are factors in dealing with the fallout. In child psychology classes, the ages of 10 through 13 are often referred to as the "vulnerable years." If children experience trauma during these years, it will affect them more than at any other time of their lives.

Trauma may become a strengthening force in an individual's overall development. It may actually become a positive force to make the person mentally stronger and more compassionate. Many who experienced early childhood trauma will "move on" in their lives by pursuing careers helping others with such problems. Many social workers, teachers, police officers, psychologists, doctors, or other "helpers" in our society came from troubled childhoods. Their compassion and understanding were developed and ignited during their past. This passion to "make it better" was planted and what blossomed was a caring strong-willed adult. But other victims of emotional trauma may never fully escape the nightmares of their pasts. These suffering and tormented victims will look in the rearview mirror for the rest of their lives. Still others may self-medicate with their drug of choice, and the most desperate may commit suicide.

With the exception of being a direct target of abuse, a child younger than 10 years of age, generally speaking, will not suffer as much due to the lack of fully understanding the situation. This age group may perceive that "something is not right" in the household or that something "bad" has happened, but a clear understanding of the stress and turmoil is not there. Obviously, each child is different, but the years from 10 through 13 are a very important stage in a person's psychological development. Most 10 through 13-year-olds have the ability to understand the issue and problem to some degree, but their coping skills have not yet emerged or are in their infancy. An older child has developed certain coping skills which will help them deal with the chaos. Most 14 through 18-year-olds have drifted away from the "nest" and a peer group is there to assist them, often becoming more important to their coping process than the family itself. Most of these adolescents will drift back to the family fold in their 20's after their teenage years and the associated "break" as they achieve a sense of self and independence. This will certainly depend on the love and strength received from the family as a child.

Each child is different in the way he or she perceives stress and copes with it. There are diverse avenues to take when dealing with the turmoil. One way to function is by living in a world of denial. But in the end you still have to look at yourself in the mirror. Denial is a defense mechanism and a way to cope, not the best way, but a way. There are also the "scapegoat" children. These children may begin to get into trouble as a subconscious attempt to redirect the attention away from the stress brought on by issues between Mom and Dad and to bring it upon themselves. They witness the stress and chaos between the parents and want it to end between them. Becoming the center of attention of the family, requiring Mom and Dad to work together to help their little delinquent, is the scapegoat child's way of pulling the parents together while redirecting attention away from the real problem. Still another child may react by becoming a "clown" in an attempt to bring humor to a seriously horrific situation. For that child the family atmosphere has become too dark and the need to laugh is a coping mechanism. Some of our greatest comedians came from totally dysfunctional home environments.

Then there is the child who becomes a great athlete, an artistic prodigy, a straight A student, or an overachiever because the family needs a "hero." Later in my career working with young people, I found many professional colleagues surprised when they learned that the students who won all the awards at school came from dysfunctional homes. At times, these hero children will take their efforts over the edge and become workaholics, suffer from eating disorders, or take their athletic efforts to extremes ending up with "overuse injuries" or abusing steroids to get an edge on what they perceive as necessary to hold their world together.

The obsessive-compulsive marathon runner, who constantly ends up with stress fractures and scars in the connective tissues, may be attempting to cope with childhood trauma emanating from a dysfunctional home or from a horrific episode outside the home. Kids reacting this way may not "succeed" and in their own minds, become "failures": turning to drugs or taking their own lives. Negative behavior can be turned inwardly on ourselves, outwardly on others, or both in extreme cases. If the stress is not dealt with professionally at a young age, the suffering may continue through adulthood.

Withdrawal or the "the lost child syndrome" is another coping skill that works for some kids. These children will spend a good deal of their time alone in their rooms or even under their beds or hidden in their closets. Games of fantasy become important as reality is too difficult to face.

This withdrawal mechanism became my crutch as a child. I did not withdraw to my room but went deeper and deeper into the forest. Sometimes I would just sit and listen to the silence or the peaceful mysterious sound of the whispering wind in the trees. I would sit by a stream or a brook to be soothed by the rhythmic sound of the water running over the rocks with the sweet melodies of the song birds in my ears.

Chapter 3
I Turn to Nature to Cope

Honor the sacred. Honor the Earth, our Mother. Honor
the Elders. Honor all with whom we share the Earth:
Four-leggeds, two-leggeds, winged ones, swimmers,
crawlers, plant and rock people.Walk in balance and beauty.

– Native American Elder

S o it was that I found myself in the woods a lot as a child. It was
my refuge. It was a different era, a time when a young boy could
still go into the woods alone. I could explore, discover, create,
fantasize and break away from the reality that was too much for
me to deal with at times. The woods were my haven, full of beauty, silence,
and peace; I would find extreme comfort there. Experiencing nature in
solitude was my sanctuary and my salvation. It was lonely at times, but
as I had my animal friends, I was never truly alone. I drove my Mother
crazy bringing home little critters from the forest, but I never kept them
long. I would bring them back where they belonged, where I belonged. I
felt comfortable there with them, and they all became my friends. I had
my turtles, frogs, snakes, salamanders and finally rabbits.

Sometimes, for even more seclusion, I would climb trees to perch
high above the stressful world below me. Other times my safe place
might be a protective rock formation or the hidden secret cave I had
found off a beaten path in the woods. I vividly recall the first time I saw
a deer step out of the protective covering of the forest and bolt across an
open meadow. Then there was that screeching hawk soaring high above
me in the sunlit blue sky, only to suddenly swoop down, grab something
off the forest floor, and then shoot back up in the sky like a rocket.

As I mentioned earlier, one of the very special places I enjoyed in my childhood was a 420-acre woodland known as Rocky Woods. The original acreage with an endowment had been donated by Boston surgeon, Dr. Joel Goldthwait, in 1942 to establish the Rocky Woods Reservation. This amazing doctor saw the value of "recreational therapy" long before the term was coined. He placed this precious gift in the hands of the Trustees of Reservations with the understanding that it was never to be developed and would be dedicated to "active recreation." In the 1950's and 1960's, this haven was a prime outdoor recreation area in Medfield, Massachusetts. His gracious gift would be utilized by hundreds of families during this time.

Rocky Woods or as Dad simply called it, "The Woods," had everything a young boy like me would dream about each night. There was man-made Chickering Lake, one of five lakes in the reservation. Ironically today such lakes could not be created due to ecological and habitat concerns. One could still cut out stumps in a marsh pond and turn it into a wonderful lake for skating, boating, and fishing. Chickering Lake had ice skating both day and night during the winter months.

The "Club House" on the Chickering Lake property had two large rooms. One had a wood stove and the other a large open-hearth stone fireplace. This haven was a place to put on your skates, get warm after being exposed to the elements or to relax. It had a snack bar serving hamburgers, hot dogs, hot chocolate and an assortment of snacks. There were large windows for grandparents to watch their little ones skate. At night, floodlights suspended from nearby trees illuminated the ice, and music was piped from the Club House. Beyond the bright lights at the far end of the half-mile lake there was darkness. That end of Lake Chickering provided an exciting mystical place filled with shadows for a child to explore, and it was also where many young romances were kindled.

Each night after the skating ended, a volunteer crew would clear the ice with small vehicles equipped with circular brushes. After snowfalls, plows would be attached to these same vehicles to clear the ice. A hole was punched through the ice along with a fire hose, and a pump would be used to spray water on the ice to insure a smooth surface for the next day's skate. This work was all done by volunteers for the benefit of children and families. This skating area was so successful and popular that after a couple of years an adjacent marsh was transformed into a hockey pond. Hockey nets were added and the ice area was big enough for two good size pond hockey games. Skates were strapped on me at the age of 3, and, hockey became my love along with exploring those woods.

Rocky Woods had rowboats for fishing or just having fun on the lakes in the summer months. There was a three-story steel tower to climb, a sledding hill, a rope tow for downhill skiing, and Echo Lake had great large-mouth bass fishing. I spent countless hours on that hockey pond as a kid and countless hours all year long in those woods. It was my refuge from all of the tension, anger and suppressed feelings I had inside. It was heaven for a child to be in this natural world of enchantment, something missing today for many kids in this country.

At age 11, my Mother began to require me to read in my room for an hour each day after lunch during the summer months. I wanted to be outside on a sunny day down in the swamp catching frogs, turtles or snakes. I would look up from my book staring out the window in the direction of Kovar's Woods, longing to be running free and chasing rabbits. So when we took that trip to the library each week, I would pick out some gems for those forced mid-day summer reads. My choices were always the same, the woods. I researched the fauna and flora in my sanctuary. I studied animal identification, behavior and habitats. I knew every animal that lived in those woods of New England. I could identify every bird, reptile, amphibian, insect and mammal. I understood all there was to know about my friends and came to realize I was just a larger mammal walking amongst them.

It did not take long before I became fascinated with the mountain men I read about: Jim Bridger, Jed Smith, "Wild Bill" Williams and other rugged explorers and scouts. I researched the rich 1820-1840 historic era of the mountain men and the fur trapping industry. These were adventurous loners with whom I could identify as I read about their explorations in the rugged Rocky Mountains. I was fascinated and intrigued by their adventurous spirit, independence, and closeness to the natural environment. Born exactly one hundred and fifty years too late meant I lived in a very different world where I somehow had to learn to cope. I came to realize at a young age that I did not fit in a world of concrete and high rise buildings. Man had destroyed much of the wilderness and the beautiful natural environment that surrounded me. I would fantasize about being one of these hardy adventurous souls from a bygone era. If I had been born in 1799, I would have been 21 years old in 1820 and could see myself going into those mountains and wildernesses. I was living in the wrong century. The mountain men were loners and lived differently by running free in the wilds the same as I did.

I read books about Daniel Boone, the Cumberland Gap, the Wilderness Trail, and other wilderness explorers. My favorite TV show was Walt Disney's, "Davy Crockett King of the Wild Frontier." I tuned in each week for Davy's next episode, collected Davy's cards, and read books about the man who wore buckskins and that coon-skinned cap. I fell in love with this free spirit from the woods of Tennessee. This was my world as a youth. Mom bought me a coon-skinned cap, a set of fringed clothing like Davy wore, and I hung my hero's picture on the wall.

I had become brainwashed as a younger child by the entertainment industry of the 1950's that portrayed Native Americans as hateful savages. As I got older, I discovered the reality of it all. The annihilation and forced relocation of certain Native American Tribes by the United States government are among the saddest episodes in American history. I would also discover later in life that my step-grandfather Rufus King was the son of Charles King, who had been dispatched by the government to fight in the Indian Wars along with the likes of Brigadier General George Armstrong Custer.

Then I began to read about the Native American Indian Tribes and seemed to identify more closely with them. They loved Mother Earth, respected her and lived as part of the greater landscape. Native Americans have always been conservationists and protectors of the natural environment as they took only what they needed and lived in harmony with nature. They were so unlike the Europeans and others who would come to plunder the wilderness in the name of "progress" only to try later to save what was left or to attempt to re-create it artificially.

Chapter 4
I Discover Maine

"I need this wildlife, this freedom." – Zane Grey

My Mother was close to the church and had confided in an elderly minister. I did not understand it all back then, but Reverend Harris was like a father figure to my Mom, given that both of her parents had long passed. One summer day when I was 11 years old she came to my younger brother and me and told us she was taking us north to a place somewhere in Maine to stay for a while.

"Come with me and I'll help you pack," she stated.

There was no way I wanted to leave my friends and the woods that summer. As she helped pack my bag, I kept pulling stuff out refusing to leave for someplace in Maine completely unknown to me.

"I don't want to go," I replied.

"No, we have to go. You'll love it," she exclaimed.

"I'm not going! I want to be here. I'm not leaving! I want to play with my friends!" I yelled with anger. The battle went on for a time until Mom broke down in tears. This was probably the most belligerent and defiant I had ever been towards my Mother. I was acting like a total brat.

"I have to get away for a while!" Mom yelled out in frustration.

I felt the anguish, stress and torment I was putting upon my Mother and burst into tears myself. I ran around the corner from the bedroom that I shared with my younger brother to the bathroom and slammed the door behind me. The floodgates were now wide open. Tears were flowing like never before, and my nose was dripping on the floor. I found myself having difficulty catching my breath. I grabbed for a handful of toilet paper attempting to clear my nose and finally splashed warm water on my face drying it off with a bath towel. I had to be that good English boy.

So after several minutes, I regained my composure and opened the bathroom door. My Mother was still crying in my older brother's room alone. Rob, my younger brother, was in the bedroom we shared throughout our childhood, standing by himself alone, seemingly confused. The shame of what I had just done set in immediately and I walked slowly back into my room in silence. Mom returned, and I finished helping her pack. Then we got into the car, pulled out of the driveway and headed north to this foreign place somewhere in Maine. I was as nice as an 11-year-old boy could be to his Mother during that long, hot car ride of silence on that sunny humid day in July. The Maine woods were a place I had never been, a foreign land to this little mountain man, who would soon discover a new paradise.

We stayed in a rustic cabin on the shores of Keyes Pond in Sweden, Maine just down the road from Reverend Harris's old family farmstead. It was heaven, and to think I kept unpacking my bag and saying all those horrible things while battling with Mom and refusing to go. This was not Kovar's Woods, the Swamp, Martha Jones, Baker's Pond or even Rocky Woods. This was something I had never seen and thought existed only in my dreams.

Maine provided a true wilderness as experienced by those mountain men whose lives I envied. There were dense forests of towering pines and hemlocks, lakes, ponds, and mountains, as far as the eye could see. We had hills back in Eastern Massachusetts, but these were real mountains, and the smell of the forest was pure and strong. I felt like I could really breathe here, the air was different and that scent of balsam was like inhaling life and heaven with each breath.

There were animals I had never seen in those woods around my home in Massachusetts. There was this smaller squirrel, chattering all the time, that was not gray but rather a tinge of orangey red. We took trips to the library miles away, as Mom still insisted I read indoors for that hour each day during the summer. That hour inside the cabin was pure torture for me. I longed to take my books outside to read sitting under a tree.

It was peaceful and quiet, so very quiet, and then this strange eerie sound would come out of the silence from the darkness of Keyes Pond. The beautiful serenade of the loons calling to their mates would croon me into the dreamland of the mountains and those adventurous and free spirited mountain men. I had found my sanctuary, my heaven on earth. I was in Maine! There is a sign on the turnpike when you enter this magical place, "Maine, the way life should be." As true a statement as I have ever heard.

The black bear, the moose, and raptors I had never witnessed back home were in Maine. But one of my favorites that first summer was the raccoon family raiding our trash barrels each night. Mom would put out the garbage with those corn cobs we had for dinner right on top, just under the lid of the trash can. If I was not awakened by the sound of the overturning trash cans at night, Mom would come wake me. We would tip toe to the door with flashlight in hand, and stand there in the darkness watching those raccoons having a banquet from our leftovers. I would watch in amazement as the talented creatures lifted the covers right off the barrels with their little hands. I loved sharing those late times with my Mom. She understood me better than I gave her credit for at the time.

I would beg my Mom and Dad over the next few years to let me have my own pet raccoon. I would have built his cage ten feet off the ground around the old maple tree in the backyard so he could climb up and down. I wanted to hold the cute furry animal in my arms and pat his little head. That it never happened is probably for the best as his place was in the woods, as was mine.

My favorite animals were the chipmunks. I watched these little mouse-like creatures with brown, black and white stripes running the length of their bodies and tails. I watched with excitement as the cute little creatures scurried around camp all day long running in and out of holes in the ground. I found books about all the animals indigenous to the North Woods at the library when we took those trips down the country road to Bridgton. I read with focused interest about what they ate, their life cycles, their habits, and what their footprints looked like. After all, I was a mountain man and needed to know everything about the animals I would try to trap. I spent countless hours each day putting out peanuts and other foods in my attempts to catch those little striped chipmunks. I tried catching them in boxes and other contraptions but never caught a single one. I just wanted to hold one of the little guys, feed him by hand, and tell him how much I loved him. Every day I tried. Again my lack of success was probably for the best.

There was a raft on Keyes Pond to swim out to and dive from after lounging in the hot sun. My younger brother and I would take out an old rowboat, follow the shoreline for a mile or more, and catch the biggest bullfrogs I had ever seen. Day after day we would grab the fat, slow bulls with our hands filling the boat with these amphibious jumping beans. Later we would retrace our trip putting each frog back in the same cove where we found it. Each day we would do it again, and we started giving each big fella a name. We began to recognize each one as we reunited with our frog friends each day.

I would end many days sitting on an outcropping of granite ledge at the edge of Keyes Pond being soothed by the lapping of the crystal clear water on the rocks, staring to the far end of the pond. On those real hot summer days in July, there would be a burst of blinding red sunlight streaming in all directions from the mountain-filled horizon in the western sky. I could feel God touching me, hypnotized by this beautiful, tranquil place, "Maine the way life should be."

I fell in love with Maine that first summer. Its spiritual hallucinogenic powers reached deep into my soul and my bones; I would never be the same. I had found my Shangri-la. Thus began a love affair with the "Great North Woods" that would last a lifetime. We would head back to the same cabin the next summer for the greatest two weeks of the year. I certainly did not fight Mom on this return visit. In fact, I helped her pack my bags with great excitement and anticipation. This time I had my buck knife, hatchet, bow and arrows, makeshift little traps, and all my mountain man gear ready to go.

I spent much of the summers between the ages of 11 and 15 either in Maine or at summer camps in New Hampshire. Camps were different in those days from most of the summer camps today. There were woodcrafts, Indian lore, canoeing, hiking, swimming, archery, arts and crafts, and nature study. There are still old camps to be found with similar activities for our children, but much has changed. Most camps today have a single focus such as a specific sport or some other kind of specialty. Kids attend camp with the expectation that they will improve at something in order to better compete. Just having fun is no longer a priority in our competitive, progressive society.

So the woods, mountains, and the natural world were forever etched into my soul. The towering hemlocks, white and red pines, spruce, birches, maples, and aspens were the surroundings I craved. The black bear, moose, loon, raccoon, chattering red squirrel, bullfrog, white-tailed deer, hawk, bald eagle and that cute little striped chipmunk were now my friends. There was no tension in these woods, just peace. As a child, I never associated my fascination for nature with its therapeutic powers and healing spirituality, of how it could soothe my soul. I have come to realize it saved me.

I would come back to that same little cabin on Keyes Pond again, a quarter of a century later to stay with my wife, Karen, and our two young daughters, Christina and Samantha. We all needed a relaxing break after a long stretch of difficult times and found the cabin still there and open for rent. It was a great time to recharge before the summer crowds arrived.

Some twenty years after that first trip to Keyes Pond as a boy, I bought my first piece of land in Maine. It was forty acres of woodland on the side of Burnt Meadow Mountain with rocky outcroppings and ledges. It was worthless for cultivation or commercial development, but to me it was heaven. On a clear day I could see the smoke from the Cog Railway atop Mount Washington in New Hampshire. I got the parcel for just three hundred bucks an acre. Forty years after that first summer in Maine, I would discover my present home on the shore of a beautiful remote lake. As the bird flies, it was just fifteen miles from Keyes Pond.

Chapter 5
My Lost Years

"That's all that drugs and alcohol do, they cut off your emotions in the end." – *Ringo Starr*

Well, I should have stayed in those woods of Massachusetts and Maine, but I hit my adolescence: the hormones kicked in and I turned to alcohol. My friends noticed before I did that I could really drink. My tolerance grew, and before long, I would down a quart of whiskey at a sitting. Decades later, I found out from a doctor I had this medical condition which enabled me to oxidize alcohol very quickly. This gave me an "ability" to drink enormous amounts of alcohol and still walk straight and talk somewhat cohererently. I am a little guy, and at this time I was maybe 5'8" tall and weighed around 140 pounds. Most people can oxidize one ounce of pure alcohol an hour, which equals approximately the amount in twelve ounces of beer, four ounces of wine, or one and a half ounces of distilled spirits. My liver oxidized the alcohol, unknown to me, at an accelerated rate.

I was also a hockey player. I had been on skates from the time I was 3-years-old, given that hockey was practically a religion in my house. Dad had season tickets to the Bruins for eight years, Section 4, Row G, Seats 1 and 2. I was one of two freshmen to make the varsity hockey team in high school. Hockey is a macho sport: score a goal, smash somebody into the boards, and get thrown into the penalty box. Then after the game, I could outdrink everyone. So here I was – a small statured and reserved teenager who could literally drink anyone under the table with a hockey stick in one hand and a whiskey bottle in the other. What did my peers think of me? Let me tell you. I was the "Big Man on Campus," "King of the Hill" and I would pay the price that comes with being those things for all the wrong reasons.

I am not going to lie; back then alcohol was beautiful. It did everything for me. It was like putting a big blanket over all my emotions. All my apprehensions, anxieties, and worries were buried when I drank. All that childhood turmoil in my "never tell or show emotion" existence would be suppressed. I became instantly popular and received attention and respect from my peers like I had never experienced before in my life. Alcohol did it all. It felt so good to get out of myself and be someone else, so relaxed, carefree and "bulletproof." All the pats on the back just reinforced my behavior.

This was 1960's America, where we grew up with a warped sense of alcohol being cool. I had a perverted view of this mysterious "forbidden fruit." What happened to me is still happening to many kids today, a half century later. Little has changed in our society related to alcohol. The only thing that changes is the specific drug that is popular at the time. It seems that heroin, as a less expensive option to prescription drugs, tops the chart right now. Alcohol, a legal drug, is always there and its widespread social acceptance by society contributes to its misuse by millions. There are still glossy billboards and magazines "encouraging" millions of young people to take the same foolish road to popularity. More people are killed by alcohol than all the other drugs combined. Later in my career as a health teacher, I held discussions with my students in an attempt to get them to recognize the media hype behind the use of alcohol. It was like trying to turn back the tide.

As is the case for many young people in America, the first time I drank with my foolish friends was with no knowledge of what I was doing. It was an experiment into the "adult only" world with absolutely no supervision of any kind. There was this guy Jack, a senior in high school who looked like he was in his early 20's. He stood about 6'4" and weighed about 260 pounds. He had fake I.D.s, which he really did not need as he was one of those guys who had a five o'clock shadow by the end of the school day.

"Hey, you goin' to the party?" he asked at lunch one day in the cafeteria.

"Me?" I asked.

"Yeah, you." he stated.

"Yeah, I'm going I guess." Part of me was forcing myself to become more social.

"What do you want?" Jack asked.

Now I did not know much at this time about alcohol, just what I had learned from TV and magazines. I had heard of this drink called a rum and Coke, so I told Jack I'd take some rum.

"How much you want?" he asked.

Everyone seemed to be ordering half pints and pints so I blurted out, "I'll take a pint of Bacardi rum." I had heard of this company figuring I would get the rum and a couple of cans of Coke and be all set.

Jack took my money saying, "I'm not sure you got enough for Bacardi, so I might have to get you something else."

I'm sure I got ripped off that day as I had no clue about the prices and Jack needed something for his troubles.

I was not driving yet, thankfully, so I took a ride with some upper-classmen that sunny day in May to the state beach before it was open to the public. I found myself in some sand dunes hidden from sight with about fifty other foolish young girls and guys. There I stood with my pint of 80 proof Caldwell's Rum, a cup, some ice and my two cans of Coke to use as a mixer. Well, I did not put a watch on it, but the rum and Coke were down my throat in no time and I was feeling something I had never experienced. The reasoning section of the brain was no longer working properly and, being out of alcohol, I began searching for more. One of my confused drinking partners let me dive into his case of Colt 45 Malt Liquor. I remember putting down five of these 12-ounce cans with a lot of junk food brought along for the party.

There is not much else I remember that day, other than being on the ocean floor swallowing seawater and thinking I was going to drown. I do not recollect ever going into the water, just being under it. If I had died that day, I would have been just another bit of data on a statistical graph. I learned many years latter that sixty percent of drowning deaths are alcohol related. What almost happened to me does happen to so many others.

Thankfully, someone saw me being knocked down continuously by the waves in my struggle with a loss of equilibrium due to the alcohol I had consumed. I found myself being dragged out of the water by two unknown teens. On my hands and knees, I left a mixture of junk food and seawater on the water's edge. In my alcohol induced amnesia commonly referred to as a "blackout," I recall nothing else about that day. How did I get home? Who was driving? How did I end up in my bed at home in the morning? I had no clue.

Upon awaking, I struggled to the bathroom and noticed my legs, arms and hands were trembling, and I had a blinding headache. I dressed as quickly as I could, realizing that I should get out of the house before my parents discovered my physical state. Over the next hour or so, I got some food and healthy fluids into my system and began to feel much better. I did not understand that I had been suffering the effects of dehydration. I knew nothing about the oxidation of alcohol and the time needed to recover. I never vomited that first time I drank except when I purged the seawater and junk food on the beach. All this alcohol did not seem to give me that dreaded hangover many others experience.

Upon returning to the corridors of my high school on Monday, I had a day like I had never had before. Dozens of kids, especially older kids, were patting this self doubting underclassman on the back. Some of the "coolest" kids in the community were shaking my hand as girls passed me in the corridor giggling and winking. They were giving me the attention every teenager craves from his peers. I later found out that it had been these older kids who drove me back to town and kept me away from my house until my parents left. They somehow found the key we hid on the porch, unlocked the door, and put me in my bed. Kids take care of kids. They share their drugs and watch out for each other. I learned fast and became one of them in a big way.

My tolerance to alcohol developed quickly, and the more I drank the more everyone liked me. I was a different person when I drank: fun to be with, not shy or withdrawn. I was happy, outgoing, and as far as a drunk goes, a nice one to have around. I never got angry or violent. I was the guy with the lampshade on his head and a clown. I would come out of my shell. At first my drinking was all about the social acceptance, but then it became more about how it numbed me and stopped the stress and pain of the past or anything bothering me at the time. It worked well for a while. I found kids like me, who just wanted to drink and get "wasted." My favorite was to drink in the woods around the fire at night. Deep in the woods away from all adult intervention, that was where we would "do our thing."

I had my fake ID at 17, and some of my friends liked to hit the bars, but I had no desire to do so. I was not into the bar scene, dancing, or "scooping" the girls. I just craved the sedation alcohol provided. Perversely, my beloved woods with all its therapeutic value now combined with alcohol to become my haven. My therapy was sitting atop a mountain in the wilderness with a bottle. I was one of the wild mountain men I had read about as a child. I knew all about their yearly celebratory booze-filled rendezvous after the trapping season. As the radical late 1960's hit, I would have my long hair, a beard, and a Davy Crockett buckskin fringe jacket along with a bottle of whiskey in my hand.

Alcohol is classified as a depressant. As an already confused, young guy, alcohol drove me deeper into a dark hole of depression. So what do you do when you cannot see any light; you hate the world and everything around you, but most of all you cannot stand yourself? By my senior year in high school, things took a turn for the worse, and I was spiraling down. All the confusion and sadness of my childhood and pressure of my future after high school was getting to me, but as a good Englishman, I struggled not to show weakness. We know now that in the mental, emotional, and physical development of a young adult, the downward spiral of mental illness is accelerated with drug use.

Chapter 6
My Life's Darkest Stretch

"The thought of suicide is a powerful solace:
By means of it one gets through many a bad night"
– *Friedrich Nietzsche*

I t all would come crashing down as I sank deeper into depression and hopelessness of that dark hole. I did not want to live. As I drank, I started swallowing aspirin, maybe fifteen that first time with no great effect. I began to lie in bed at night thinking about different ways to end my life. This went on for months. With no sleep, I walked around in a daze. The school eventually made a call to my Mom, and she asked me what was happening. "Everything is fine, Mom," I explained. Parents are always the last to know. Suicide was my way to end it all and rest in peace. I saw nothing but the dark side of life. It seemed to me that going to bed one night and never waking up was a good way to go. Just give me peace!

All life and the colors of autumn were gone. It was November and in New England the trees were bare; the leaves were strewn over the ground, brown and dead. In nature autumn is a time of hunkering down, hibernation, and preparing for the sleep of winter. I counted out fifty aspirin and thirty chlorine tablets, and swallowed them down one at a time alone in the bathroom. I settled into my bed to die.

Most teens in deep depression, as I was, are not fully committed to end their lives. There is usually some part of them that wants to survive, and their suicide attempts are cries for help that they somehow cannot utter. Their difficulty is the feeling of hopelessness and not understanding how to reach out for help. If I had really wanted to die, I would have taken the whole bottle, not fifty. There remains a faint ray of hope that some how, some way, someone will save you and bring you back; that someone will understand and help you out of the darkness. I lay awake in my bed waiting for the end in my state of insanity.

Dawn broke and I stumbled into the bathroom, shut the door, and vomited into the toilet. I remember it being a Wednesday and went off to school after breakfast. As soon as the day ended, I bolted from school and ran home. It sounds strange even today that while running down Clapboardtree Street, a lonely country road surrounded by woods, I heard voices from the devil telling me to join him in hell. At the same time I felt another pull to fight for life and stay alive. It was a strange hallucinogenic feeling of conflict I will never forget.

Upon entering my empty home, in a bout of insanity, I began searching for something to swallow. I eventually found myself in our dirty unfinished cellar near the washing machine. I grabbed a dirty old glass, filled it with laundry bleach and took a big swallow. The burning in my esophagus was excruciating. My eyes, nose and mouth were pushing a massive flow of mucus out of me, and I vomited into the dirty old sink next to the washer. I gasped for air and had trouble breathing. I attempted to hold on to the sink to steady myself but collapsed to the dirty cellar floor. In that moment, reality of what I was doing hit me. The pain of that burning bleach and the horrific physical shock of it hitting my body slammed me into a moment of sanity.

My Mom entered the house within the next hour, and I asked her for the keys to the car. She asked me what was wrong with my voice and where I wanted to go. I told her I had to see Dr. Fisher, our family physician.

"I'll go with you," she said.

"No Mom, this is something I need to do alone," I replied.

Dr. Fisher was not just any doctor. He was special, and I had known him since childhood. He made house calls for a decade after any other doctor in the area did. He was a most caring man with a wonderful bedside manner. He had a fatherly image and always made you feel comfortable when seeing him. I entered the empty waiting room and heard Dr. Fisher say through the open door of his office, "Come on in son."

No one was there because he never had office hours on Wednesdays. We were alone. I walked in seeing him in his usual position behind his big desk in his office. After your visit in the examining room, he would always invite you into his office and sit across from you on the other side of that big desk. He would take the time to speak with you, and he really listened. In my experience, that is pretty much a lost art in medicine today. You always were offered a piece of chewing gum, usually Wrigley's Doublemint. I felt comfortable with this wonderful man and sat down.

"What's wrong, son?" he asked. I sat in silence for the next few minutes trying to find the words. He waited.

"Make me a man," I finally blurted, taking off my glasses and tossing them in the air in a hopeless manner. I look back upon this almost a half century later and still believe I could not have said it better. It was my first time reaching out for help, but coming from that stoic Yankee culture, doing so meant I was not a man. As a lost 17-year-old kid, I said what I wanted without understanding it at the time. I wanted him to fix me.

"What have you been doing to yourself?" he asked. I explained my destructive behaviors and fleeting attempts at suicide. The next day I found myself at McLean Hospital in Belmont, Massachusetts on a psych ward with someone by my side around the clock. I was locked inside from November 17th until December 24th, at which time I was asked if they could do anything for me given that the next day was Christmas.

I had pleaded many times to let me go outside, but in vain. No one would listen or understand that a mountain man had to be in an outdoor environment to function. I felt like an animal locked in a cage, being watched, poked, and prodded. In my frustration, I would take a running start and jump at the large windows, bouncing off the heavy screen mesh to the floor. This action certainly did nothing to help the situation I found myself in, trapped on the second floor. After several attempts, I surrendered but ended up on continuous 24-hour supervision. Someone would sit in my room at night with a light on to observe me. All day and all night long there was someone by my side pulling "special" duty.

On December 24th it was snowing. I kept asking to be let outside for my Christmas present. That evening a freakish winter thunderstorm rolled in for Christmas Eve. In the thunder and lightening, I continued to plead my case, which confirmed my insanity to the working staff. Finally after the violent storm was over, I was allowed to go outside accompanied by two large staff members who walked on either side of me. They were bundled up with heavy coats, hats and gloves to go out in the wind and now falling snow. I felt the cold winter air in my nostrils and could breathe again for the first time in over a month. It felt glorious to have the wind touching my face again, and I welcomed the coldness I felt in my bones. I was finally outside again!

I began touching the bark on a towering oak tree. I felt its strength, its toughness and natural beauty. I caught snowflakes in my bare hands and felt them melt from the warmth of my body. I stared into the sky and watched the flakes swirling round and round before finally hitting the earth. It was beautiful. I unzipped my coat to feel the cold and snow more directly, and was advised to zip it up by Matt, one of the giants walking the grounds as my bodyguard.

"Don't worry, I'm okay. It feels so great to be out here!" I yelled out. I was the animal at the zoo that had escaped his cage and was basking in all the glory of this moment of freedom. I looked at all my outdoor surroundings and wanted to stay out all night long. However, Matt and his partner kept telling the mountain man that we had to go back inside. I pleaded for more time as long as I could but knew they were in charge of me and my freedom. So I thanked them both for bringing me outside, even if it was for just a short time. I told them both that I hoped I could do it again soon, like tomorrow for Christmas. Christmas Day came and went and I did not get to go outside. Eventually, I was allowed to go out now and then, always accompanied by staff.

Given that it had been pounded into me my whole life to keep my emotions in check, and that it was a sign of weakness, to not open up; my therapy sessions were useless. I never worked things out or said much to the psychiatrists and psychologists who were all strangers to me. All I did was complain to them that I wanted some type of activity to do outside, but no one was listening. I played card games, checkers, ping pong, watched TV, and generally sat around counting the days that all blended together in a monotonous sameness.

Finally, finding an old typewriter, I spent a day typing how I felt about being there. I included the analogy of the animal in the zoo and explained how I would never get any better until I could be outside. I walked in for my morning session with my assigned psychiatrist and his two colleagues and handed them what I had written. I told them I was done trying to communicate orally with them, and maybe they would understand the written word. They did not take me seriously, and after this my sessions were mostly conducted in silence.

Dad's insurance finally ran out in February, and with a heavy heart, he told me I would have to be transferred to a state hospital in a neighboring town. Ironically, it was in Medfield, the same town as Rocky Woods, my old stomping ground. He felt so bad about what had to be done. I kept telling him it would be okay, and that I was excited just to get out of McLean, which was considered one of the best psychiatric facilities in the country and is to this day.

I was transported by my parents in their automobile with Matt sitting beside me in the back seat. Medfield State Hospital was a little frightening in the beginning as I was only 17 years old on an adult ward, but after a few days, I adapted. I was asked in the first few days if I would like a job in the kitchen operating the large dishwasher. I jumped at the opportunity and worked 7 days a week, 6 hours a day (2 hours after each meal) for a weekly total of 42 hours. My pay was two packs of cigarettes. I began to smoke cigarettes thanks to the Commonwealth of Massachusetts and their hospital system to get me well. I have always found this interesting, but learned later in life that the American Red Cross delivered smokes to the soldiers during World Wars I and II. I eventually became a two-pack a day smoker.

Albert DeSalvo, "the Boston Strangler," was housed in another Massachusetts facility, Bridgewater State Hospital for the Criminally Insane. During my stay at Medfield State, corruption and horror stories at Bridgewater ended up on the front page of all the papers in Massachusetts. Bridgewater was cleaned out and these insane criminals were scattered throughout the state in other hospitals. We slept in barrack type bed situations, and I suddenly found my 17-year-old self on an adult ward. I was sleeping in the open; surrounded by murderers, rapists and other criminally insane inmates. So while I slept with one eye open, I had the freedom to walk the grounds, got out of lock-up to work in the kitchen three times a day, and began to be allowed home visits for a day or two. I found a psychologist I could talk to about some things, but I never communicated about my real problems or feelings.

One day I walked off the grounds unnoticed and got myself to my old childhood haven, Rocky Woods. I went to my old secret cave and watched a gray squirrel scurrying around. I sat alone on a large granite boulder and listened to that wonderfully familiar sound of the whispering wind in the trees. Later, I sat by a brook being soothed again by that joyous gurgling of the water running over the rocks. I thought about all the wonderful childhood adventures I had in these Woods and walked by my old fishing spot at Echo Lake. My prayer was to get back here someday soon.

I returned in time for my evening dishwashing and was questioned as to where I had been between lunch and dinner. I explained it was such a nice day that I just walked the grounds for hours. I was told not to do this again or I would lose my opportunity to wash dishes. It was kind of like slave labor, but I was not going to argue. Anything was better than being locked up all day again.

Finally by April, it was time to go home for good. As Dad drove me home, he asked about my plans, as it was too late to go back and finish high school that year. I told him I planned to get a job, finish up high school the following year, and play hockey. Dad had already checked with Mr. Chase, the principal, and my case would have to go before an administrative board to decide whether or not I could play hockey again. Thankfully, they approved my rejoining the team. Sometimes I think if the vote had gone the other way, it may have been my end.

Coach Peter Case, my mentor, was the greatest and most positive asset I had in my life at this time. He was soft spoken, compassionate and on my side, not so much as a hockey coach, but as a person. He had a way with "at risk" kids, and he was good for me. I had taken his U.S. History class two years earlier and observed how well he handled the toughest characters in the school. His demeanor worked well with these kids. He taught me a lot in life and was there for me at the right moment.

We would reconnect over forty years later. My only remaining connection from high school and the hockey team had notified me about the loss of Coach Case's wife to cancer in 2009. In my attempt to locate him to send off a sympathy card, I discovered he was living alone, less than a ten minute drive away in the next town from mine. We have seen each other constantly since, going to breakfast, hockey games and family gatherings. I owe this man more than he will ever know. I would go on to become a caring, compassionate track coach myself. After my own retirement, I realized that it was all due to this fine man and his mentoring. Pete Case was my role model as I encountered many "at risk" young people during my career, and I honored him best by striving to make some type of positive difference in their lives. I believe I may have changed a life or two for the better. This is all a teacher/coach looks for as a reward for years of service. Thanks, Coach!

Chapter 7
I Am Still a Party Animal on the Loose

"I have absolutely no pleasure in the stimulants in which I sometimes so madly indulge. It has not been in the pursuit of pleasure that I have periled life and reputation and reason. It has been the desperate attempt to escape from torturing memories, from a sense of insupportable loneliness and a dread of some strange impending doom."
– *Edgar Allan Poe*

The lessons learned from my attempt at ending my life, being locked up with so many troubled adults, and Coach's mentoring would sit dormant for sometime within me. Later these experiences and lessons learned would surface to serve me well. But at the time I was a 17-year-old wild animal free of his cage. It was time to get back with my friends and party.

I took up drinking right where I left off and the hard partying became more frequent. I sedated myself most of that summer and beyond. I hooked up with an even more hardcore crew and would eventually go on to engage in ever more dangerous and self-destructive behaviors. These guys would enter a world of heavier drug use and misery. This was the group I chose to associate with after I got out of the hospitals. In fact, my theme song would become "Born to Be Wild" by Steppenwolf. I have come to believe that coming close to death, in the long run, makes you more appreciative of life. But at that time I could not see how my world would ever be any different. From my warped perception of life, living it to the fullest meant my only recourse was to pursue ever more dangerous thrills.

Along came Crazy Billy and Joey. We were three stooges in Billy's 4X4 jeep, drunk out of our minds in the dark, flying up and down Duxbury Beach. Joey and I would cling to the front fender or lie face down spread-eagled on the roof as Crazy Billy screamed and laughed maniacally from behind the wheel. I never thought about the consequences. There were so many times we would be speeding down Strawberry Lane, a winding country road, at incredible speeds going sideways around corners in the opposite lane. Billy liked to drink and drive fast wherever he went, and I had that seat belt on so tight I could hardly breathe when we went on these joy-rides. I had all the whiskey I wanted as the two of them would constantly break into houses or the country club in the neighboring town cleaning out the bars. They would always hide the liquor under blankets on a dead end road and cover it all with leaves. I got quarts of booze for just two bucks so I always had plenty to drink. I was not interested in the thrill of the criminal activity, just drinking and living wild.

My time with these guys all ended in the dunes of that same state beach where my drinking had all started. Crazy, as he was now called having dropped the Billy from his name, was drunk out of his mind and attacked me with a broken whiskey bottle. He was bigger and stronger than I, but I was faster so I ran. We were heavily intoxicated, stumbling and falling, but he finally gave up the chase. I spoke to him the next day from a good 20 feet away in case he did not like what I had to say. I told him I was done with him because he was losing control.

"You're losing it. I'm not hanging with you anymore after yesterday. You're going to kill someone, end up in jail for a long time or die before you're 21," I said.

"You're nuts, just like everyone says and don't know what you're talkin' about," Crazy said as he laughed at me.

Sadly, my prediction came to pass. Ten days before his 21st birthday, Crazy died in a car crash on a winding road on the way into Boston. I heard that he had so much heroin in him at the time that he probably felt nothing as he crashed. By some miracle, he did not take anyone else down with him. I can still hear that sickening, sadistic laugh of his ringing in my ears. Joey, the other kid with whom I drank my "brains out" for two years solid, flunked out of college after just one year because of drugs. He made it all the way to age 30 before someone found him with a rope around his neck.

I finally crawled out of high school at age 19 in 1968, arguably, the worst twelve months in American history. In February, there was the Tet Offensive and the escalation of the Vietnam conflict. Two months later on April 4th, Martin Luther King, Jr. was murdered; followed just two months later by the assassination of Robert F. Kennedy. In August, the Democratic National Convention was held in Chicago.

Mayor Daley gave his police force the order to quell any peace demonstrations and protests outside the convention center. This led to the riots where protestors and innocent bystanders alike were beaten by police.

This was a time of race riots, protest marches, the burning of draft cards and the public desecration of American flags. There was the lottery to determine who would be drafted just as the American public learned that we had been lied to by our government as to the number of casualties in Vietnam. It was an insane time, and to deal with it all, young people turned to drugs in numbers never seen before in American history. It was the beginning of the escalation of the drug culture and its destructive force that is still with us today. The guts of America were ripped open during those twelve months, and in my opinion, this country has never totally recovered.

As young people wanted to go on a "trip" to fantasy land to escape the reality of the times, LSD and psychedelic mushrooms were everywhere. For others of this angry and rebellious generation, marijuana became the drug of choice. Other drugs would follow, and it was not long before high schools were infiltrated with addiction problems too. The destructive force of drug abuse got a real foothold, and has only intensified since, leaving us with a multitude of social problems.

I was practicing for my high school graduation ceremony on a football field with an old transistor radio plugged in my ear when it was reported that Robert F. Kennedy had been pronounced dead. I relayed this message to my classmates that day on the field in the sunshine, as we continued with our preparations.

A private prep school on the north shore of Massachusetts, with the intervention of Coach Case, had offered me a partial scholarship to play hockey. I wanted to go to improve my game, and knew I was not ready for college. My parents, however, wanted me to apply to college to determine if I could get accepted anywhere. So I sent in six applications and got five rejections, as I had not applied myself as a student.

Then Barry Urbanski, the hockey coach at Salem State College, called my house. He was a former goaltender for Boston University.

"Hey kid, I saw you play the other day and would like you to come to Salem State and play for me."

"Great!" was my reply.

"The problem is you're no student, and I don't think you'll get in. I want you to re-apply to major in Social Studies. That way maybe I can put a bug in Admissions ear to let you in," Barry explained.

"I'm not sure I want to study Social Studies," I replied.

"Kid, do you want to get into college and play hockey for me?" he asked.

I figured I would be there until January, and once semester break came and grades came out, I would be done. So I went off to Salem State College figuring I would play hockey and drink for a few months. As it turned out, I had to attend classes as Coach Urbanski would check attendance. I did not study or apply myself until it was almost too late. I liked being on campus and away from home. So I made a big decision to study and to stay for my whole freshman year at least. I quit playing hockey and studied for the first time in my life. Studying did not come easily to me, and I just barely slipped by that year.

Every Friday, I would cut a small article out of the Boston Globe stating how many guys died in Vietnam that week. These articles with the past week's casualties became the wallpaper in my room on campus. When I was 20 years old, a close drinking buddy who had spoken constantly about being a gunner on a helicopter, headed off to Vietnam. I had seen too many young guys come home in body bags. I had learned by this time what to do with my madness and sadness. I was a bourbon and beer man, and my goal this crazy day was to put more alcohol in my body than I had ever done in my life. I succeeded. My friends kept count as I guzzled it down for the next thirteen straight hours. After awhile, I did not want to be with anyone. I just wanted to crawl into a hole. Instead I crawled into a car, alone. I do not remember getting in the car, driving on the highway or crashing on that night.

Those who have experienced an alcohol induced "blackout," know that they are freaky. You get up the next morning not knowing where you are, how you got there, or what you did. You could find yourself in a court of law standing in front of a judge. You are telling the judge you did not do anything because you do not remember doing anything. There are many people in prison cells today who committed crimes when they were high, and have no recollection of what they did. Still others are left to write a letter of apology saying they are sorry to the victims' family.

When you are a young alcohol abuser, you do not think about anybody else. Your whole world revolves around you. You are the center of the universe. It is a very selfish time of life. How is my hair? Do I have the right shirt, shoes? Do I walk right, talk right? I certainly did not set out to kill anyone that night. The fact was that I was not thinking of anyone else.

Well, apparently I was going pretty fast because I blew out all four tires when I hit the curb. As I already stated, I have no memory of the crash. Someone unknown to me pulled me out of that car. I did not have a cut, a scratch or a broken bone despite the fact that I did not wear a seat belt on that miserable night. Thankfully, it was a one-car crash. It would be another ten years before I got it through my thick skull what I could have done that night. I do think about it now.

I could have killed someone that night, robbing a family of their children and would have never known until later. Drunk driving is a hideous crime committed every day. It is hard to believe that more people have been killed by drunk drivers in just the last century than all the American soldiers that have died fighting for this country's freedom since 1775. Memorial Day is our national holiday to honor our military dead. What day do we have for all the victims of drunk driving? The victims' families and friends are often left to mourn in silence. This is one of the most pathetic, hideous tragedies of America.

Chapter 8
I Meet the Love of My Life

"Sometimes a rose is destined to love a thorn." – *Unknown*

Around this time, I met an 18-year-old girl. Karen is a second-generation Italian-American beauty with the dazzling blue eyes of her mother's family from northern Italy. That she fell in love with me is something I have never fully understood. Karen saw the goodness in me that no one else saw, not even me. It was in my second year at Salem State when I met this newly arrived freshman after just a couple of weeks on campus. She was involved in the unsettling revolution of the 1960's and was engaged in her own private rebellion. The fighting and bombing in Vietnam had intensified and so had the protests and unrest in America in 1969. But Karen had more to reconcile in her own mind than most of us.

Her father was Brigadier General John William Antonelli, U.S.M.C. After he graduated from the U.S. Naval Academy in Annapolis, Maryland in 1940, he was commissioned a Marine second lieutenant. He reported for duty with the 1st Battalion, 5th Marines, later designated the 1st Raider Battalion. In May 1942, he was promoted to captain. He served as a company commander at Tulagi, Guadalcanal and Savo Island. As a major, he became commanding officer of the 2nd Battalion 27th Marines, 5th Marine Division. He led the battalion during the Iwo Jima campaign, where he earned the Navy Cross for extraordinary heroism and the Purple Heart during battles from February 19th to

March 16th in 1945. Karen was and always has been justifiably proud of her father.

Somehow I had caught her eye. Karen wasted no time before she invited me home to meet her family. With the hubris of a radical 20-year-old, I was eager to engage the General in a discussion on Vietnam. I was ready to do battle. So during the first visit to Karen's home, I asked the question I thought necessary to begin the attack.

"So, General, what do you think of the mess in Vietnam?"

"Well, we've gotten ourselves into a hornet's nest, and we're trying to get out," he replied. He knew what I was attempting to do and diplomatically was not about to take the bait from his daughter's new boyfriend. Later in the day, after sharing some Chianti, I again tried to ignite a confrontation.

"I'm planning to take Karen to the Boston Common for a peace rally on October 15th where the 'dove', George McGovern, will be speaking. What do you think of that?"

"I think it's good to become involved with what is happening in our country at this troubling time. Keep an open mind and look at both sides of the issue learning as much as you can. If you take Karen with you, understand there will be thousands of people, drugs, and the potential for trouble. Please keep your eye on my daughter, if she is with you, and keep her safe," he answered.

I wanted to salute him saying, "Yes, Sir, I will keep her by my side and will not let any harm come to her." That peace rally on October 15, 1969 was the biggest gathering in history on the Boston Common with over 100,000 in attendance. I did as the General expected and kept his beautiful daughter safely by my side.

So Karen Marie Antonelli, my beautiful girl with her Italian name and heritage became the focal point of my life. She came from a totally different culture. She helped me to begin to open up, and to begin to realize for the first time in my life that it was okay to express my emotions and inner feelings. I remember our conversation after my first dinner at her home with her family. We stepped out into the driveway as I asked,

"What was that all about?"

"What?" she asked.

"Everyone was drinking wine at dinner and yelling at each other."

Karen looked at me strangely and said, "No one was yelling."

This home, unlike mine, was verbally expressive. After having dinner at my home, Karen said that no one communicated how they felt. The conversations were interesting, polite exchanges of information, but they seemed "sterile" to her. The differences in our two homes were extreme, and emotionally speaking, we came from opposite cultures.

Karen was also intelligent and a real student. Her influence helped me to become more serious about college and my studies for the first time in my life. She helped me to believe in myself, but I was still fighting my past and my culture. We argued about one thing. Coming from that cosmopolitan Italian home where they educate their children around the dinner table to use alcohol as a beverage to accompany good food, she could not understand the use of alcohol as a drug. She was not tempted and has never viewed alcohol as some sort of forbidden fruit. Kids in America are now taught how and when to eat cookies. "You can't have any cookies until you eat all your vegetables." But in most homes, we do not have any proper instruction on the use of alcohol, the drug that causes more misery and problems than all other drugs combined.

But I was a slow learner. I wanted Karen and I wanted to drink my way. I wanted it all. She asked me more than once not to get drunk, but never to stop drinking. Being intoxicated made and makes no sense to her at all. At the time, I could not understand her sensible appreciation and use of alcohol, but today it is so clear to me. Karen stuck by me even through another stint in lock-up. She always saw the positives in me and showed me love and understanding.

As soon as she turned 21, I asked her to marry me. She was in her junior year of college, but there was no way I wanted to lose this beautiful young woman who loved me. Her birthday is the 29th of March, and that year Easter fell on the Sunday one week later. After everyone else left the Easter dinner table, I asked the General, formally, for his daughter's hand. I was sitting across from this highly decorated war hero, who was already in the history books, with my long hair, beard, beat-up old jeans, Davy Crockett fringe jacket, and the remains of a burnt draft card in my back pocket. Unbelievably, that was my attire for Easter dinner on the most important day of my life to date.

I will never forget his response after a brief conversation, "You do not have my permission to marry my daughter..." There was a brief pause at which time I could feel words of disappointment and anger welling up inside me when he continued, "... but you have my blessing." He knew I would not have asked him unless Karen wanted to marry me and she was of legal age. I found out many years later her maternal uncles had written Karen letters urging her not to ruin her life. She took a big chance on me. Thank God she did.

We got married in October of 1972. We lived in a basement apartment that year in a student rent district of Salem, Massachusetts close enough to Salem State for her to walk to classes. I took our beat up old Volkswagen Bug to my job, which ironically, was in a liquor store. I had promised the General his daughter would graduate from college, and she did the following spring of 1973. We never attended her graduation. It was a nice weekend, and we took the old tent and headed to our favorite camping spot in New Hampshire instead.

At that time, my mother was a secretary for a principal at an elementary school. Mom kept telling me to go back to school to get certified to teach at this level. I took her advice and completed an intensive program of study and student teaching. The divorce rate in America had escalated after the radical 1960's. Divorce had been a foreign, whispered word when I was a child, but by this time, it had become common. Many children were being raised in homes where the father was not present so there was an increased need for male teachers in the classroom. This was especially true for grades 4 through 6.

I searched all over northern New England, and finally in late August of 1973 landed a 5th grade classroom position in New Hampshire just south of the White Mountains (the Whites). We lived in a three-room walk-up apartment in a formerly condemned building. The pay was at the poverty level, and we went through that first winter with no stove. I had bought a two-burner hot plate at a yard sale for five bucks and we used a toaster oven we had received as a wedding present. Karen gave birth to Christina Marie in February of the winter of 1974. Karen and the baby slept in the kitchen for the rest of the winter. But I loved that we were close to the woods and the Whites.

Marriage didn't change me much. Karen broke my bottles of bourbon and beer, cried, and slammed doors. Please understand that those first three years of marriage were not all bad. We had some great times, and I loved my wife and daughter with all my heart. I do not know how good I was for her, but she was great for me coming from that Italian culture where feelings are expressed and all problems are out on the table for discussion. She was helping me along in life a little at a time, but it was an uphill battle for her as I was still fighting my past and my Yankee culture.

I had found my life's love, but there was still something missing. Fate would now intervene, and my direction in life would be changed forever. My existence would now have true meaning and I would now begin to discover the road to fulfillment and happiness. It still amazes me how one encounter can forever alter one's direction and purpose in life.

Chapter 9
The Chance Encounter that Forged My Dream

"In everyone's life, at some time, our inner fire goes out. It is then burst into flame by an encounter with another human being." – *Albert Schweitzer*

We were living a somewhat gypsy life, running from one dumpy apartment to the next, and then when I was 26-years-old, it happened. That lure of the woods and the wilds was calling again. That urge to experience the soothing calmness of nature had never left me. It was in my bones and beckoning for me to return. So I took a job in that summer of 1975 to work in the Whites. I grabbed my wife and our 18-month-old daughter, Christina Marie, and headed off to the mountains and the woods. This is where and when the encounter that changed my life happened.

The stranger with his long hair and beard did not say much, and he pretty much kept to himself. Everyone else at work thought he was strange and kept their distance. I on the other hand always had the attitude, "Why be normal? It's boring!" I gravitated toward this mysterious lone wolf-like character. I wanted to find out what he was all about. Well, it took some time, but one evening sitting around the fire he started telling me about an adventure that had taken him over 2000 miles up and over mountain after mountain through fourteen states on a path in the wilderness. He simply referred to his trek as "the trail." As he spoke in a somewhat mysterious, reverent tone, I noticed the reflection of the flames from the fire in his widening, glowing eyes.

How his story excited me. Every time he spoke about the trail, I sat up with my attention focused on his every word. He told me about the things he had seen, the people he had met, and other encounters on his long journey. Tales of the trail were told around that fire on many evenings, and he shared old photographs of his adventure. I sat mesmerized with the stories of his journey through the wilds. I had never heard of this trail and at the time did not realize that I had encountered one of the pioneers of the Appalachian Trail (hereafter, the Trail or the AT).

As that last summer campfire burned down, I stared into the dying glowing embers and made a secret pact with myself. Some day I was going to take this journey and hike the Trail. My encounter with this introverted stranger in the White Mountains of New Hampshire in the summer of 1975 would be the spark that would ignite a new me and cause me to be reborn that summer. I would never be the same person again.

My love and life-long therapeutic connection with nature, Rocky Woods, my childhood fascination with Davy Crockett and Daniel Boone and the rest of the free spirited mountain men, my love of the Great North Woods of Maine made sense now. This adventure and journey would be the culmination of my life. But how could I do it now? I had a wife and a kid. I was trying to be a good husband and father. Plus, I was no hiker. Not by a long shot.

At the time, my outdoor experience consisted of paddling my rawhide seated, mahogany ribbed canoe upstream for a few miles, then turning that "baby" around, cracking open the cooler, drifting back downstream, and sucking down as many "cold ones" as I could. I had christened the canoe "Six-pack" with a beer bottle, and my wife had given me the nickname, "The Dough Boy," as she poked her fingers into my soft midsection.

We moved again. Almost like it was meant to be, my neighbor was one of those crazy marathon runners. As the months went by I would see this skinny guy running all over town, and then I would look at myself in the mirror. I was shaped like a beer keg with arms and legs coming out of it. I began to think about my direction in life. I thought about my future with Karen and my baby daughter, Christina. It was about time.

There were also my genetics to consider. My father had a heart attack at age 44, my paternal grandfather died of heart disease at 49, and I found out later that my great-grandfather's heart gave out at age 53. Quite the gene pool, and it gets worse. My maternal grandmother died of a stroke before I was even born. My maternal grandfather died when I was just 3-years-old, and my mom's brothers met their demises at early ages of the same disease as their mother. Great... heart attacks and strokes! With my genes, I was a train wreck waiting to happen.

Well, everything started to add up, and the dream of someday experiencing the adventure of hiking the Trail was constantly on my mind. Six months after I met the stranger in the White Mountains, New Year's Day was approaching. I decided to change my life and get in shape. This would be my New Year's resolution for 1976.

January 1st came and went, and I never got outside. It was cold that day; plus I had another hangover. I continued drinking beer and taking a shot of Wild Turkey now and then. I knew I had to do something with myself. Hiking that Trail from Georgia to Maine and the tales I had been told had become entrenched in my psyche. I dreamt about it throughout the cold nights of January.

February 1, 1976 was unseasonably warm for New England. I cannot recall if it was Saturday or Sunday, but I remember it was the weekend. I decided this was a day to do something. I did not know when I was going to hike this Trail, but I figured you had to start somewhere. If I ever planned to hike the Trail's over 2000 miles, one mile seemed a good place to start. I went out in my Chevy Chevette and drove around our neighborhood in Bellingham, Massachusetts using the odometer to measure that mile. Back at the house, I dug out my old high school sweatshirt and sweat pants. I laced up my old black high tops and yelled out to Karen that I was off to run a mile. She went along with the whole thing and did not laugh.

As I jogged along that first half mile, I felt pretty good about myself. It was a partly cloudy day without much sunshine, but warm for February 1st, probably close to 50 degrees. I thought I was doing pretty well for someone living on bourbon, beer and potato chips. As I moved into that second half mile, everything started to change radically. My breathing became labored, and there was a wheezing sound I had never heard before as I inhaled. I seemed to be having difficulty getting enough air into my lungs. It was a frightening feeling. I began to panic, and my breathing became erratic. I was sucking air through my nose and mouth, but mostly pulling in as much oxygen as humanly possible by mouth. It was wide, wide open. I started to get a little dizzy and lightheaded. I could feel my heart pounding in my chest ready to explode. My legs were now aching, feeling kind of rubbery and not my own.

I stumbled on a small rock on the road and caught myself before falling to the pavement. What was happening to me? My knees, ankles, hips and back were barking at me to stop. My pace slowed, there was a pounding in my head, the dizziness increased, and I grabbed onto a parked car to steady myself as the world was spinning in front of me. I stood there as the unsteadiness finally started to dissipate. Hunched over, I began retching all over the road splattering vomit on my high tops.

I did not finish that one mile jog. I could see my place in the distance and limped along, dragged myself up the steps to the front door, grabbed a beer out of the fridge and collapsed on the couch. It was a day of great discouragement and a wake up call. That first year of jogging was actually quite comical, as I look back on it. After all, I was still drinking heavily. Hard-headedness has always been part of my personality. I did not understand at the time how this stubbornness would be an asset for a hiker, especially a thru-hiker on the AT. Anyone who hikes the Trail up and over mountains for over 2000 miles has to be one stubborn pack mule. In addition to being a slow learner, I often found that personal experience was my only way to learn and accept new things. It was a tough first year or so before the realization that drinking and running just do not mix. Eight beers and a shot of bourbon each night, and then attempting a 3-mile jog the next morning was not going to work. I got sick on the road more than once by running with hangovers.

That day, February 1st, would change my whole life. I would come to cherish this day each year eventually more than my own birthday, and I now thank God every February 1st for what happened that day in 1976. Although I did not realize it for many years, it was the day I finally began to accept that I could not be the drinker I was and become a marathon runner much less a thru-hiker on the Trail. The desire to pursue my dream was forged that day. It was the chance encounter with that pioneer of the Trail that changed me. My days of alcohol abuse to suppress emotions and feel good about myself were coming to an end. The dream meant more to me.

Chapter 10
My Dream of Many Steps

"It is good to have an end to journey toward; but it is the journey that matters, in the end." – *Ernest Hemingway*

The first steps in any journey toward a dream are always the toughest, and this first year was no exception, but I kept dreaming and dreaming. This focus on some day hiking the Trail continued to get me out the door most days. Things moved slowly, but change was happening. Any radical lifestyle change is never swift and not without pain and suffering. The beginning was tough, but I had a real goal in life. Motivation is the key to any transformation and thankfully this is what I had in my dream to hike the Trail. It all takes time, and persistence is necessary.

One day running down the road I saw a path that led off into the woods. Suddenly, I found myself back where I belonged in the first place, but this time I was running with a dream and that dream would grow and sustain me as I ran in the natural world around me. A walker or runner notices the transition of the seasons, being close to nature day after day. I could smell the closing of the dark and dreary winter, and it ended each year on February 15th according to my internal calendar. While we might get a cold day or two after this or even a foot of snow some years; it would not last once the repositioning sun of spring popped out.

There were spells of running on the road now and then when my woods were blanketed with snow and ice, but most of my time was in those woods on the animal paths chasing rabbits. I would notice the beginnings of the budding on the trees and witness animals emerging from their winter slumber. Spring would be recognized during a late day run as the sound of the peepers announced winter's door closing for another year. The warmth of the summer sun combined with smell of a baking forest floor would spur me on during my runs. The first autumn color of a leaf on the ground would stop me in my tracks, and I would take the time to pick it up. Anyone who spends time in the woods like this on a daily basis will become connected with nature's beauty, magnificence and mystery. Nature is a powerful thing.

I spent as much time as possible running off-road in wooded areas away from unleashed dogs and drunk drivers on the road. It was calming and spiritual. I was finding myself again and finally feeling like I was back where I belonged. It is not natural to run on pavement and concrete I told myself. This all made perfect sense to me, as I also reasoned that off road running would also be better on my knees, back and the rest of my body. I was also slowly drifting away from my old set of friends and acquaintances; none who could understand me. For most macho men any form of "working out" was respected. This meant that I was not actually hassled too much by this group of guys. But to others, as my beard and hair grew and my weight dropped, this obsession with running meant I was losing my mind.

In April of 1977, Karen and I drove to New York to visit Mike and Carol, a couple who had been our neighbors in one of the ramshackle apartment buildings we had lived in during our first years of marriage in New Hampshire. They ended up living in that same building, in the unit above us, when their car broke down on a wayward adventure around America that had begun on the west coast. For most of that year, Mike received welfare checks from the State of California, and he worked only sporadically. The rest of the time was a vacation of tequila and "grass." Mike and I had split a few worms back then as we drained those bottles of tequila. Karen and I had not seen Mike and Carol since we had moved out of that building two years earlier. At the time of our visit, they were living in a coastal town a five-hour ride south of us in yet another dump. Not much had changed for Mike while my life had changed radically over the last year.

I got up early that first day of our visit and went out for a 4-mile run. I remember running and exploring the coastal town on that warm, sunny morning as everyone slept. It was also the third Monday in April. At exactly noon the gun would go off in Hopkinton, that little borough west of Boston.

Until 1969, the Boston Marathon (hereafter the Marathon or Boston) had always been on April 19th, my birthday. Then Massachusetts changed the Patriot's Day state holiday to the third Monday in April. I have always been a bit resentful about this change as I liked having my birthday off every year on what I called "Marathon Day." My parents used to take me to see the Marathon as a young boy in either Wellesley or Newton. I can still remember running along side the top runners on the side of the road. I would sprint with all I had for a hundred yards or so as those super humans continued to expand the distance between us. I would slowly come to a stop gasping for air and staring in amazement as these athletes disappeared from my sight. It was inconceivable to me, that anyone could run 26.2 miles at that speed. Who were these people and how did they do such an inhuman thing? They did not seem to me to be like the rest of us; rather they seemed like some aliens or freaks. As the years went by growing up in the Boston area, I was always interested in this annual event but knew little of its history. I would often see a man in our town running the roads. Dad would explain that he was a milkman who ran the Marathon each year. He did not look all that young and the mystique of this milkman and the rest of the runners always intrigued me.

As I ran that morning watching the sun come up glistening over the ocean in Mike and Carol's town, I thought about the Marathon. Later that day we went to the beach. I searched on an old transistor for the radio broadcast of the race. It was a freakishly hot, 98 degree day in the Northeast. I even dove in and out of the cold ocean because it was so unseasonably warm. According to the broadcast, they were "dropping like flies" back on the streets of Boston. As it turned out, the 1977 Boston Marathon was one of the hottest of all time.

Even Bill Rodgers, who had come out of nowhere and set the course record back in 1975 with a time of two hours, nine minutes and fifty-five seconds (2:09:55), had dropped out in Brookline around the 23-mile mark. Bill would go on and win the event the next three years in a row... 1978, '79, and '80. Only the immortal Clarence DeMar had surpassed Bill's feat by winning it seven times. Rodgers came to be known as a runner who did not perform well in hot weather. The heat would always zap his energy. His kind of Marathon Day was 40 degrees with an overcast sky or a light drizzle. Under those conditions he loved those hills.

The Marathon challenge really caught my interest that afternoon sitting in the sun on that beach with Mike, Carol, Karen, and our little girls. I also thought about how much my life had changed in the last fourteen months given the path I had chosen to pursue. It had been an amazing year for me with this new passion of running and dreaming about the Trail. While walking along the shore line alone, I daydreamed about running the Marathon that afternoon in the sunshine as the waves broke and the foamy surf swished around my feet. Could I do Boston's 26.2 miles? Was it possible?

All Mike talked about that day was the party we were invited to go to that evening. He was practically foaming at the mouth telling us about the nurse who would be there. She worked at a local hospital and had stolen an oxygen mask. He was so excited to experience smoking dope from a Turkish water pipe through the mask. The big problem of the day was finding a babysitter for our little Christina. Now, I had gotten to know Mike pretty well that year we lived in the same apartment building and was not eager to see him without his dope. Marijuana is not physically addicting, but for many it becomes "necessary" psychologically. I had always known when Mike was out of grass. You would not want to be around him during those times. Mike would pick fights, proverbially kick the dog, and overall be one miserable guy. His routine that year we knew him had been to work for a while, live on peanut butter and jelly sandwiches and save money. Once he had enough saved, he would get laid off or just quit and go on a vacation of smoking pot and drinking until all the money was gone.

Nothing much had changed in his life, except he now had a baby daughter. The night of the party there was no one to babysit our two little girls. Karen and I stepped forward. He kept telling us we could not do this because it would not be fair for us to miss the party. We both explained that as the party meant so much to him, we were fine about missing it. Truth be told, Karen and I had not been comfortable at the thought of a stranger looking after Christina, and we were relieved not to go to the party. So despite our having traveled over ten hours round trip to visit them, Mike left us to babysit that night while he and Carol, at his insistence, went to the party. That spoke volumes of the hold alcohol and drugs had on him. As we pulled out of their driveway the next afternoon to head home, I said a prayer for their little girl. We never saw or heard from Mike and Carol again. Our lives were heading in different directions.

Karen and I had lain awake the night before discussing how much our lives had changed. I was also becoming fixated on the Marathon and had made up my mind to be in Hopkinton next April when the starting gun went off. I had never run more than 4 miles, but the dream of running 26.2 miles was now planted in my brain. I was so filled with excitement at having made this decision that I barely slept a wink.

Being from the Boston area, the only race I'd ever really heard about was the Marathon. So to run Boston as my first race made perfect sense to me. It seemed completely logical to run a 26.2 mile marathon as my first race given that I one day planned to hike the Trail's 2000 plus miles. I kept this idea to myself for most of the next year, as it made no sense telling anyone until the goal caught up to reality. So while staying silent about my running in the next year's Marathon, I planned to train slowly to increase my distance. I had no idea when I would hike the Trail, and the motivation of training for the Marathon, an event I had been in awe of since childhood, would be another log in the fire to keep the dream of the Trail alive.

When you have a long range dream, it is best to cut it up in segments and develop short term goals along the way. Staying motivated is the key. Otherwise, having to look so far into the future for such a long time inevitably leads to the thought of quitting. It is all a head game to keep any dream alive. My goal now was to concentrate on adding miles rather than pace. It became a contest of doing this without suffering from overuse injuries. Marathon training, I would discover, was all about preventing injury. If you are not injured then you can train. Being "on the shelf" prevents you from training. It was as simple as this in the beginning. By that summer's end I was running 6 to 7 miles a day, five days a week.

Chapter 11

My Emergence as a Marathoner

"If we did all the things we are capable of, we would astound ourselves." – *Thomas Edison*

My serious training did not start until January 1978, which was no picnic living in New England. Then the big snowstorm hit, the first week of February. "The Blizzard of '78" was a historic event. The school where I was now teaching in Massachusetts was closed for a couple of weeks. In fact the entire eastern half of Massachusetts was shut down, but I only missed two days of training. I shoveled a path from my front door to the road, figuring tomorrow once the snow ended the plow would come down my street to clear us out. There was no sense hurrying to shovel the driveway as I knew the schools would be closed for a while. I just wanted to walk down that deep shoveled path and get to the road for my run. It kept snowing and the plow never came. The next day there was still no plow. I sat in the house crazed with cabin fever, eating, tending to the wood stove, and reading. The utilities had been knocked out, and we were left with no central heat or electricity. Governor Mike Dukakis had called a State of Emergency.

Finally in the afternoon, I announced to Karen that I was going out. I put on some work boots, layered up and headed out. I trudged through waist deep snow for a half a mile in the streets of our neighborhood, as I was curious to see if Route 126 had been cleared. It was exhausting battling through that deep snow for nearly an hour to finally find it with one lane cleared of snow. There was not a car in sight, so I crawled down out of the snow bank and began shuffling down Route 126. Only emergency vehicles were allowed to use the roads under these conditions given the Governor's order.

There was no pavement to be seen, just a hard packed layer of snow on the road. My pace was slow and cautious with short choppy strides. I certainly did not want to fall or pull a groin muscle. There was not a sound to be heard but the crunching of snow underfoot. It was a soothing, rhythmic sound that went along with my breathing. I watched my breath slowly dissipate before my eyes as I moved along. I was at peace with this world of silence, and it was wonderful to feel the crisp air on my face and cold sweat on my body cooling me. I unzipped my windbreaker and continued my shuffle.

The silence and tranquility of that late afternoon was now interrupted with the rumbling of a vehicle approaching. I could not see it, but the break in the quiet alerted me to it. I finally saw the car creeping toward me, probably at 10 mph. I moved to the high snow bank and let the car pass. I received a strange look from the solo driver and proceeded on my way. After another mile, I found myself running on the overpass of Route 495, a four lane highway. As far as my eyes could see there were stranded cars, buses, and 18-wheelers. As I gazed down upon this parking lot of snow covered vehicles, I chuckled to myself thinking when will I ever be able to run down a four lane highway again in my lifetime? Life was at a stand still, but I was still moving.

The entrance ramp was cleared and I could see some areas of pavement on 495. I trotted down the ramp and began my running adventure down that highway. I was exhilarated and felt more alive than I could ever remember. As I ran, I passed by State Police cruisers, tow trucks, snowmobiles, and people still stranded in their cars. The looks and stares I got that day were priceless. The rest of the world was stopped in their tracks, and I was moving. I felt super human that day. As I shuffled back home to sit by the warm fire, I realized the power of what I was doing with myself. My thinking and behavior were "out of the box," and I realized that with a healthy conditioned body almost anything was possible. I was filled with confidence after that day and thought that the Marathon's 26.2 miles seemed like it just might happen for me.

Running became easier after this experience, both physically and psychologically. In southern Massachusetts winter on my internal calendar usually ends around February 15th. There will be cold days now and then, but you can smell and feel spring coming. I had read an article about running "doubles," as a way to increase mileage. It seemed easier to me to run two 5-milers, than a 10-miler straight out. It would be a good way to increase my base mileage. I decided to run back and forth to work each day, if I could arrange to take a shower once I arrived at school each morning.

I finally found a small locker room that referees used on occasion. It had a shower and everything I needed. With the help of my principal, Tom Collins, I had been issued my own key to this facility. Tom was an ex-Marine and respected what I wanted to do. I would take my longest runs on Sundays and then use Mondays as the day to drive to bring my box of food and clean clothes for the week. Mondays would also be a day off from running, after the long one I did every Sunday. On Tuesdays through Fridays, I would run doubles of 7 and 7 miles. This gave me 14 miles for the day. I kept this schedule up for most of the eight weeks remaining before Boston. I missed now and then due to pouring rain or if my body started telling me to back off and just run once or not at all that day. It was good hard training.

One day in the second week of March, I added 4 more miles to the late afternoon 7-mile run home. When I got there, I danced in the street realizing I had completed 18 miles for the day. My confidence kept growing, and my ability to run that 26.2 miles seemed more and more real as the days passed. In retrospect, I should not have been so excited and full of vinegar, as it was my first straight out run in double figures. It had been only 11 miles that afternoon in the late winter sun. I would still have 15 miles more to go on Marathon Day to complete the 26.2 mile race. But that day I did not dwell on that; the only thing in my mind was that I had done 18 miles.

My plan to run the Marathon in April was still unknown to anyone, including Karen. She had not seemed to pay much attention to what I was doing or the time I was spending on the long runs. I had read an article in "Runner's World" magazine that your marathon training should include at least three long runs of 18 miles or more, so I went out that Sunday in mid-March to do my second. After I finished, I walked up the stairs with a salt-stained face, sweat smelling like ketones, and looking like a rung out wash cloth. Karen met me at the door. I was unaware that Margaret, a neighborhood friend of hers and the neighborhood sentry, had made a visit to speak to Karen while I was out for my run.

"Where have you been?" Karen asked with a look on her face that could stop a stampeding herd of buffalo.

"Out running," I replied with a confused expression.

"You have been gone for over two and a half hours. What have you been up to?" she nervously asked.

"I have to get a drink of water. What's this all about?" I asked as I moved to the kitchen with Karen following close behind.

"Margaret came over after you left and told me she has been noticing how long you have been going out running and thinks you must be having an affair!" Karen said angrily.

I started laughing hysterically, replying, "Yes, I am having an affair. It's a love affair with my running that's all."

"You can't run for over two hours without stopping. What else is going on?" she asked.

"Yes, I can now run this long and I'm in pretty good shape," I confidently answered.

"Why are you running so much?" she puzzlingly inquired.

"Well, it's about time I told you what I'm working on here. Next month I'm going to run the Boston Marathon," I explained with pride.

Karen was somewhat taken back by this whole idea and asked if I really thought I could do it. I spoke with confidence telling her it was something I had fantasized about doing since I was a child, and with another month of good training I hoped to finish. She was quite confused with the idea, but supportive none the less. She was concerned with my health and well being.

The running boom that came from Frank Shorter's winning the Gold Medal in the 1972 Olympics was in full swing, and I had been swept up with this whole new generation of runners in America. I was in the middle of reading Jim Fixx's number one best seller, "The Complete Book of Running," and was fixated on the Marathon. There was not much that would stop me, except for an overuse running injury. I was playing the game of nursing wounds in training and backing off when need be, but still training as much as possible. I look back now at what I was doing and wonder how I got through it without serious injury. My knowledge of marathon training was limited to what I read in a book or magazine, and I was backing off only when I felt it necessary. My workouts were erratic to say the least. I would run 36 miles one week, followed the next week by 72, which was my high mileage week during this crazy training.

Motivation was my greatest ally in making it to the starting line. My self confidence just kept growing the more I pushed myself. But I have since come to question my thought process. I had trouble containing and disciplining myself, as I ran with raw emotion fueled with the thought of the Marathon approaching. In the week following that jump to 72 miles,

I could only manage 32 miles. I climbed upstairs backwards to my bed each night. By morning I could again stand on my feet, lace up my Nike "Cortez" running shoes and hobble down the road to work. It was an amazing adventure, and I enjoyed the struggle of getting myself ready for the starting gun in Hopkinton. Those early morning runs were magical, and I felt so alive with the new me.

We were invited to Sunday dinner at my parents' home the next weekend. Sunday dinner was always at 1:00 PM. That morning I told Karen I would be leaving around 11:00 AM to run over my parents' house some 13 miles away. She questioned what I was doing as I put a bag of clothes in the car. I told her I would get there in plenty of time to take a shower and be ready for dinner. I always liked point-to-point runs versus running in circles, and this was a great opportunity. After all, the Trail from Georgia to Maine is point-to-point. Karen told me she would be leaving well after I did but would find me on the way to bring me some water. She met me about 9 miles into my run with that refreshment and kept asking if I wanted to get in the car.

"This is your last chance. Are you sure you're okay?" she nervously asked.

"I'm fine," I replied with a smile of confidence to reassure her.

"Please be careful," she said looking very concerned

I laughed out loud to myself, as she drove off with Chrissy's perplexed face pressed against the car window. Our four-year-old must have been totally confused as Mommy drove off leaving sweaty Daddy on the side of the road. She kept staring out that window until I could no longer see her little face. The day was starting to become interesting with little knowledge of what was about to happen once I reached my parent's house. As I took the corner, I looked down the road at the small Cape Cod style house where I grew up, third on the left, to see Karen holding Samantha, our two month old baby, in her arms. My parents were also out front and Chrissy was walking around the front yard. I was finally in view of my Mother's look of horror, my wife's stare, my Father's concerned face, and Chrissy still trying to figure out the whole scene and questioning if her Daddy had lost his mind. I chuckled to myself noticing Dad had an orange cut in quarters and Mom was holding a glass of water. I slowed to a walk as I heard Mom's frightened voice.

"Are you alright? Do you need to sit down on the front steps? What are you doing this for? Karen told us that you plan to run the Marathon. Have you lost your mind?" After pleading for a shower and cooling down, it was time to eat. This is when all the interrogations and cross examinations really got into full swing.

"Mom, can you please stop all this discussion? I didn't come over here to have dinner with you and Dad and argue. I came over with the family to enjoy the day, and I'm hungry and want to eat," I said.

Remember, my Dad had a major heart attack at 44, another at 50 and again at 55. He was taking handfuls of pills every day just to stay alive, and just 10 months prior had undergone a quadruple by-pass. Heart by-pass surgery in 1977 was relatively new and not performed routinely as it is today. Mr. Landry, a neighbor, had the same operation a month earlier and left his wife and three daughters. He never made it off the table. This was not all of it. As I mentioned earlier, there were generations of heart disease and strokes on both sides of my family.

Mom was scared. I was not enjoying this Sunday dinner with my parents. I was reassuring Mom that I was fine and kept attempting to change the conversation with no success. Finally, as calmly as possible, I explained if this line of questioning continued we would be leaving. We eventually got off the subject, but Mom was tense and uneasy for the rest of the day. The following evening the phone calls from Mom began. They went on right up to the day of the Marathon.

"Don't you understand the genetics? I think you have a death wish and need to see a psychiatrist again. You have a wonderful wife and two lovely little daughters. Can't anyone talk you out of this?" The best of all was the night she asked, "Do you have enough life insurance?"

As Marathon Day approached, I was starting to lose sleep over all these dire warnings and became somewhat concerned myself. Both my brothers had seen Dad's cardiologist, Dr. Mike Klein, at University Hospital in Boston, but I had not. I called to make an appointment a few weeks before the Marathon. I explained to his office staff that I could only take one day off from work and would be more than happy to spend the entire day undergoing tests to determine my fitness to run the Marathon. I arrived at 8:00 AM and would end the day with the consultation with Dr. Klein. Doctors had discovered a murmur in my aortic valve when I was 17, so I started the day with an echocardiogram. A stress test was scheduled for late afternoon, hours after my lunch would be digested.

I was very interested in the stress test because I wanted to make sure my heart was okay under heavy exercise. I showed up with my running shoes and shorts in my attempt to "beat the machine." I had read about stress tests in the running magazines and was up for the challenge. The technician wired me up, and I told the doctor overseeing the test that if my heart rate reached 190 beats per minute that I wanted to stop. I explained that was about my maximum heart rate for my age and did not want to damage the muscle. I knew the normal max is 220 minus your age.

The technician laughed and said, "Okay."

"We might be here for a while," replied the doctor.

My blood pressure was in the normal range until the treadmill was turned on to begin the test. The tech mentioned it to the doctor, and I replied, "Sure it went up. I'm excited and want to beat the machine."

The treadmill was moving at just one mile an hour, but every three minutes it would reprogram itself and speed up. What I was not aware of was that the incline also became steeper. After twenty-six minutes I was covered with sweat, running at a full gallop with all kinds of apparatus strapped to my chest and wires shaking all over the place. My blood pressure was being taken at every reprogramming. The doctor was laughing and called someone into the room to see what seemed like a freakish performance to them.

I told them gasping, "All you see is sick people. There are many runners in much better condition than I am."

I was ready to drop when the doctor said I was approaching 190, and they had seen enough. I was then told that my blood pressure had dropped to 90/57, which frightened me.

The doctor explained the health lesson for the day. "If you are in poor cardiovascular health your blood pressure would just keep rising and the test would have to end. Healthy blood vessels retain their elasticity because they do not have much plaque build up. They readily expand, and the blood flows through them faster and easier. Therefore, blood pressure drops. Your vessels are in great shape."

Dad later explained to me how his stress test would end after a short duration of walking when his blood pressure would start to elevate toward that heart attack number of 210/110. Once I became more educated with this exercise physiology and cardiovascular health, I would always use the analogy of this expansion of healthy vessels with that of a rubber verses plastic hose. When the water is turned on and runs through a rubber hose it expands, whereas, the cheap plastic hose splits eventually, as a result of the lack of expansion. When the plaque accumulates in arteries, usually due to a diet rich in saturated fats and cholesterol, the vessels not only narrow, but also lose their healthy elasticity.

I finished the day with my consultation with Dr. Klein, which was most enlightening. The conference started with the doctor asking me if I was active in some type of cardiovascular exercise.

"Mr. Cook, you are in great health compared to your two brothers. Are you doing some type of regular exercise?" Dr. Klein asked.

"This is why I'm here," I answered.

"What do you mean?" he asked.

"I have been running and training to run the Boston Marathon next month and people at home, especially my Mother, are driving me nuts with their concerns. Do you think I'm okay to do this?" I asked.

Dr. Klein sat back in his chair and very intelligently asked, "What have you done to prepare for this?"

"I have been running back and forth to work three or four times a week, 7 miles each way and have taken two long runs of 18 miles. I have read that taking at least three long runs of 18 miles or more is the minimum required to finish and plan to do one more long one," I stated.

"It seems as though you have thought this out logically and have worked hard for this race. I see no reason, medically, for you not to do this. Your murmur is something we should keep track of, but not something to be concerned with at this time," Dr. Klein replied.

We finished the consultation with me asking, "Do you have a business card?" Dr. Klein handed me his card, and I asked, "Can I have people back home call you, if they need reassurance that I'm okay?"

The doctor laughed saying, "That would be fine. Just keep doing what you're doing. You're on the right track and understand that most of those at home will never figure it out. Send me a postcard about how the day went."

Chapter 12
I Just Want to Finish

"You simply have to put one foot in front of the other and keep going." – *George Lucas*

t was April and my anxiety and excitement was intensifying. I read anything I could find about this historic event. I bought a short paperback with a brief history of the Boston Marathon from the time of its origin in 1897. It was filled with pictures and interesting facts. I was captivated with this amazing sporting event, started by a New York running club after the resurrection of the modern Olympic Games in Greece, in 1896.

The Boston Marathon has been held annually without interruption every April since its inception. World Wars, boycotts, storms, nothing had ever stopped the gun going off at noon in Hopkinton sending the herds of runners east to the streets of Boston. Although there were races that actually started in Ashland a few times in the beginning years, the starting line was finally established to be in Hopkinton for the 26 mile and 385-yard official distance of a marathon.

I read about the immortals of the great Boston like a child reading about his sports idols. The printer from Melrose, Clarence DeMar, who placed first in the event an astonishing seven times was my favorite; his last victory was at the unbelievable age of forty-one. He would have won more races, but did not run the race for several years due to doctors explaining he had "heart problems." The confusion was likely due to the doctors never having witnessed a heart with a left ventricle stroke volume like DeMar's. I have read that he had a resting pulse of thirty-five beats per minute where as the average American's heart beats seventy-two times. He also missed other races due to his humility and religious beliefs that seeking the fame and accepting trophies was sinful.

I was now daydreaming nonstop about running in this most renowned and prestigious race, participating together with some of the greatest distance runners in the world. My excitement was overwhelming, and sleeping was becoming a problem. I was like a little kid waiting for Christmas. I was filled with wonder and magic, as I counted down the days to that third Monday in April 1978. I was filled with bravado. I felt powerful and confident finishing up the last few miles one afternoon of my second 7-miler for the day when I suddenly found a runner next to me. He shocked me, as I never heard his footsteps from behind. Where had he come from?

I now know that an experienced distance runner has no heavy footsteps and does not waste energy. A good runner is soft footed, something I was not aware of at this point in my running career. I did not know who this character was running next to me or how he had managed to sneak up on me so fast. It was also the first time I had met anyone running on my journeys to work and back. The loneliness of the long distance runner was now interrupted.

He asked very politely, "How's it going?"

"Pretty good," I answered.

"How many miles you running?" he asked.

"I'm finishing up my second 7-miler today. I run a lot of doubles," I replied.

"Wow! What are you training for?" he inquired.

"The Boston Marathon!" I responded like a bragging child.

"Are you a qualified entrant?" the stranger asked.

"No." I humbly answered his question with a respectfully soft voice. It was like letting the air out of a hot air balloon. This guy was somebody. I had figured out that he was a runner and knew what he was talking about as he ran along side me. I was immediately humbled. I now understood that this guy probably had run the Marathon more than once. But at the time, I did not know with whom I was conversing on that day.

"Then please respect the hard work the official runners have done and get at the back of the pack at the starting line assuming you just want to finish," the stranger requested.

"Yes, just finish," I responded like a child who had just been caught with his hands in the cookie jar.

I then told him that I was going to take a left soon to head home. He asked me how far off Route 126 I lived, and I told him that I lived about a half mile away. He said he would go with me and swing back to 126 later.

"If I can give you some advice?" he asked.

"Please do," I replied with total respect. The pace had picked up dramatically and I now found myself chasing him from behind. The stranger knew he had me in his back pocket. I wanted desperately to talk with him, and I was digging deep to keep up. He was giving me a lesson. "Speed kills! Start out slowly and don't get sucked into the crowds and all the excitement of the day. Focus on your pace and what you are doing. When you get to the finish don't cross the line, as you will cause confusion with the officials," he stated.

"Thanks," I gasped, feeling my left hamstring beginning to cramp. "I live right up there, so I'm done." I struggled to finish the sentence, sucking in as much oxygen as my nose and wide open mouth could pull into my lungs.

"Good luck," the mystery runner called back, as he stepped up a gear and flew out of sight. I broke into a walk feeling dizzy with legs that were not my own. In anaerobic debt, I finally crouched over with my hands on my knees in a stationary position feeling like I was about to retch.

Turns out this stranger would place 1st in the Masters Division at Boston that year, competing against the best runners in the world. This was Ken Mueller and his time of 2:25 would humble me even more, being 11 years his junior. I've always wondered what pace he was running when he came up behind me, the arrogant turtle, that day we first met on the road. I would take all of Kenny's advice except for one thing. If I made it to the Prudential Center, there was no way I would not cross that finish line. Part of what he said would save me that day in April, and I have never forgotten his helpful words. While it is important to train for distance in preparing for a marathon, a runner also trains to establish paced intervals which are adjusted according to the conditions on race day.

A new sports store had opened in Millis, a town in my daily running route. I got to know the owner, Larry Olson. He was an extremely quiet person who was initially difficult to engage in conversation, but I persisted. It seemed odd to me that this introverted individual would be running a store. He did not seem to have the right personality for such a venture. I later learned that Larry was another marathoner and a friend of Kenny Mueller. In his early 30's, that year Larry would finish Boston in 18th place overall, crossing the finish line at 2:18. He would go on to be one of the best senior (over 50) runners in the world. He never really slowed down like the rest of us. Unfortunately, Larry would suddenly drop dead on a run when he was just 63. The running community and the world lost a wonderfully kind and remarkable person.

I tapered my training over the last week, reducing mileage, getting more rest and increasing the carbohydrates in my diet a few days before race day. I had recently read an article on carbo-loading and was enjoying pigging out as part of my preparation. I spent many hours lying on the couch during the weekend in anticipation of Monday's race, eating and increasing hydration. I went over in my mind what would happen that day and tossed and turned in bed at night. It was almost here. I would be taking the line at the Boston Marathon running shoulder to shoulder with the greatest runners in the entire world. As far as I was concerned, this would be like playing in the World Series, the Super Bowl, the NBA Championship and the Stanley Cup Finals all at the same time.

I read in "Runner's World" years later, that anyone who runs a marathon as their first race would have to be insane. Over the years I have looked back on this and am so happy I started with this insanity. It would become a magical day that I will never forget and could never repeat in a lifetime. This was my first high on the journey of getting "high on life" and a giant step toward hiking the Trail some day. It all made sense to me, as I viewed hiking the AT as my life's marathon.

Chapter 13
The Magic of My First Boston Marathon

"If you want to win a race, you have to go a little berserk."
– *Bill Rodgers*

I t was a day a marathoner looks for, 45 degrees with cloud covered skies. I was certain that Bill Rodgers would be smiling this morning after the inferno of the previous year's race. But to me, being a beginner, it seemed sort of cool. I kept going outside in the morning trying to figure out what I should wear. I was nervous and confused, finally selecting a cotton sweat suit. It turned out to be a big mistake!

The marathon back in 1978 was nothing like it is today. We left our place in Bellingham at 10:30 AM to make it to Hopkinton for the noon start. Karen drove me right up to Hopkinton High School about a 1/2 mile down from the starting line. This is where the majority of runners would be trying to calm their nerves, rest for a while, drink fluids, begin their personal warm-up procedures, and finally head down to the start.

I hugged and kissed Karen good-bye. I had talked her out of going into Boston for the crowded finish. Samantha, our baby daughter, was only a few months old, and Karen also had to take care of Christina. I did not want to put her or anyone else out.

"Are you sure you want to do this? You don't have to do this you know. I'll be worried about you," seemingly as nervous about the day as I was.

"I'll be fine," I said confidently. "I'll give you a call from Boston when it's over. Just understand I'll need to eat and get some fluids in me when I finish before I can get to a pay phone," I said.

As the little Chevy Chevette drove off, I questioned for an instant what I was about to attempt to do, but then it was time to prepare for this long awaited joyous day. Before heading to the start, we all used the woods and farm fields adjacent to the high school to empty our bladders and bowels to lighten the load. I would watch a television special about the Boston Marathon with my parents later that evening. It included helicopter shots of a bunch of entrants squatting in those fields.

My Mother asked horrified, "I hope you weren't one of those disgusting baboons."

"Oh no, not me, Mom," I grinningly replied. To do any physical endeavor like a marathon, athletes have to be in tune with their body right down to squatting in the fields. Not understanding the needs of the body at the appropriate time and its biorhythms can ruin six months of preparation and training on race day. I have seen it happen to athletes.

Unfortunately, I took Ken's advice and lined up at the back of the pack of 4700 runners that day. I gave those official qualifiers respect and kept out of their way. At that time Boston was the only marathon in the world that you needed to qualify for besides the Olympics. For those under 40 years of age qualifying meant completing a certified sanctioned 26.2 miler in under 2:50 within the calendar year before. This was equal to running at an average pace of under 6:29 per mile.

Then off went the starting pistol, a sound I will never forget. It was not only the start to my becoming a marathon runner; it would eventually lead to a career change to become a health educator and a track coach. I would eventually work in a city with thousands of troubled youth, hoping to inspire them to set their own goals and to believe in the power of their dreams. I certainly did not understand where the sound of that gun would lead but did feel that sound was the start of a whole new way of life. It was also the sound that would bring me that much closer to my own personal dream of hiking the AT from Georgia to Maine some day.

It took me almost five minutes to reach the painted starting line on the road as I had lined up so far back. I realized now that I had made a big mistake and would be limited to walking much of the first mile down the long hill after reaching the start line. On my left was some guy sucking wind with blubber shaking all over the place, and we had not even broken into a run yet. I started to notice others around me who clearly did not belong in any road race and figured most would not make it past the 5-mile mark. I found out quickly that under these crowded conditions I could not run anything close to my planned pace. I kept tapping people on their shoulders trying to squeeze by to pass them. It took me fifteen minutes after the gun sounded to hit the first mile marker. We entered Ashland at mile 2 and hit the 5-mile mark fifty minutes into the race finally seeing the sign "Entering Framingham."

With the Marathon being a point-to-point race, you feel like you are going some place when you keep passing through towns along the way to Boston, similar to thru-hiking through the fourteen states of the Trail from Georgia to Maine. At 7 miles, I was down to a tee shirt and those heavy, now soaking wet, sweat pants. By the time I reached the town of Natick, I could finally run without worrying about stumbling over people. There were musical bands playing on the rooftops of buildings. There were places for grabbing cups of water, sliced oranges, and ice from the supporting crowds. There was magic in the air. The beta-endorphins, norepinephrines, cortisols, adrenaline, and other hormones were really kicking in now. I felt like I was floating on air. There were runners from all parts of the world around me, the size of the crowds were increasing and their screams and encouragement fired me forward.

I quickly remembered the advice Ken had given me. "Focus on your pace and what you are doing." I toyed with the crowd, but kept cautiously in control of my emotions. Ken's warnings kept ringing in my ears and would pull me back into focus. It must be noted that I had never run in front of a crowd or for that matter run with anyone except for Ken that day in March. The excitement and experience was overwhelming; something I will cherish and hold dear forever. I was no longer the lone runner. I had literally come out of the woods and off the lonely country roads to run in the greatest footrace on the planet.

I could hear the cheers a good quarter mile away. I had read about this part of the race. I let my emotions go as the young coeds had come into the road and narrowed the race path. The Wellesley College girls were out in force! This had to be one of the greatest highs of my life. I let go and took it all in emotionally. The sound of the screams were deafening but exhilarating. It went on for another quarter mile or more. Those girls should be blessed. Their excitement and encouragement lifted me off the ground, and I so appreciated them. My pace quickened, and running became easier now. It was unbelievable how this jolt of adrenaline would carry me. I was now half way to Boston and feeling good.

Next came the infamous and dreaded hills of Newton. There are many things that make the Boston Marathon challenging. Mid-April in Boston can bring any type of weather. The race has been run in high humidity and temperatures in the high 90's. It has also been run in the cold and snow as well as in heavy winds and pouring rain. The weather conditions play a big part in the success of the day, and you never know what to expect.

My first marathon was run on the kind of day most marathoners love. I was lucky in that respect. However, I foolishly was wearing the pants of a cotton sweat suit which were getting heavier as the miles clicked away. The cotton fibers had been collecting perspiration ever since the gun went off, and now there was a drizzle in the air. When I took the turn on to Lake Street, entering the first of the Newton Hills, those pants weighed a ton. I dragged myself up that first long hill, struggling. This is actually, in my mind, the toughest hill. They say there are three hills, but there are actually four. This one is the longest and seems to go on forever because it curves to the left as you climb and you cannot see the crest. The hills are located between 17 and 21 miles, right at the point when most people are "hitting the wall." This is the point physiologically where you have depleted your reserves of carbohydrates as a fuel source for firing your tired muscles. You are now converting stored fat as your energy source or are eating away at your own body. If you have not done the required long runs activating this energy source you will hit the infamous wall and have great difficulty functioning both physically and psychologically. Next to me there was a runner wearing his white running suit with the rising sun on his chest crawling up this last hill. We were somehow communicating, he in Japanese and me in English, and I was hallucinating. What we call the "runner's high" had taken over with all the hormones flowing through my bloodstream to my brain.

A debate would start in my hallucinating mind. A voice in my head was saying, "Get rid of the pants and you'll be able to fly." Then another voice would caution, "You cannot do that because you'll be on the news, probably the national news!" You see there was one major problem; all I had on underneath was a jockstrap! I was getting sucked into the crowd with my left hamstring barking at me as I limped up "Heartbreak Hill." I was hitting the wall with those heavy leggings. The biggest crowds I had seen were screaming and the stench of beer and vomit was in the air. "Pull off those pants," the voice in my head screamed again. The crowd will love it! You'll look like Pheidippides running down the street with a loin cloth." Then what was left of the rational part of my brain kicked in, "No! Karen will leave you this time and never come back!"

This hallucinogenic debate would continue off and on, as I finally struggled over the Hills and started the long, gradual downhill into Cleveland

Circle. This was what the late Johnny "Marathon" Kelley had labeled the "Haunted Mile." This is the point in the race where many runners believe the tough hills are now over and it is all down hill to the finish. However, your energy and reserves are now spent, and cramps, muscle spasms and dehydration set in as your quad muscles now take over most of the work and pounding. As I would learn, the race starts at mile 20. Blood sugar levels would drop and rise and comfort levels would correlate with those ups and downs. A runner can feel good at mile 23 and be confident of floating in over the next 3 miles to the finish. A mile later that same runner may be struggling to finish, ready to collapse with spasms and a lack of energy. Such is the mystery and challenge of any endurance event.

"Hang in there!" the crowd would continually scream as twitching hamstrings, quads and calf muscles would dictate my pace. The CITGO sign near Fenway Park was visible in the distance. It was beckoning me on just as Mt. Katahdin calls to a thru-hiker in Maine at the end of the Trail. I knew this sign was where I wanted to go, and it looked as though I would never reach it. Those cotton sweats were weighing me down and the debate kept raging on in my head. But hanging on to hope and persistence, I would keep inching along. I finally reached Kenmore Square and knew I had just a mile to go. I now noticed that the runners ahead were suddenly disappearing from sight. As I ate up more turf, I suddenly realized they were taking a sharp right turn.

Once I took that dive to the right up Hereford Street the continuous yelling of the thickly packed crowd behind the barriers was deafening; their screams of encouragement were bouncing off the high brick buildings on this narrow street. There was a kick of endorphins blended with a shot of adrenaline giving me a lift to the mobbed finish line, which I crossed as the clock above read 3:47. As I said before, I was not taking that one bit of advice from Ken Mueller. There was no way I was not crossing that line.

I immediately came to a stop, which was all wrong, but how was I to know? The relief of finally stopping was more than I can describe, but this feeling was short lived when I started cramping all through my quads and hamstrings. Limping into the underground garage of the Prudential Center, I got what was left of the traditional beef stew. I have always treasured this moment as it all changed the next year. No stew and the Boston Marathon went the way of the rest of the commercial world into an "all about the money event." Traditions of the Marathon would be forever lost as the years went by all in the name of progress. My greatest marathon and race was this one—the first marathon and race of my life.

It would never get better than this day.

Sitting down on the pavement in a corner of the damp, cold garage to eat my warm stew and rest from my efforts felt so good. The problem was after eating, I couldn't get up! There was no strength left in those bird legs of mine and every time I struggled to rise, holding on to the wall for support, my hamstrings would tighten and knot up. Fellow runners finally noticed me groaning in pain and assisted getting me to a standing position. There were no aluminum foil reflecting sheets that year, and I was wrapped in a wool blanket handed to me at the finish. Thank God for that blanket! The plan was to call Karen and tell her I was alive and well. I wasn't quite sure of the "well" part because I had no idea of what would happen after finishing. I had no post race plan in place because my only focus had been to finish.

I had no clue of what I was in for in the hours that followed the finish. The vomiting began as I crawled out of the Prudential Center. I felt a blast of cold, damp air. The temperature had plummeted, and it was now raining. I wrapped that life saving blanket tight and limped along the sidewalk in search of a pay phone before I hit the pavement. I was shivering uncontrollably now, not understanding I was suffering from hypothermia.

Yet through it all, I found myself that day. I had a feeling of self-esteem that I had never known before in my life. I do not think I ever felt this high after a race again. It was the beginning of a new and more confident me, a happier me, and I would never be the same again. The emotions of the transformative experience I went through from February 1, 1976 to completing Boston 1978 is something I cannot adequately put into words. I would come to discover that most of the greatest moments of my life would be moments alone, those of solitude, self-discovery and of personal triumph. No one was at the finish line that day, and no one would be at most of the finish lines of the hundreds of endurance events in my life time. I wanted it that way. It was also understood that if I ever made it to the summit of Mt. Katahdin after hiking north for over 2000 miles I would also be alone. I have come to believe that many of the most meaningful moments in life are solitary moments. In those times alone with tears of happiness and pride comes the understanding of the need for sacrifice and perseverance. It is the recognition of the value of a challenge to make it through the journey of hope to the completion of a dream.

Karen was waiting for my call at her parents' home. I reported in with pride, as I could hear her Dad, the General, cheering in the background. I also explained how I was okay and feeling fine to my worried, concerned, and loving wife. As I hung up the phone, I began calculating how I had covered the last 21.2 miles in less than three hours with heavy sweat pants on, but would realize days later that the slow start probably was one of the reasons I finished at all. Ken said to start out slow and being so far back in the pack at the start forced me to do just as he had advised.

Karen would meet me at the end of the Orange Line, part of Boston's transit system, in Forest Hills. I gave her a time to pick me up, which would be long after I arrived, again not wanting to put her out. Walking down the subway stairs backwards I moved painfully toward the train. The heat felt so good when the doors shut, and I could now rest collapsing onto an empty seat. When the doors opened at the Dover Street transfer station, I crawled off that train, as quickly as a wounded Spartan could hobble, and promptly vomited on the waiting platform. The doors closed and the train sped off, as I stumbled to a bench to wait for the next train to Forest Hills. My fellow waiting riders stared at me wrapped in that wool blanket shivering alone on that bench. Anywhere else I may have been taken for a homeless drunk but this was the third week of April in Boston, and the natives know a marathoner when they see one.

I finally made it to the end of the line at Forest Hills and took one step backward at a time down the stairs to the street, as my quads were being stabbed with daggers of pain. By this time it was dark, cold and raining hard. I had over thirty minutes of time to kill waiting for Karen to arrive in a heated car. I crept into a liquor store to kill time and keep warm. How ironic to now find this place as my safe haven, a liquor store of all places. The warmth felt so good but did not last long.

"Hey buddy, if you're not buying anything you gotta move on," the store manager growled at me.

So I stumbled outside into the cold, rainy night looking for another safe shelter as my teeth chattered, my head spun from dizziness and my muscled weakened. I hoped I would not fall to the gutter. As I went in and out of stores and stood in doorways out of the rain, Karen finally pulled up. Rolling down the window, she saw my condition: the pale skin color, blue lips, the shaking and slurred speech. Bursting into tears, she said she should have been at the finish for me.

Struggling to get into the front seat, I felt the warmth of the car's heater. I was so thankful to now be warm and sitting. Then when my left hamstring cramped with a knot that would not cease, I gritted my teeth squirming, groaning and wishing that Karen was not witnessing my pain.

"What should I do?" Karen screamed.

I pushed the seat back as far as possible attempting to straighten my leg and grabbing for the knot.

"Why didn't you ask me to meet you at the finish?" she yelled.

"I didn't want to put you out with the girls and all. I had no idea this would happen," I growled with clenched teeth my muscle seizing in pain.

Through it all, I discovered who I was that day. I was on my way! Before too long, I was running three marathons a year. I also joined a running club, the "Marshfield Road Runners" after moving to Kingston, Massachusetts. I was meeting all kinds of high impact individuals. I was now running on a weekly basis with doctors, corporate vice presidents, CEOs, and an Assistant District Attorney of Plymouth County. I was meeting an assortment of wonderful, amazing people as I embarked on a journey full of adventures, challenges and happiness.

Another wake up call in my life came one day when I returned home after a Sunday run with this amazing group of people. I received a phone call informing me that one of my former high school drinking buddies had just gone over to the other side. There have been so many over the years who died early from car crashes, overdoses, suicides, and murders. There were also those who found themselves locked up in institutions or in rehab due to drug abuse

Of all the guys from that old group, I only have one friend left. He has not had a drink or a drug since June 14, 1992. That means he has over twenty-four years of sobriety and counting. He still goes to his A.A. meetings and sponsors young people. I am very proud of this guy. Sometimes I shudder to think of where I would be today, or whether I would be here at all, if it was not for that young girl who became my wife, that stranger in the woods, and the dream of hiking the Appalachian Trail.

Chapter 14
My Career as a Health Educator and a Track Coach

"The greatest good you can do for another is not just to share your riches but to reveal to him his own."
– *Benjamin Disraeli*

Through the self awareness realized by becoming a marathon runner, I had found my niche. Six months after my first Boston Marathon, I returned to the college campus to pursue a graduate degree in Health Education. I attended classes at night for the next five years and became a health educator and track coach in a city with a genuine need for someone with my life experience. Brockton, Massachusetts had become a troubled city, like many cities in America. I would coach at the biggest high school in New England, training State and New England champions, along with an All-American miler.

Motivating and mentoring thousands of adolescents would become my calling and passion in life. I aspired to give these lost and confused teens hope and to assist them in their quests to have their own personal dreams for happiness and fulfillment in life. Teaching from my heart, I came to be known as a patient young teacher, who was asked many times to take on the "troubled student." I would welcome this type of kid, whereas many others would do anything to keep them out of their classrooms. It is ironic to think that someone who had not been a great student, had unhealthy self-esteem and once had no interest in school had become a teacher with great understanding and compassion for his students. As a teacher, I was determined to use my own troubled past to fuel my passion to teach and assist those students who were depressed, rebellious, and who harbored that same dislike for the classroom.

I worked with so many kids already dismissed as "damaged goods," but still I would try. There were times when my colleagues would tell me to let one of these kids go because they believed him or her to be too far gone. It became a numbers game. There were so many abandoned kids as the years went by, and society's problems increased. The family structure in this country was falling apart. Over the course of my thirty-five year career, I witnessed the erosion of family values. It got to the point where many kids had no clue as to who they were because their own senses of self and individual identity were lost in a culture of just trying to survive from one day to the next.

By way of an example, I remember back in 1980, when Kathy, a student in my classroom, came in one morning and placed a court order on my desk with an explanation that her name was being changed to Carol. I spoke with Kathy/Carol about how this might be confusing to the other students having to suddenly address her as Carol and not Kathy. She did not seem to understand the point to our conversation, explaining that her mother's new boyfriend liked the name Carol. This was over thirty years ago, but it is no different in many respects today. Many of today's kids have no family structure and no knowledge of their roots. Millions of our children are confused, feel lost, and have no idea of who they are and where they fit in this world.

I certainly could relate to their pain and torment, and my career became my love. Teaching was never just a job. It was a way to see myself and understand the pain so many of our young people are experiencing. It was never just about the classroom and the books sitting on their desks. Being more than a teacher and a coach, my greatest satisfaction would come from being a mentor trying to save lives, as mine was saved when I met that stranger in the woods in the summer of 1975. So it is with pleasure and pride that I tell you about Robert Morales.

After many years of absence from the track in order to spend more time raising my daughters, I had returned to coaching. That first day of practice was a brisk late fall afternoon as I stood at the top of the football bleachers looking over the 90 plus high school runners as they circled the track. I always started practice with this four lap warm-up mile. I had explained to the hopeful athletes that this was not a race and that I might yell down asking them to shout out their names to me. By doing this day after day in the beginning of the season, I could begin to assess each athlete's bio-mechanics and in which events they would be most successful, a mile or a sprint.

My eyes became fixated that first day on a young man moving with such flow, grace and with a naturally perfect running form. He floated with effortless ease through space, and I immediately approached him after coming down from the top tier asking,

"What's your name?"

"Robert Morales."

"What year are you?"

"Junior."

"Have you run track before?"

"Yes, sir."

"What have you been running?"

"The 300."

"Really, what else?"

"Just the 300."

"Have you been on the track team in the spring?"

"Yes, sir."

"What was your event?"

"I ran the 400."

"Anything else?"

I couldn't believe any coach would do this to a kid. There seemed to be no endurance building events, no "peaking" and any runner would become bored and stale running the same distance over and over again. I realized right away he wasn't a 300 or 400 runner to begin with anyway. I asked him about his best times. Not surprisingly, his clockings were mediocre and I left him saying, "I couldn't keep my eyes off you. You move like a deer, you're a runner, but your best distance is not the 300 or 400 meters."

This is the way it started with Robert. He told me years later that he had thought I was just some crazy old guy who didn't know what he was talking about that day. Ten years later he understood, and we were the best of friends. He was a kid looking for a mentor to help fulfill a pipe dream. I had been impressed with Robert immediately that first day, not just with his God-given ability and talent to run, but his politeness. I checked around and found that everyone from the principal to the custodian liked Robert Morales. He was a kid with a smile on his face and a soft spoken manner. This was a young man with a burning desire to reach a dream. I knew he had inborn talent and seemed to be coachable for age 16.

It was now time to see if he had the third component to become a champion. He had never run anything but the 300 or 400 meters. So the first meet of the season I threw him into the 1000 meters. Instead of running one and a half laps around the 200 meter Reggie Lewis oval in Roxbury, Massachusetts, he would have to circle it five times. He shot out like a missile before the smoke cleared the starting gun. I stood nervously hoping he had the third component necessary to be that top runner. On the last lap his knees began to buckle. That initial killer pace was taking its toll. His first place finish dropped to second and on the last straight away he found himself battling for third. He stumbled out of his lane, but continued to reach for that finish line not giving up on placing. Little did he know he was already disqualified (DQ'd) for stepping out of his lane. He was now running and competing with nothing left but intestinal fortitude and sheer will. His rubbery legs gave way and he slid belly first over the finish line ripping his Brockton High singlet running jersey and bleeding from his chest. I climbed down from the stands with great excitement asking him, "So how do you like the 1000?"

In anaerobic debt struggling to stand and to get air into his lungs he managed a weak, "What? Do you hate me?"

"Walk around, get the oxygen back into your body, get yourself a drink, and see me after you cool down. I'll be sitting up in the stands."

After a good fifteen minutes he climbed up to see me with a nervous smile on his face. I asked him to sit down next to me.

"Robert, it takes three things to be a champion. What are they?" Confused at the questioning and my motives, he finally answered.

"Talent."

"What else?"

After a short pause, "Effort."

"Good and what's the third?" None of the young athletes ever get this one.

"The last one is the toughest to find in a high school kid, coach-ability," I explained.

"Most kids your age are too immature to be coached. They read an article in some running magazine and think they know it all. You have amazing talent and move like a deer. I think you're also mature enough to be coached, and tonight I found out you have the other necessity to be a champion. I watched very closely how you ran that 1000. You had no idea of pace and ran on emotion and guts. Did you know you were DQ'd?"

"What?"

"You stepped out of your lane. I don't care. I was looking for the fire and guts of a champion, and kid you've got it! Now we can go to work and make you the champ you are, but only if you are willing to give your heart and soul to this old coach. Do you want it?"

"Yes, sir, coach!"

I put out my hand and he gave me that nice firm hand shake. Our pact was made that evening in Roxbury to take it as far as we could go.

He bought into my program and worked like a beast on the track, on the snow covered roads of New England that winter and in the weight room. I cautiously worked him up to the 600 meters that first winter, and he finished the indoor track season on the podium, as one of the top runners in the state. We became close, and he constantly talked about his dream of being the first in his family to graduate from college. I took the time to check out his academics and curriculum. I found he wasn't even college-tracked.

I spoke with his special education teacher, Mr. Doyle, "Listen, this kid's different. He puts in a tremendous amount of effort, and I think if we could get him college-tracked he just might do it. He has a reading comprehension problem, but with his dedication to his studies, I believe he can overcome this handicap."

Many high schools in America have one guidance counselor for every five hundred students. Most counselors are so over stretched with that many students that it is difficult to give any of them the time and real guidance they need. With Brockton High being the biggest high school in New England, it was easy to get lost in the crowd. Even before entering high school, Morales had been tagged as "special ed" due to his delayed reading skills. He was just another kid falling through the cracks of the system.

"Robert Morales has been talking to me constantly about his dream of being the first in his family to graduate from college. I'd like to see this young man placed in the college prep program." I explained to the Guidance Office.

"You're wasting your time. Robert Morales is not college material." I was told.

"So do you want me to go back and tell a 16-year-old boy that his dream is over? I don't care if this kid has to go to night school for ten years. He wants to give this a shot. Please give him his chance." I replied, keeping my tone pleasant. Through persistence and diplomatic means, Robert finally got placed in the college prep curriculum.

Another runner, Mike Gomes, was a sophomore and Robert's rival on the track. They both had been 300 runners. But by the spring track season I had coached them to run the 800. My plan was to work with these two hard working athletes and combine them with a two miler and a miler, the latter, Kevin Gill, happened to be an All-American, to make up a 4X800 Relay Team. Mike and Robert competed in practice on the track, the roads and in the weight room. They were close friends. As it happened, Mike Gomes was also academically number one in his class. He would go on to Harvard after graduation.

"Mike, I need to speak to you about something very important and in complete confidence. Can I talk to you alone, and no one else will know?" I asked one afternoon after practice.

"Sure coach, what do you need?" he asked.

"Mike, we got Morales college-tracked, and the kid has a dream of being the first in his family to go off to college and graduate."

"That's great, coach!"

"Mike, you got everything going for you in life. You're talented in so many ways. Morales doesn't have all this, but he can run like a deer."

"You don't have to tell me, Coach. I wish I could catch him."

"I want you to encourage him in his school work. Talk academics when you guys are out doing your road work and in the weight room together. Check his homework. I don't want you to do his assignments for him or anything, just help the kid along a little."

"You got it, coach. Let's get him into college!"

The hardest thing to find in any sport in high school is a good 800 meter runner. I was looking for four I could mold into a relay team. Here I had two sophomores and two juniors to work with for another year. I hoped to have four solid coachable runners by next track season. It's hard to find one good 800 runner, and I had found four who were mature enough to work the program. The following year, when Robert was a senior, we went on to win the New England Championship in the winter. During the spring track seasons these kids set an all time state record in Massachusetts and went on to place in the top ten in Nationals.

Robert Morales made the honor roll his senior year and got into four colleges. He went off to the University of Massachusetts and graduated with honors. He then went on to receive his Masters degree in Criminal Justice. I had been invited by his mother to attend his undergraduate graduation ceremony as a surprise to him. While his Mom was outside taking pictures of her proud son in his cap and gown, Robert turned to me and asked, "Coach, you know who I'm going to show this diploma to first?"

"No, who?"

"The Guidance Office back at Brockton High."

"Why's that?"

"At first they laughed when I said that I wanted to go to college."

Disgustingly, I stepped away saying, "Really."

Should I or shouldn't I, I thought. No, he's a man now and I returned, "So they laughed at you too."

"They laughed at you too, coach? That's all wrong."

"Robert, you're a big boy now and understand there's a lot of wrong in the world. I think you should go back and show them your college diploma. Go back there in a suit and tie and be polite about it."

"Coach, why are you telling me to be polite? I'm always polite," he said with his face looking confused. I smiled. I hadn't needed to say anything. The kid didn't even understand what I was getting at because his mind never went that way. His thoughts were never negative and resentful.

"I guess you fell in love with my son because he was such a good runner," his Mother said to me one day.

"No, I fell in love with your son for another reason," I returned.

"What's that?" Mrs. Morales puzzlingly asked.

"He's the most polite young man I've ever met in my long career as a teacher and a coach. He had a dream of going to college. It was my pleasure to work with your boy. He works hard, is determined, disciplined and had a burning desire to make his dream come true."

"Mr. Cook, you came along at the right time in life for my boy. Most all his friends are either dead, on drugs or in jail." his mother said with tears in her eyes.

"Don't sell yourself short. You did a wonderful job as his Mom nurturing and raising this polite, hard working young man."

Robert Morales is like "Bruce Wayne/Batman." He has seen too much tragedy and lost potential in the city streets, and he has buried too many of his classmates. He wants to help others who are lost and confused find their own dreams and ways out of the darkness. Robert believes in "justice for all."

Robert is presently a member of the Philadelphia Police Department. His personal dream now is to be in the FBI. Whichever branch of law enforcement he serves in will be the better for having this amazing man among its ranks.

Chapter 15
My Arrogance and Ignorance as a Hiker

"Pride goeth before destruction and a haughty spirit before a fall." – *Proverbs 16:18*

It was ten years after that encounter with the pioneer thru-hiker, one of the first to ever hike the Trail from Georgia to Maine, and I was into some heavy duty hiking myself. I was the worst type of hiker imaginable, arrogant and ignorant. I thought, what's the big deal about hiking 15 miles in the White Mountains of New Hampshire? After all, I told myself, I am a marathon runner!

Nick Howe's masterpiece, "Not Without Peril," is a compilation of stories of hikers who lost their lives in these beautiful, rugged mountains. It is a series of short stories chronicling some of the many deaths in this region. It should be required reading for anyone before they ever set foot in these mountains. He did a splendid job demonstrating how arrogance and ignorance spells death. I feel lucky that I am not a chapter in the pages of his book. For a slow learner like me, it took not one, but two life-threatening episodes to become humbled and to truly start my education as a hiker. Running marathons and hiking are two different things, and it would take some time for me to come to this realization.

If you run into difficulty during a marathon, such as an injury, dehydration, or sickness, there are first aid stations, people around, phones and nearby hospitals. Hiking solo in the Whites, as I did, you are on your own. When taking the lone wolf approach to hiking, it's just you and the elements. So if something goes wrong, you have only your own wits and skills to survive. If you have a serious problem you'd better understand how to handle it, or you risk becoming the mountain's next casualty. Your body may be found in the spring. There have been individuals who ventured into these mountains, who never came out and who have never been found.

It was Columbus Day weekend 1984, a very popular three-day weekend in October for hikers. "Bagging" 4000 footers was a goal that many hikers attempt to achieve in these mountains. My goal was to "conquer" as many such mountains as I possibly could that weekend. Inconceivably, with no map, no compass and no real knowledge of the trails, I took off at a gallop to climb Crawford Path. There was no note of my hiking plan left on the windshield of my old pickup, although I had given Karen and my older brother Steve a quick outline of where I would be headed. The weather was crisp with clear skies.

Being a frugal Yankee at heart I had on my back one of those little packs in which to tote around an infant. I had it lined with a trash bag. Basically all I was carrying was a good sleeping bag that my brother, Steve, had loaned me, power bars, water and a few essentials. I charged up Mt. Clinton and then over to the summit of Mt. Eisenhower. There I found at least a dozen hikers lunching on the summit in the sun. I wolfed down a raisin and peanut butter sandwich on whole wheat that I had made that morning, as I enjoyed the view and the warmth of the sun.

"Hey, is that Washington I see over there?" I asked the group.

"Yes, that's Mt. Washington," someone replied.

"How far off is it?" I inquired.

"You're not heading over there at this time of the day are you?" a hiker asked.

"No big deal. I'll be there in no time," I boldly shouted out running away from the group. I can only imagine what this group of hikers thought that day. Still a slow learner, I needed direct experience to be humbled and to learn some respect for these mountains. That was to come all too soon.

I charged over Mt. Franklin, bagged Mt. Monroe, and then went on to tackle the "Big Daddy," Mt. Washington. I read the sign about the highest winds ever recorded on earth on the summit. It read that on April 12, 1934 the winds had topped out at 231 miles per hour. That sign did not register with me. I filled my belly with as much water as I could hold and then my water bottle at the cafeteria on the summit before running off to tackle Mt. Clay next. Then I was off to Mt. Jefferson. As I came off the summit of Jefferson, daylight was waning as the sun was setting.

The cold was beginning to set into my tiring body.

I was alone but in the distance could see a group of hikers moving along together with their headlamps illuminating the growing darkness. I wanted company for the evening and figured they were probably headed for some campsite. I struggled to keep them in view cautiously making the descent. I felt sure that they knew where they were going. I finally caught up with them.

"Where are you guys headed?" I asked.

"The Perch," they answered.

"What's that?" I inquired.

"A three sided shelter and campsite area," someone said.

This sounded good to me. I liked the idea of having a place to rest with people around. I felt comfortable and secure knowing I was in good hands and would find a place to bed down for the night. I followed the other hikers and welcomed their slower pace to wind down from my day as we made our way to the Perch.

Upon arrival I found out that this crew and others had already set up camp. The three-sided shelter was full and not a piece of flat ground was to be found. It was now as dark as midnight and cold, and this place did not look appealing for my weary bones. Someone told me there was another shelter maintained by the Randolph Mountain Club called the Log Cabin about a mile away. It was cold standing there, and I decided to move on, as the Log Cabin sounded like a better option anyway. All I could picture was a nice cabin with four walls, a roof and a fired-up wood stove. I would find out years later that it was nothing of the kind.

I walked alone down the path for quite some time with my little flashlight in hand. I suddenly came to a fork; not knowing which way to go. I debated what to do and finally decided to go back to the Perch, before I got lost out there with a dead flashlight. A few hikers were still up as I rolled out my brother's sleeping bag on the hilly ground. I put on every article of clothing I had and was ready to bed down for the night. A hiker came over and strung a line between trees and placed a small tarp over my sleeping area for some added warmth and protection from rain. I thanked him for his kindness and crawled into my sleeping bag chomping on a power bar. The temperature plummeted, and I shivered all night. My knees, lower back, ankles and whole body ached. My muscles were cold and sore. It was a sleepless night I will never forget. Hypothermia was on my mind, and this part of the adventure was not making me happy.

As soon as dawn broke, I decided I better get up and start moving.

My head hit the low hanging tarp and sheets of ice rained down upon me. The vapor from my breath had frozen solid over night. I struggled to get to my feet with the pain in my shaking legs and body. Some hikers were already up cooking some hot food and they were all staring at the shivering ill-equipped fool on the ground. It was humiliating.

"Hey, you want some hot oatmeal with raisins?" someone yelled over.

"Thanks for the offer, but I'm fine and am heading out," I shouted back with foolish pride. Shaking all over, I slowly fumbled to pack up. Out of no where, a hiker handed me a bowl of that hot porridge and insisted I eat it before heading off.

"Thanks, I appreciate it," I said with chattering teeth. It really hit the spot. It felt so good to get some warmth in my freezing body. I gobbled it down and headed out attempting to bring some warmth to my body. "Just move fool, move. I've got to get the motor running to get warm," I told myself. I moved, on to the second highest mountain in the northeast, Mt. Adams, my maternal family namesake. After a good thirty minutes, I started generating some heat and my shaking finally ceased as the sun was also doing its job. Although exhausted from yesterday's effort and the lack of sleep on that cold ground, I was still moving along. I hit the large cairn of rocks known as, "Thunderstorm Junction" and began the final ascent. Alone on the summit of Mt. Adams, I sat to rest my bones in the sun before heading off toward my next challenge, Mt. Madison. I sat there with weary legs and absolutely no reverence for these rugged mountains. It was about to all come tumbling down.

I would now learn that the descent is much more treacherous than the ascent. If you take a spill running up a mountain the fall will probably land you flat on your face, but on the down slope you will continue to bounce around on the rocks until your momentum finally ceases. The summits of the Presidential Range are covered with slabs and boulders of hard granite, the result of glacier movement during the Ice Age. The footing is horrendous. I wondered how many 4000 footers I could do today on these legs as I ran off the peak of Mt. Adams.

Years later a doctor explained to me that a joint will give way when it is over stressed, as a natural defense to protect itself from further overuse and damage. My ankles, knees, hips and back were aching from yesterday's hike, compounded by a lack of sleep in shivering cold last night. I charged down Mt. Adams still filled with bravado, maybe not as much as yesterday, but still an arrogant fool who had not yet had enough to bring himself to reason. As I said earlier, twisting an ankle or coming up with an injury while running a marathon is not life threatening, but out here in the wilds alone it could mean never making it home. I was about to find this out.

My left knee buckled and twisted on a jagged piece of billion-year-old granite. Flying into the air, my momentum from the downhill run turned my body into the sphere of a pin ball machine. I was bouncing around from side to side off giant slabs of granite finally coming to an abrupt halt when my torso slammed into a hunk of hard rock. As I laid there motionless, a lightening bolt of excruciating pain shot through my body. I let out a blood curdling scream heard by no one. It could just as easily have been my head instead of my torso that hit that last boulder. Once again dumb luck was a factor in my survival.

Struggling to sit up, I was now aware that the most critical damage was to my left knee. Had it been to the cruciate ligaments, any further movement would have been next to impossible. With four ligaments to support the vulnerable knee joint, the two cruciates, which criss-cross under the knee cap, are the most important for support and lateral movement. The collateral ligaments situated on the inside and outside of the joint are not as important to mobility, and I knew it was the outside lateral collateral ligament which was damaged. I attempted to organize my thoughts and to pull myself together. As I sat there alone, realizing what I had done, my prayers now were to get up and to get down to a road as soon as possible.

If I had acted rationally, I would have hunkered down where I was and bundled up to stay warm. It was Columbus Day weekend, and someone would certainly have been climbing this popular peak that could have helped and guided me in the proper direction. Remember, I had foolishly set out with no compass or map of the network of trails. My arrogance had now vanished, and the sun was still in the eastern sky. I had started my descent toward Mt. Madison when I fell and had now managed to limp along until I came to a sign pointing down. It read the Buttress Trail. My moronic adventure suddenly was about to go in another direction.

I just wanted to get down, so I followed the Buttress descent. The problem was I had no clue that I was heading into a restricted wilderness area of some 5552 acres of National Forest. This was the Great Gulf Wilderness, the deep valley between Mts. Washington, Adams, and Jefferson. It is part of the National Wilderness Preservation system, established in 1964, and a permit was required for its use at the time. It is an isolated area and I was alone with an injury, all because of arrogance, ignorance and a lack of respect for these mountains. I would discover just how dangerous a situation I was in once I reached the valley's bottom.

Eventually finding myself below the tree line, I began to search as I crawled along at a turtle's pace, for a small branch to make a splint. I finally found the piece I needed and broke it into two fairly flat splints. I ripped my bandana into two strips and tied them onto the inside and outside of my knee for support. As walking became somewhat easier and less painful, I would continue to adjust and tighten the straps as I descended.

If I had known the trails I would have come off Mt. Adams and headed toward the closed Madison Hut and then descended the gradual slope of Valley Way to Route 2. This is also a very popular trail, and I would have certainly seen people all day to help. So following the Buttress descent was mistake number one. I would now make another, not understanding the area. Continuing along the Great Gulf Trail would have taken me to Pinkham Base Camp and Route 16, but I came upon a sign directing me to the more familiar sounding Mt. Jefferson. Sitting on a rock to rest, frustrated, in pain and totally disoriented, Mt. Jefferson seemed like the better option to me.

The Trail goes up the knee of Mt. Jefferson Ravine. Ice and snow can still be found in summer here, and it is steep with a capital "S." The ascent was a relief after all the downhill hiking, and it may have been part of my reasoning to go up. After climbing for quite some time, I came upon wooden ladders bolted into the sheer vertical cliffs. I should have turned around, but had hiked for some time and refused to retrace my steps. Anger and stubbornness were now added to my frustration, and I proceeded on by doing pull ups, dragging my bad leg as I climbed to the next rung. Was there some reason the name of this monstrous trail was named Six Husbands? Panic brought my progress to a crawl, as I listened to the whistle blast in the distance of the Cog Railway. That sound had been beckoning to me all day. In my disillusioned mind, I believed that if I could reach it in time some tourist would give me a ride down Mt. Washington. I now had a mission and fought on wondering where everyone else was given that it was Columbus Day.

Taking a break I evaluated the little food I had left and began to ration, thinking I may be in these mountains for another night. I realized everyone would be heading home as it was the end of the long weekend. I had to make it out before dark. I started to think about my wife and daughters, especially little 6-year-old Samantha. Would she be too young to remember me? Would I see her grow up, graduate from high school? I kept telling myself not to slip or fall or it would be over for me. I felt like a stupid jerk and kept up the conversation in my head. "Come on hang in there. You are going home tonight to hug Karen, Chrissy and Sam." I could feel myself going into a panic and had to tell myself constantly to relax.

I was elated breaking tree line and continued searching the open distance for another hiker. It was getting late in the day, and I thought that everyone had already descended and headed home. Fear set in as I was still all alone, as I had been all day. Would I be lying down on these rocks exposed to the elements tonight? Would I freeze to death? Would I ever see my little girls again?

Walking for a time, I finally saw two hikers in the distance. I began screaming, but there was no response. I scrambled over the rocks, as fast as possible hoping they would hear my cries for help. No luck. I then noticed one of them stop and look my way only to turn and continue hiking in another direction away from me. I hobbled at a quicker pace with as much caution as possible. His partner looked back, and I began frantically waving my arms shouting with all I had left.

Thankfully, they started moving quickly my way. After not seeing anyone all day, it was comforting to meet these other hikers at last, and I hoped to stay with them and hike to a road. However, these two Canadians were on national holiday and would be staying the night. After evaluating my situation and listening to my pleas to get out, they suggested moving along the flat Gulfside Trail to try to reach the Cog Railway. If I could reach the track at an extremely steep descent point, the train would be moving so slowly I might be able to jump on the back of it.

My hope was to reach the last train run of the day down the mountain. On the way toward the beckoning train whistle that had been teasing me all day, I decided that if I missed the train I would walk the tracks in the dark to the parking lot. Could I make the train? I moved along in the remaining sunshine of the day with all I had left, thinking how different things had been just twenty-four hours ago. Emotionally, I had taken a 180-degree turn from arrogance to total humility and now just wanted to get home to my family.

After some time I could see the tracks but no train. I moved more quickly, finally reaching the tracks. I began looking for a very steep area in hopes of hopping the train. I settled in to wait and see if I could now hitch a ride to safety. It was late in the day and darkness was closing in quickly. I heard the whistle from up above and knew I was in luck. The old steam locomotive was slowly approaching and I planned my leap to see my family again. As it reached me, it was moving so slowly there was no problem grabbing onto a hand rail of that last train. Hopping aboard I received a stern cold look from the conductor, but he looked away seeing the crude splints on my leg. The only way I would have ever left this life boat to safety and home would have been to be physically thrown off. The conductor signaled me into the car. With the seats all taken I stood amongst the tourists and all of them were gawking at this hobbling "hiker."

"What happened to you?" a tourist asked.

I humbly answered, "I fell coming off Mt. Adams this morning." But then things changed when a young couple began talking to me.

"Are you parked or is someone meeting you in the parking lot?" the guy asked.

"No, I'm parked miles away in Crawford Notch," I answered. We talked for a while, and then they offered me a ride to my pickup.

I now understood that marathon running and hiking are two very different things. One false step can change everything in an instant, and your own resources may be all you have to survive. Yet inconceivably, I would have to be "kicked in the teeth" one more time to understand with true humility that no one ever "conquers" a mountain. The only explanation for arrogant hikers to ever make it to a summit is because the "Mountain Gods" looked kindly upon them that day.

Chapter 16
I Nearly Die in the "Whites"

"Do not go gentle into that good night but rage, rage against the dying of the light." – *Dylan Thomas*

The weather had been good to me during the Columbus Day episode of 1984. I realize today that if it had been cold and wet, that weekend could have had a tragically different outcome. Weather is everything, and it would take another horrifying hike for me to finally get it. The result would change me forever from an arrogant, ignorant hiker into one of total humility and respect. I came to realize that no matter how much you know about hiking, there is always more to learn.

Brockton's Westside was predominantly Jewish, which meant there was no school during the Jewish holidays of September 1987. As Karen flipped the calendar to September, she saw hiking written in all four boxes, September 24th – 27th.

"What's this?" She asked.

"Oh, I don't have school those days because of the Jewish holidays," I told her.

"You're kidding me. You have Thursday and Friday off from work? She inquired.

"Yes, it's great." I replied.

"You can't just take off hiking for four days," she declared.

My definition of a good marriage can be summarized in one word, compromise. We debated the situation for a while and decided to spend all day Thursday doing whatever Karen wanted to do. I tagged along for a day wandering through gift shops, taking a walk along the water in Plymouth, and touring some of the historic parts of the town. We rounded out our day taking in a movie and having dinner at her favorite restaurant.

I planned to set off early from home on Friday morning and then hit the trail after a four-hour drive to the Whites. My early start was delayed as Karen did not want to see me leave. So we ended up going out to breakfast before I left.

"Please be careful and call me as soon as you get out of those mountains," Karen nervously said, as we hugged and kissed each other and said our good-byes.

"Don't worry, I'll be fine. I'll call you when I get out sometime late on Sunday," I reassured her. The late start also put me in Boston's commuter traffic that Friday morning causing a further delay in my arrival in New Hampshire to begin my hiking weekend.

In my hiking excursions to date, I had yet to make it over to the Randolph Mountain Club's cabin, Gray Knob, so that was my destination for the day. I planned to take a long, tough hike to Gray Knob figuring it would be a good workout. After all, I had increased my running distance to 80 miles a week. I was running doubles four days a week, and most days averaged around 15 miles. Hiking in from Dolly Copp Road by way of the Pine Link Trail would be no big deal. So I thought.

It was just before 1:00 PM when I started off from my parked truck. It was several hours later than I had planned to set off, so I moved along quickly to make up for lost time. I was wearing old blue jeans and carrying an exterior framed back pack that I had purchased on sale a few years earlier. My older brother Steve always had the best gear, and he had lent me his winter sleeping bag. I was feeling pretty good and secure about this weekend's hike. The fall foliage of yellow, orange, and red leaves was mixed in with the various greens of the coniferous trees. It was gorgeous. It felt refreshing as I hustled along with a chill in the air. I had a spring in my step and was feeling so free. I felt the need for this time to recharge my batteries after working with troubled adolescents in the city.

After about an hour, a light rain began to fall. I thought it was nothing to be concerned about at the time. Gaining elevation, I had reached the split to the Howker Trail on my climb toward the summit of Mt. Madison when the light rain turned to sleet. Again I reassured myself that it was no big deal. I told myself that I was fit and strong and could move along more quickly to get to Gray Knob cabin for the first time. I was looking forward to an adventurous long weekend, and I so wanted to see this old cabin that I had read was built in 1905. The sleet picked up and now was mixed with snow. It was only September 25th and I convinced myself that this weather would not last long. As I broke out past the tree line, I was pushed back by a blast of powerful wind and cold. I moved on with determination and that marathon spirit.

Summiting Mt. Madison started to become a struggle into the wind. I figured I had better move quickly off the cone and down to the now fogged in Madison Hut. If things got hairy, I thought I would jump into the hut and get warm and dry. I also figured that there would be the option to hunker down here for the night if things did not let up. I kept telling myself that I would be fine. I "reasoned" that I was a hardcore marathoner.

Ice began sticking to my blue jeans, and I brushed it off with the gloves I found at a ski area after it closed last year, always the frugal Yankee. I was happy to have these nice gloves on that day thinking how warm my hands were feeling. I only wished I had something for my face, as bullets of ice pellets were drilling off my nose, chin and cheeks. I pulled my hat down tighter toward my eyes. I was afraid I might lose a contact lens so I resorted to squinting to see ahead through the snow and ice.

It seemed like I was in a wind tunnel as I approached the top of the mountain, obviously not understanding updrafts at this point in my hiking life. Once I made it to the peak, the wind began moving my body around and staying steady on my feet was becoming impossible. Suddenly, a strong gust threw me to the ground, which freaked me out. I steadied myself holding on to a hunk of granite to get back on two feet. The wind was coming in strong and I moved along slowly and as sure footed as I could trying to make headway off the cone. The updrafts had probably increased the wind speed by at least another 20 miles per hour. I knew I had to get off this cone and move down toward the hut.

I crouched down like a football lineman to search for better balance. Each step became more dangerous, as the placement of my feet never seemed to be where I wanted them with the wind shifting me around. Another gust hit and took me down really hard. I caught myself just before my head would have otherwise hit a boulder. I knew that I had to get down off this mass of granite boulders. Almost on all fours and holding on wherever I could, I finally started to make the descent in the mist and fog toward Madison Hut.

I would be so happy and relieved to get into the warmth and out of this wind and pelting ice. I started to move easier and hit some little spruce trees about thigh high and the trail seemed to narrow out. There was now a little protection from that wind but not from those pellets striking me continuously in the face. I kept asking myself how I could protect my face from all this wind and ice. When I could, I used one of my hands to cover my face, but needed both most of the time to hold on to rocks or spruce bushes to steady my progress. As I got closer to the hut the wind speed continually dropped and walking became easier. It was a relief to get off that mountain and I could feel myself calming down. I would soon be protected from the elements in Madison Hut.

Through the blowing and moving mist I caught a glimpse of the shelter. Ah, warmth and comfort was close at hand or so I thought. As I struggled closer, I asked myself why there were no lights on during this dark and dreary day in late September. It was like a dagger in my heart when I finally could see that the windows were boarded up and that the hut was closed for the winter. "This cannot be." I said to myself. It was only September 25th. Again, ignorance would play its ugly card; I did not know that Madison Hut had been closed for the season weeks ago.

I looked for a place to crawl under the building to get out of the cold wind and the now heavier snow and ice. I walked around the hut looking for a place to take refuge. I crouched down to get my thoughts together and to re-gather myself to ward off my panic. Should I huddle in this corner and spend the night on the hard ground in this storm? Should I attempt to move on into the wind and decreasing visibility to try to find this place called Gray Knob? Should I retrace my steps to the summit of Mt. Madison and attempt to make it back to my truck?

Again my ignorance of the area and trails combined with my arrogant refusal to bring a map would cost me dearly. I could have used Valley Way, a tame trail, to Route 2 and safety. But as it stood, all I could do was contemplate my options. There was no way I was going back up Mt. Madison in this raging storm, and the thought of staying here in this dark cold gloom was not appealing. I ate some food, drank some water and rested for a few minutes before moving into the wind and pelting ice to search for Gray Knob cabin. Poor visibility was becoming a major factor to my survival. I had to make it to Gray Knob before dark or I would be in serious danger with the temperature dropping. How much longer could it snow? It was still September!

Just like before a marathon, I began to psych myself up to face the battle I was about to confront. It would be a battle for my life. "What have you gotten yourself into this time, Cookie?" As I posed this question to myself, I took out a bandana and tied it to cover my face thinking I must look like a bank robber from an old western movie. Now only my eyes were exposed. If I had only equipped myself with hiking goggles, things would have been different. But I was unaware that such goggles even existed at this stage of my hiking life.

The battle began in this raging wind, snow and ice and all my mental strength as a marathon runner would become my greatest ally. I struggled into the wind and made the ascent to climb out of the Madison Hut area. From past hikes I knew that the Gulfside Trail would soon level off and it would become a relatively flat walk across a boulder field of billion-year-old granite. It would be like this all the way to Thunderstorm Junction, a place with which I had become acquainted. My immediate goal was to make it to this familiar ground and then to find Gray Knob cabin.

I struggled up and out of the crater to that flat trail, sheltering my eyes with my hand and still squinting so I would not lose a contact lens. If this ever happened given my eyesight, visibility would be cut down further in this soupy mess of a storm, and I would be in even more serious trouble. Moving along in the steady headwind was difficult, but it became even more dangerous when there would be a sudden gust or during a momentary let up of wind. If the wind speed had remained constant I could have pushed forward into it accordingly, but these sudden changes of wind speed would suddenly throw me forward or back. Staying upright was next to impossible. It had become a game of widening my stance and crouching at times to stay on my feet and not be thrown to the hard ground. I moved as slowly and as cautiously as I could across this flat area, and I could finally make out the ten foot high pile of rocks, known as Thunderstorm Junction. I felt the excitement of making it this far toward Gray Knob.

Several trails meet at Thunderstorm Junction, and I searched the posted signs to send me in the direction of Gray Knob. After some time, I found the wooden sign reading the words Gray Knob. I was elated and started moving along, as the snow piled up on the ground in this raging wind. It was not just the gray of the day and the falling snow that made visibility so difficult. The snow was swirling off the ground in this heavy wind. How long could this last? It would also be dark soon. I looked at my watch and realized I had not seen anyone for almost five hours. No one else was stupid enough to be out in this storm.

After a short time, the trail split. There was a Randolph Mountain Club sign signifying two trails, Lowe's Path and the Spur Trail. I took a moment to decide which trail to take. Again, ignorance would play into my calamitous hike. If I had taken the Spur Trail I would have been into the protection of trees within 3/4 of a mile, but it was a tenth of a mile longer. Being uneducated, I chose to take the shorter Lowe's Path to Gray Knob which totally exposed me to the elements the whole way.

I moved on into the cold wind to continue the battle for my life. Visibility was waning. As the darkness deepened, and the freezing cold was beginning to envelop me into its death trap, I began to feel myself panicking and my breathing became erratic. Taking long deep breaths I tried to calm myself by saying that I was okay and that I was almost there. Over and over, I chanted, "Hang in there, and keep moving forward." I was working my head as much as my now trembling body. My blue jeans had become frozen to my thighs and I understood the signs of hypothermia. I was slowly going down for the count. Again I resorted to talking to myself, "Keep moving! You're one tough son of a bitch! Come on, Cookie, you can do it. Think of your kids! Karen! You're only thirty-seven. You have a great life to fight for so you keep moving!" I started doing what I would always do in the tough last 3 miles of a marathon. I would hold every breath for an instant and on the exhale say the word "calm" out loud to myself. "Work the head, baby, work the head," I said repeatedly. I could now fully understand how people panic and lose control of rational thought.

I was working with all I had to keep my sanity at this point; squinting and praying not to lose a contact lens. "Keep going until you can't see anymore. You've got that winter bag Steve let you borrow. You'll be fine. Just don't get off the trail. People die because they get lost. You're still on the trail. Keep following the cairns. It has to stop snowing soon. It's September for God sake! How much more can it snow?" I stumbled and in my weakened hypothermic state the wind took me hard to the ground. I fought to get up, but the wind threw me down again, this time on my side. I again realized I was in the fight of my life and there was no way I would let a September storm win. I crawled on all fours to a boulder for support and managed to get both feet on the ground. I crouched down in that football stance again and made it to the next rock. Pushing against the wind from boulder to cairn became my goal in the challenge to make headway. I fought with all I had left in me.

Suddenly the trail started descending. I was heading down. At least I was moving on to lower elevation and hopefully there would be less wind. Having trouble walking properly in my uncoordinated hypothermic condition, I finally came upon a small spruce bush, then another. I felt a jolt of adrenaline and with tears in my eyes I told myself that I would live. As I descended further, the spruce became more numerous and taller. I told myself that I would be able to put my bag amongst the bushes and huddle under them for protection. I held on to bushes for support in the wind, moving with renewed life and hope. I came upon an open area of ledge and questioned which way to go.

In the blowing wind and snow I noticed another trail heading into the taller spruces, I stepped into the protection of the trees and walked a short distance. My God, the scent of a wood stove! It would be like a Hilton. The scent of burning wood became stronger as I took a few more steps down the trail in the trees. Tears of joy ran down my face and my pace became easier. It was Gray Knob, an enclosed little cabin with a wood stove burning! Warmth, protection, and life were waiting for me.

I pulled my trembling body up the few steps to the door and tried to open it, but it was a struggle given my loss of strength and in my frozen condition. I banged my shoulder against the door and fumbled with the handle at the same time. The door sprung open. There was the caretaker; I practically fell into his arms. Laughing out loud, he yelled out, "Another blue jean death!" and pulled me into safety.

I owe my life and the beginnings of my hiking education to that caretaker, Sean Irlbacher. He knew what to do that day, and within hours the wet and cold of death was transformed into the dry and warmth of life. That September storm did not blow out for over twenty-four hours, and it blanketed the ground with over 5" of snow and ice. Sean was radioed a weather report each morning from Mt. Washington. We learned that I had battled through 13 degrees, winds steady at 60 miles per hour with gusts up to 99 producing a deadly wind chill. Every type of precipitation had fallen from the sky that day. I was lucky to be alive, and Gray Knob cabin became and still is my favorite place on earth. Is it no wonder?

It took these two life threatening experiences to transform me from that arrogant, ignorant hiker into one of total humility. So began my real education as a hiker. Almost thirty years later, I am still reading and asking other hikers advice in my quest for more knowledge. As I said before, I could have easily been another chapter in Nick Howe's book, "Not Without Peril," just another one of those hikers who lost their lives in these beautiful, rugged White Mountains.

Sean taught me a great deal, and I thank him for my beginnings as a hiker. The Randolph Mountain Club is a hardcore group of individuals who have great respect and knowledge of hiking in these mountains. The club became my learning ground and my love. The club was formed over one hundred years ago, and I was pleased to be able to attend their 100th anniversary in Randolph, New Hampshire. Sean taught me about winter hiking, and solo hiking in the Northern Presidential Range became my greatest thrill over the next quarter of a century.

My favorite mountain became Mt. Adams, the second highest peak in the Northeast. One of my goals was to stand atop of this mountain of ancient granite every month of the year at least once. December was my most challenging month. There have been times that I have turned away from the summit after hiking 4.6 miles to reach the top and with just .2 of a mile to go. I now know that there will always be another day, and only the self-absorbed, egotistical hiker continues on when there is the risk of never coming home. When my hiking days finally come to a close, I have asked that my ashes be thrown in the sky atop Mt. Adams. I have left instructions for my son, Tom, not to throw them into the wind if it is blowing more than 50 miles per hour southward. Although I am a marathoner, I do not want to end up in the streets of Boston!

Marathoning and my efforts to educate myself as a hiker were two giant steps that brought me closer to my dream of some day thru-hiking the Trail. Over the next two decades, I would continue to hike with humility and respect and learn as much as I could about hiking and living in the wilds. To educate myself as a thru-hiker, I started doing sections of the Trail in Maine, New Hampshire and Vermont during the season the north and south bound thru-hikers would be coming through these mountains. I would go out for three to five days and do sections of the Trail. I would ask the hikers I met about their experiences, and I would study their equipment to learn what I could incorporate into my own hiking style.

"Hey, would you like a nice juicy apple?" I would ask.

This was an oasis to a thru-hiker because they do not usually carry fresh fruit. It is too heavy and a delicious ripe apple was never refused. I carried apples with me, not bananas, as an apple takes some time to consume.

"I'll give you a delicious apple under one condition. You sit down next to me on this rock and tell me about your adventure from Georgia," I would negotiate. Thus, the question and answer session would begin. I would ask about packs, tents, diet, water treatment, hiking footwear, socks, clothing, food and anything else I could think of to learn about how to make it all the way from Georgia to Maine. These adventurous souls were most helpful in transforming me into a thru-hiker over the years.

In those days, my AT sectioning took me from Shelburne Pass in Vermont north through the beautiful and challenging Bigelow Range in Maine. I never ventured farther than this as I wanted to leave this northern stretch of Maine and the "100 Mile Wilderness" for my own thru-hike of the Trail.

Chapter 17
"Hankshwa"

"If a child is to keep his inborn sense of wonder, he needs the companionship of at least one adult who can share it, rediscovering with him the joy, excitement, and mystery of the world we live in." – *Rachel Carson*

After sixteen years of marriage with two loving daughters, Christina age 14 and Samantha age 10, a miracle happened on July 9, 1988. Karen and I were blessed with Thomas. He was born two months early and spent the first three weeks of his life in an incubator. I taped a sign to that incubator that read, "Gray Knob or Bust." Karen and I visited him every day until we finally brought him home. The neonatal nurses told us that we were the only parents that visited every day; that other parents were younger and so scared they just couldn't "take it." Karen and I were astonished. There is nothing we couldn't or wouldn't "take" for one of our kids.

Would I have a little hiker on my hands? Given the bugs, snakes and an assortment of other inconveniences, camping and hiking were not something my girls had come to enjoy. I love my daughters dearly, but my boy, I would soon discover, was and remains a different animal. I put Tom in a backyard tent for the first time when he was just 2 years old. We camped overnight on our own property down in the towering pines on the edge of Forge Pond. I had bought a little tent for just thirty bucks at the local department store and built a crude fire ring with rocks I had found in the woods. I found the right green stick to carve into a point, making a nice marshmallow and hot dog stick.

My young son was so excited that first time we cooked our treats over the open fire. He still cooks hot dogs over an open fire to this day, whenever we go camping in the woods. It all started decades ago. He used to drive me crazy in those mornings down by Forge Pond. Like every young child, Tom loved playing in the tent. So we would end up spending hours in that crowded little tent every morning. All I wanted to do was get up, get out, and start the day. But I did not rush him. I knew that it is important to put a child's pleasure and pace first, particularly if the child is to come to love something for a lifetime.

I had a long range plan for my son to develop a love of the outdoors. I must have done something right. Now grown and married, he lives in Maine, and he enjoys going camping, hiking, skiing and fishing every chance he gets. We found ourselves many weekends down by the water's edge in our little department store tent over the next two years. Finally when he reached age 4, I felt he was ready to camp out away from home. I planned his first night in the tent away from home for the night of August 31st in 1992. After putting the little guy to bed the night of the 30th, I took a trip to the supermarket and shopped for his favorites: Gummy Bears, Reese's Pieces, Pepperidge Farm Goldfish Crackers, and Snickers. An old hiker I had met the year before wandering around in the Northern Presidential Range in a snowstorm gave me some good advice about hiking with little ones. "If you want to get your kid into hiking, pack a bag with a lot a candy," was his advice.

It worked. As the years passed Tom came along to the store with his old man. He loves to hike to this day and on occasion tells me that some of the greatest times of his life are those he has spent hiking with his Dad. Hiking all these years with my son knowing that he values our close connection and the power of nature means the world to me. One of the greatest rewards of our hiking was that there were no televisions, electronic devices or toys to interrupt this "quality time" between father and son. He had my attention 24-hours a day with no interruption. I cannot think of a better way to spend time bonding with your child.

Karen was perplexed and puzzled with this whole idea of taking Tom, who had just turned 4, overnight in the woods of New Hampshire to camp out in that little tent. As I packed the old pickup in the morning she kept asking me, "Are you sure you know what you're doing? Don't you think he's a little young for all this? Do you think he's ready? All I can say is you better have a lot of patience with him." The questions and lecturing went on as we both hugged and kissed her good bye and backed out of the driveway.

Tom never left my side as we sat around the fire that first night out in the New Hampshire woods. This was a scary adventure in the unknown for the little guy. I almost tripped over him in the dark when adding another log to the fire we had built. There were shadows from the light of the fire, wind in the trees, and an occasional moving leaf to contend with that night. It was sort of spooky for a 4-year-old, but once snuggled in his sleeping bag lying next to his Dad in his familiar little tent, he calmed down and fell into the deep slumber of a child's sleep. I stayed awake most of the night, so grateful to be with my little guy away from home in these beautiful woods of New Hampshire for the first time.

It is no exaggeration that it seemed like a dream to be with Tom at this moment. He had been born ten years after our younger daughter Samantha, after four miscarriages during sixteen years of marriage. I have always known how lucky Karen and I are to have him. I love my two beautiful accomplished daughters with all my heart, and am very proud to say that they are both incredible mothers. It is just that Tom has always been different from his sisters, and I thought even back then that I might have a little hiker on my hands. I knew I would have to be patient with him tomorrow during what I planned to be his first hike. "You better have a lot of patience with him," Karen's admonition stayed with me. I did not know how much patience I would need that first day in September with my little four-year-old son.

I had hiked Rattlesnake Mountain in Holderness, New Hampshire years before with Christina, my oldest daughter. It is a great starter mountain for children because you can park your vehicle at about the 1000' elevation mark and then hike up an old bridle path with a mild elevation gain of maybe 200' to the open summit. On a clear day it has a breathtaking view of the countryside overlooking Squam Lake, which is the lake in the movie "On Golden Pond" that starred Katherine Hepburn, Henry Fonda and his daughter, Jane Fonda.

We were lucky. It was crisp and clear, not a cloud to be seen, just a blue sunlit sky as far as the eye could see. September 1st in the White Mountains has the very beginnings of the autumn colors of the approaching foliage season, and there are no bugs to annoy you. It is perfect for hiking. So it was, as Tom and I set out on our first hiking adventure. Just for kicks I had started my stopwatch. If I had been walking alone at a leisurely pace I would have been on the summit in less than twenty minutes. Obviously, I had no idea how long it would take Tom. He had no clue of what we were doing and why we were there. Things got interesting very quickly when after just five minutes I could not find him. I circled my eyes 360 degrees and no Tom. Just as I was about to panic, I finally saw him behind me sitting on a boulder on the side of the trail.

"There you are buddy. What's going on?" I asked walking back towards him.

"I've had enough of this hiking, Dad. I'm tired," he answered.

I thought again about the advice Karen had given me, "All I can say is you better have a lot of patience with him." I sat down on the large granite boulder next to him saying, "Yeah, I'm a little tired too," and proceeded to take the day pack off my shoulders. Without another word I started emptying the pack of its contents. The Gummy Bears, his favorite Goldfish crackers, candy bars and other assorted treats were on display.

"Can I have some, Dad?"

"Sure, what do you want?"

As we sat munching on junk food I said, "Tom, you know whenever we go hiking together Dad will always pack stuff like this."

"Really, Dad?"

"Yes. Dad will always brings your favorites," I answered.

After another few minutes of snacking, I just packed up and without a word, flung the pack over my shoulders and started slowly heading up the trail.

"Hey, Dad where are you going?"

"Up to the top of Rattlesnake Mountain," I said as I bent over picking up a fairly straightened tree branch and breaking off a section. As Tom climbed down off that boulder, he asked me what I was doing with the big stick.

"Making myself a good walking stick."

"Dad can you get one for me?"

"Let's keep moving up the trail, and we'll find a real nice one for you."

As I coaxed him along, we kept searching for that perfect walking stick.

"No, I think there will be a better one a little farther up," I would say.

I finally stopped and got him his perfect stick. A short time later I noticed Tom lagging behind. I stopped and turned to see what he was doing and found him poking his walking stick in every root hole he could find.

"Hey Buddy, what are you doing with your walking stick?" I asked.

"I'm looking for rattlesnakes, Dad," he yelled back.

"What? There aren't any rattlers here in New Hampshire anymore," I explained.

"This is Rattlesnake Mountain, Dad. They're here in these holes," he replied.

"No, no, that's just the name of the mountain," I said.

This debate went on for a while and Tom was convinced he would find a rattlesnake soon. We stopped two more times for snacks until finally he told me, "Dad, I've had enough hiking" and sat on a rock again. My patience was wearing a bit thin, but Karen's words still echoed as I sat down next to him, again taking out the candy.

"Tom, we can take as many breaks for rest as you need, but we have to get to the top of this mountain," I stated.

"Why? What's up at the top?" Tom asked.

"Oh, you'll see. It's really neat. It looks like you're up in an airplane looking down below. The boats on the lake look so tiny and people look like ants. You'll just love it," I explained.

"Okay Dad. Let's get up there," Tom said with excitement.

Less than ten minutes more of hiking and Tom was whining and dragging his feet saying, "Pick me up! My legs are tired."

We sat down again on a rock eating more candy as I explained, "Tom, when you go hiking, Dad can't pick you up. Every hiker has to make it on their own. We can rest as many times as you want, but your own legs have to get you to the top." I kept thinking if I can just get him up to the summit everything will be fine. He will love taking in the view, sitting on the cliff, and resting as we eat the lunch that I had packed for us. Be patient and just keep prodding him along, I thought.

We finally made it to the summit in just under an hour. It was wonderful to be up here finally with Tom on this glorious sunny day. It was crystal clear, and the view was fantastic from this rounding granite ledge. I sat down and started to set out our lunch when suddenly I saw Tom running after a butterfly. In panic mode I jumped to my feet and ran after him yelling, "Stop, Stop!"

I finally caught up to him with my heart pounding in my chest and breathing heavily. The jolt of adrenaline had lifted me to him in an instant. I took hold of his wrist and brought him back to sit down for lunch.

"Tom, we need to make a rule. Whenever we are at the top of a mountain, you sit down when Dad does, and when you want to get up Dad will get up and hold you by the wrist. We must first walk around the top and make sure it is safe so we won't fall off. Okay Tom?"

"Sure Dad. Hey, what's for lunch?"

Tom did not seem interested or excited about the view and spent most of his time looking for bugs and more butterflies. The whole hike seemed disappointing to me and felt as though it was not working for the little guy. The trip down was much less challenging and we only made one stop for five minutes or more when Tom discovered a Daddy Long Legs. He loved playing with the spider and wanted to bring him home with us, but I finally convinced him that his spider had to stay in the woods where he belonged because the mother spider would worry and miss him. He finally realized it was best for the spider to stay in the woods. So we said our goodbyes and moved back on down the trail to the pickup truck and started the long drive back to Massachusetts.

Tom fell asleep next to me in short order and slept the rest of the way home. I thought about the adventure we had just had together and felt discouraged that he did not seem to enjoy the hike or the view all that much. I tucked him into bed that night and went to work the next day to prepare for the incoming students and the beginning of another school year. When I returned home from work, Karen kept telling me how Tom had talked her ear off all day about our adventure.

"What he seemed to like best was standing on the top of that mountain. He said standing out on that cliff was kind of scary, but he liked it, especially when the wind blew," she said. I realized in that moment that I had a little hiker and the patience Karen had cautioned me about had paid off.

Tom would hike his first 4000 footer in the "Whites" when he was 6 years old. When he was 7, he would summit Mt. Adams, in the Northern Presidential Range, after sleeping at Gray Knob for the first time. He was a hiker and the two of us could not get enough of the mountains and the woods. A bond between a father and son developed without all the interruptions of our fast-paced society. It does not get any better.

That same year we first hiked Mt. Adams together I brought along my 6" buck knife, which Tom had never seen. Settling into camp one late afternoon, I pulled the old knife out of my pack and without a word threw it at a large white pine. It stuck into the tree on the first throw. With his mouth wide open Tom yelled out, "Wow, Dad, can you do that again?"

I replied, "Well, don't just stand there. Go pull it out of the tree." Tom ran with excitement to the big pine and yanked on the knife. "Dad, it won't come out."

"Twist it back and forth as you pull and you'll get it."

The little guy finally released the blade from the tree and started running back with the knife in his hand.

"Stop, don't move. Okay, now slowly walk back to me with that sharp knife." I took the knife from him and began showing him how to pass it safely and gave him some instruction on its use and safety when he asked again if I could throw it. I figured I better not press my luck with my little guy in awe of his Dad saying,

"Aw, I could do it all day. Why don't you give it a try?"

"Really, Dad. You'd let me throw it?"

"As long as you follow all the rules and only use the knife when Dad's around."

"Okay, Dad."

Tom spent the better part of that weekend learning how to throw the knife. I explained to him that the Indians threw it mostly overhand and the mountain men would usually fling it underhand. As we hiked out of the woods at the end of the weekend Tom said, "Dad, I get the knife to stick more when I throw it overhand, so I think I may be part Indian."

"Really, well you didn't get any Indian blood from me. Do you think Mom could be part Indian? You know how her skin is darker than mine and she has that black hair? In fact, when she puts her hair in those braids she really looks Indian. I think, maybe you have some Indian blood in you from her side of the family."

As we continued to head back to the pickup truck, the little 7-year-old piped up saying, "Dad, I think my hiking name will be Hankshwa."

"Where did you hear that name—on TV or something?"

"No, I just made it up."

"You're kidding me. Where did you hear it?"

"I just thought of it. Don't you think it sounds kind of like an Indian name?"

Amazed at the name my 7-year-old son had created I said, "I think it does sound kind of like an Indian name, but it also has a little bit of a French sound too."

I went on to explain to Tom about the French trappers and the influence of the French that settled in the New England area. I told him stories about the French and Indian War in the 18th century on our long drive home. Thus, "Hankshwa" was born and the hiking name somehow stuck for my son.

Chapter 18
Sharing the Dream

"Dare to live the life you have dreamed for yourself.
Go forward and make your dreams come true."
– *Ralph Waldo Emerson*

Brockton, Massachusetts changed like many cities in the late 1980's, when cocaine hit the streets of America. "Crack" became the curse of this country, and I watched my classroom and this city begin to erode away. Gangs, drugs, guns, drive-by shootings and "crack houses" invaded this small city of about 100,000. Too many kids got lost in this spreading cancer and in the crossfire. I attended too many funerals. It was incredibly sad to witness it all.

The Brockton Police Department sent some officers out to Phoenix, Arizona, a city plagued with street gangs, drugs and a high death rate of teens dying from violence. The officers went out there to research and study an anti-gang program instituted in Phoenix in an attempt to save its young people from the urban brutality. School administrators, elected city officials and parents want to believe that their schools are safe, free from drugs, gang members, and violence.

The sad reality is that our schools are a reflection of their neighborhoods and culture. If someone wants drugs, the fastest place to find them is in our high schools and prisons. Our schools were once purely educational institutions. But with more and more single parent homes and the economic need for both parents to work even in homes where both parents are present, schools are now expected to take on a myriad of societal issues facing our youth. The schools are neither equipped nor funded to take on these added responsibilities. Attempting to do so distracts school systems from their initial purpose, but that is not a reason to deny or ignore the violence caused by the drug culture and poverty.

The Brockton Police wanted to place the Phoenix-based anti-gang initiative in the city schools to help with the problems. Through a series of negotiations between the Police Department and the school system, and with the help of Principal Bartlett, a man dedicated to Brockton's youth, the program would be "piloted" in my health classes in 1991. I would be partnered with Officer Steve Ferris from the Brockton Police Department to implement the program. It was not long before the city decided to place it in schools throughout the system. I am very proud of the part my classroom played, and I have been told that this program saved many young lives.

There was a section in the anti-gang curriculum about having a "vision of hope" to have a goal or a dream, as most gang members have no vision or hope. The more we discussed this lesson with the young people, the more I began to dwell on how having my own secret dream of hiking the Trail had changed me. I had never shared my dream with anyone, not even with Karen and my kids. It had been sixteen years since I first encountered that stranger in the White Mountains, and I came to realize by this time that it really didn't matter if I ever hiked the Trail at all. What transformed my life was the path upon which I had journeyed because I had a dream. It is the journey that has made all the difference.

So I taught my students that the power of having a dream is that it keeps you moving forward, opens you up to life's possibilities, and keeps you focused to figure out what is really important to you. I wanted them to understand that it did not really matter if they ever attained their dreams. The important thing to convey to them was how it is the journey in pursuit of the dream that can change them and save their lives.

Our children are taught in this country that what is important is winning and reaching a goal or destination. We cite the old adage to them, "For when the one great scorer comes to mark against your name, He writes not that you won or lost, but how you played the game." But words and actions are two different things. Once they reach a certain age, and they do not win whatever competition is at hand, they see how upset their coaches and parents become over the loss.

Playing the game of baseball was fun but not anymore. So many kids toss away their gloves and bats and never want to play the game again. It has become a metaphor for why so many kids give up on their dreams, drop out, and for some go on to engage in destructive behavior.

Adults get swept up in their own emotions and desires and in doing so take the fun out of what used to be a game. It has now become all about the competition and winning at all costs. How many of our young athletes have taken the steroid route to find "success?" We have too many kids sitting on the sidelines in life who are afraid to "play the game" for fear of "failure." It has become easier and safer to sit and do nothing rather than simply to try their best. When their best is viewed as a disappointment, is it any wonder that some become discouraged, depressed and turn to drugs and gangs for acceptance.

I also cautioned my students that once you start comparing yourself to others you are setting yourself up to lose. Find your own yardstick to measure your success in life. Our kids need to understand that the only way you are guaranteed to lose is by quitting the game because of someone else's definition of what it means to win. Hope is a good thing, a necessary thing, and anything good is worth hoping for in life. I wanted to give hope to these kids, many of whom were living in seemingly hopeless situations battling against the odds. Hope is a powerful thing and something to cling to when the going gets tough. Once you lose hope, it's "game over." Kids need to believe in their dreams and realize they are worthy of them.

When I hit 40 I started becoming very concerned about hiking the Trail. I needed to design a more definitive plan to find the best time in life to do the entire thru-hike from Georgia to Maine. It was time to get serious and take action. I better get this done before I turn 60, I reasoned. When you are 40 years old, 60 seems old. Fifty-nine seemed like a better number, and I began to focus on retiring and fulfilling my dream. Tom had also been born the year before I turned 40, and he had entered my dream. I designed a plan that now included Tom and had calculated that he would graduate from high school the same year I planned to retire and fulfill this dream.

I figured money might be a problem and thought of ways to save so I could retire and do this thru-hike. Having just paid off the three-year note on my pickup truck, I decided to continue salting away the amount equal to my payments. With the desire and discipline to reach my dream, like a squirrel gathers nuts, I began adding money to this monthly savings. As the years passed, I took the money and started a tax-sheltered annuity. I refused to ever buy a new vehicle and continued adding money to this nest egg. A vehicle to me was always just a means to get from point A to point B, so this was not much of a sacrifice. I began to realize I just might be able to walk away from the working world to fulfill my dream, if I continued on this path of investment. It is amazing how the money added up by just refusing to buy a new vehicle.

I kept wondering how else I could save money. It bothered me to see the woods littered with empty beer cans and bottles around those fire rings on my Monday runs. Weekends of teenagers drinking in the seclusion of the forest would leave it a mess. I started tucking a trash bag or two in my running shorts and would stop to pick up those nickels and dimes. If I did not fill the bag with the empties, I would stash it out of the way behind a big old white pine and would fill it after the next weekend bash. I was cleaning up my "home away from home" and at the same time squirreling away more "acorns" for retirement.

Then it was going to the football game or any other venue where there were loads of empty containers. Upon climbing out of the stands after the game, I would simply pullout the whole trash can liner, and being the nice guy I am, would re-line the barrel. I would head home, pick out all the empties to redeem the nickel deposit and would take the rest of the trash to the dump. I put up a barrel for my track athletes to throw their containers in after school. I was grabbing empties all the time. Nineteen years of nickels and dimes can really add up. Between them and what would have otherwise been truck payments, I saved over $100,000 in nineteen years. I was determined and dedicated to reach my desired dream, and the part of my journey to make it financially possible was well worth the required discipline.

I found it easy to accumulate enough money, a necessary evil, when it is all around you in this throw away society. This is particularly true if you are not interested in the superficial, materialistic, trinkets pushed by the marketing tactics of the business world. I believe that with ingenuity a person could exist on others' waste. There are thousands of homeless struggling but existing on what others discard. Living on the necessities and forgetting about or having no desire for all the meaningless frills can make it easier to save.

I call my philosophy the 4Ds: Desire, Dedication, Determination and Discipline. With the 4Ds almost any mountain in life can be climbed. I had a dream to fulfill, and it gave my life the focus to make it become a reality. There were so many wonderful things happening to me just because I had this dream. I realized this journey to pursue my dream required a positive lifestyle. The journey was helping me in a multitude of ways and would continue to do so whether or not the dream ever came to pass.

Realizing what the power of having hope and a dream had done to transform my life, I decided to share my dream with my students.

This was not an easy decision by any means. Officer Ferris and I had already discussed goals and dreams with these kids and asked them why it might not be a good idea to share personal dreams with anyone. The kids told us that some people might make fun of you, discourage you, steal your dream, try to stop you from reaching your dream, or in the city get jealous and shoot you. We agreed as a group that dreams should be kept to yourself for many reasons.

Before I shared my philosophy of the power of a dream with them, I thought my students would laugh at me. They saw me biking back and forth into the city from my home in Kingston, a 40-mile round trip to school. For decades they had witnessed me running around D.W. Park and in the city streets. Now, I intended to tell them that my dream was to hike up and over hundreds of mountains, through fourteen states in the wilderness from Georgia to Maine some day, and I had been planning for years to do it.

To these city kids it would be like going to the moon. I thought that they might not understand and would think I was crazy. But I also thought that maybe one of them, just one of them, would make sense of it all. Teachers need tough skin and will do just about anything to have their students learn. So finally one day when Officer Ferris was absent, I stood in front of those kids in the anti-gang program. I took a deep breath and began my story.

"I care about you, and because I care I'm going to break a rule today and expose a dream, a secret dream that I have kept to myself for the last sixteen years. It's a dream that I have never spoken of to anyone, not even to my wife and kids. It's a dream that forever changed my life and probably saved my life. Why am I doing this? It is because I want you to understand what a dream is all about, its value, and its power! Understand that it is not important if it ever comes true, but how having a dream can make all the difference in life."

I went on to explain a little of my former life including my troubled childhood, how I had found solace in nature, my lost confused years as a young man, and even my abuse of alcohol to sedate myself. The conversation went on with my rediscovery of the woods and my chance encounter with the pioneer AT thru-hiker that ignited the spark which is burning in my soul.

"Please open your ears, eyes and heart and realize a dream is about a journey not a destination. See, it really doesn't matter if I ever make it from Springer Mt. in Georgia to Mt. Katahdin in Maine. What's important is that I took this path at all, just trying to get to the trailhead in Georgia some day. It's about the adventure, the experiences I've had and continue to have, the interesting people I've met along the way, my health, my life, my happiness. I would not be your teacher today, if it wasn't for this dream," I stated with emotion.

The kids watched a short six minute video of a place I winter hike in the Northern Presidentials. I passed around pictures of hikes, and I hung a topographical map of the United States on the chalkboard displaying the Appalachian Mountain chain. An annuity account of mine, minus my address, social security number, and contract number was also distributed with my name and monetary amount highlighted in yellow.

"Look at all the money he has! Why you drivin' that old pickup? You could buy a BMW or something real cool," someone blurted out.

Laughing, I responded, "I have no desire for that car. I'm driving the old pickup so I can save money to retire early and get to Springer Mt. in Georgia to hike."

"Oh, so it costs a lot of money to hike this trail?" someone else asked.

"No, it doesn't cost much at all. When I hit 40, I became concerned about when I was going to find the time to thru-hike the Trail. I figured I better hike it before I turned 60. See, when you're 40, age 60 seems real old. Age 59 sounds better to me, so I'm saving money to retire early and get it done. I also paid off my pickup truck at age 40. Because I'm disciplined and have this desire, I decided to start putting away the amount of my truck payments and I've kept adding to them. I'll never buy a new vehicle. In our throw away society, you'd be surprised what you can find in junkyards and how much money you can save," I explained to the class.

"No offense, Mr. Cook, but you'll never make it. You'll be too old," someone said.

Many of these kids were from families that placed little value on personal health, and because of it, died early in life from heart disease, strokes, diabetes and its complications. Therefore, doing this at age 59 seemed impossible to them. Again, my position as a role model was important. I wanted to demonstrate to them that if you became educated in the subject of health, worked at taking care of yourself, took advantage of the advancement of modern medicine, and got lucky anything was possible.

"Don't you want to teach us? I thought you loved to teach," another student yelled out.

"I love you guys, but to be totally honest, my dream of hiking the Trail means more to me. This is my dream of a lifetime," I answered.

Taking a hike through the Appalachians was totally foreign to these city kids. I felt like I was a visiting astronaut and realized they have little connection with the woods and nature. In fact, many have never ventured off the city streets into those woods. No wonder we are having so many problems in this country today.

"Aren't you afraid out there in those woods?" I was asked.

"What should I be afraid of?" I returned.

"Bears!" several shouted out.

"The black bear is native to the Appalachians and is afraid of humans. I just hope I can get close enough to one to take a good picture," I laughed.

When presented with an opportunity to teach my students, I went on to explain that the American black bear is the largest omnivore that may be encountered on the Trail, and it inhabits all regions of the Appalachians. Bear sightings on the Trail are not that common; they are naturally afraid of humans, and with the number of hikers on the Trail, I might not be lucky enough to see many and get that picture. I told my students that there are other large mammals on the Trail I might be lucky enough to come across including deer, elk, wild boar, coyotes, the red wolf, and moose, which are commonly seen in northern New England. I also explained that being from the north I was excited to witness for the first time the timberback rattlesnake in the wilds. My biggest fear was being taken down by the most dangerous animal in those woods, the deer tick. There are many pests to contend with besides ticks. I wasn't looking forward to mosquitoes, black flies, gnats, poisonous spiders and mice that inhabit the three sided shelters along the Trail looking for hiker's food.

The conversation went on, and to my surprise, no one laughed. I broke the group up into pairs to list all the wonderful things that would happen to me because I had this dream, even if I never made it to the trailhead. They were to list what taking this journey did for my life in a positive way. I wanted these kids to understand that it is all about the journey not the destination or outcome. It is having and pursuing a dream that can transform or even save your life. Having a dream gives you a "constant" in your life. No matter what variables in life may come your way, you can always hold on to your dream.

I shared my dream with the kids in the anti-gang program for the next fifteen years and never in front of another adult. The dream became our little secret in the city and opening this journey to them produced incredible outcomes. Then the most beautiful thing started to emerge. Many of these at risk kids began sharing their secret thoughts and dreams with me. My ears became a safe place for them to open up and share their inner feelings, hopes and dreams. I was never critical or judgmental. I just let them believe that they were worthy and that their dreams were important. I believed in them just as they believed in me.

The most farfetched and craziest dreams I ever heard came from my students. The one I will always remember was about creating the real "Jurassic Park" by a straight "A" student at the genius level. It was frightening at times to listen to him, as his eyes had a burning glow of passion, explaining about DNA and the required science behind his dream. His intellect on the subject was beyond me. At times his lectures made it seem almost possible. I never laughed or swayed him to believe his dream was not grounded in reality. My thoughts were that some day he may go on to higher education to attain a doctoral degree as a research scientist in gene therapy or stem cell applications even if that meant that somewhere down the road he came to realize that "Jurassic Park" was not his destination. This wild dream of his would bring him to wonderful places, and he would experience and meet other people of science and genius.

I encouraged, not discouraged, my students to take their dreams as far as possible and along the way discover that they were a lot better than they ever imagined that they could be in life. Never quitting became my message of hope, and the kids gave me the nickname, "Real." I tried to live up to my nickname as these young people had seen enough phonies in life. As the years passed, I would be seen running down in the city park by many former students who were now adults. The following conversation was typical during such encounters.

"Hey, there's my old health teacher. I can't believe you're still running. Have you done that hiking dream thing yet?" one asked.

"You didn't listen well enough in class. I'm still working on it," I replied. I then turned the conversation on to him saying, "So that's enough about me. What's going on with you?"

"I just got out of lockup and am taking courses at Massasoit Community College," he answered.

"Great for you! You're on the right path now; keep the journey going towards your own dreams," I would reply.

Hiking the Trail became more powerful as the years went by, and I began to realize the influence and importance of it all. Making it all come true and the trek on the AT from Springer Mt. in Georgia to Maine through the wilderness was more than just a hike. I constantly reminded myself and my students that it is the dream that provides a positive journey in life. I knew that if I did not hike the Trail, these kids would just see me as another "blowhard" they had met in life. If I was truly "walking the talk" as many of them expected of me, I had better see this through to the end, or everything I had done and said would be worthless. I had a great desire to hike the Trail anyway, but now it was everything.

Chapter 19
Holding on to the Dream through Adversity

"If you're going through hell, keep going." – *Winston Churchill*

Keeping a positive focus at times can be extremely difficult, but taking one step at a time and concentrating on just this one step can lead to your dreams. My focus and hope would be challenged during a five-month period in 1992. In an instant on June 23, 1992, my whole hiking world would be radically changed forever.

It was the last day of school, and as I did many times in decent weather, I was riding to work on my high tech triathlon bike. Shortly after leaving my home at 6:00 AM, I was flying down a long gradual hill at a good 35 miles per hour on a quiet country road. As usual, I was exhilarated and feeling the freedom of the open road. It was the beginning of summer, and I was in heavy training mode to do my first 1/2 Iron Man triathlon (swim 1.2 miles, bike 56 miles, run 13.1 miles) in late August. I was full of excitement and looking forward to a full summer of hard training to make this happen.

A good bike makes no noise, and it was a beautiful, peaceful morning jetting down that big hill without a car on the road. The only sound I could hear was the wind whistling in my ears when suddenly a large hunting hound stepped out of the woods directly in front of my charging bike. I do not think the dog ever saw me coming. It happened so fast there was no time to react. I slammed into the dog's broad side and went down hard with my left shoulder taking the initial blow on the pavement before the left side of my head hit and twisted my neck. The impact split the helmet in two, leaving me with a concussion, fractured clavicle, broken humerus, cracked rib, and torn rotator cuff; but the greatest injury was to my upper spine. I am lucky not to be wheel chair-bound or worse. Damage was done to my cervical spine (C-5) and my brachial plexus nerve running behind my left shoulder. Most of these injuries would not be recognized for months and the fracture to the humerus bone in my upper left arm was not discovered until eighteen years later during surgery to my shoulder.

The spring of 1992 had already been a rough one because my brother Bob's youngest child, his 6-year-old daughter, had almost died from liver failure. He has four children, great athletes, who would all play college sports at an extremely high level. Their youngest was a kindergartner on the Walpole Swim Team in Massachusetts when an aggressive virus, Alpha 1, from out of nowhere, took her down hard in just three weeks to a Stage 3 coma. There are only four stages.

At the time only one child out of twenty-four waiting for a liver transplant was lucky enough to get one. We were all watching her die with less than twenty-four hours to live when the miracle happened. She received a liver from a 4-year-old boy who had died in Wisconsin. If the parents of that child happen to read this book, please know that the entire Cook family will always remember what you did during your time of profound grief. I wish there was more I could say, but thank-you, for saving a wonderful girl's life. She has gone on to make the most of your sacrifice. We thank God each and every day for your compassion and generosity.

As if this was not enough, Karen's Mom, having been diagnosed with a brain tumor was then given two to six months to live. My wonderful wife stepped forward to take care of her Mom through a horrific and agonizing death. She lasted eighteen months, three times longer than the doctors predicted. Karen would not leave her mother's side even as the hospice nurses were lecturing me to get her to take a break, as it was not emotionally healthy for her to be there around the clock. Eighteen months into this ordeal, I left Karen for my weekly trip to our house to bring her clean clothes for the next seven days. That is how it came to be that my tough girl was alone in the room when her Mom passed. I call my amazing wife "St. Karen."

June was a tough month, but it was not yet finished dealing out the pain. My Mom and Dad had come up from Florida to help out at Bob's and his wife Janet's house as their little 6-year-old was flown out to the University of Chicago Hospital by jet ambulance to receive the liver transplant. She remained in Illinois fighting for her life for the next four months. My parents were in their 70's, and Dad had his first of many heart attacks at 44. My brother, believing all the stress caused my frail Father to die from his final cardiac episode on the last day of June, although he should not, still feels some guilt today. So there was my niece's life-saving liver transplant on April 29th, Karen's Mom passing on June 7th, my bike accident on June 23rd, and Dad dying on June 30th. Unbelievably there was more to come that summer of 1992.

A neighbor and friend, who never spoke about the dangers in his job, would lose his life two months later in August at age 42. He would leave his wife, my son's Godmother, and two wonderful sons of his own, Billy, Jr., age 18, and Brian, just 13. His death would be played out on television as the whole country watched the national news. Bill was a retired colonel in the Marines, a decorated U.S. Marshal, and the head of S.O.G. (Special Operations Group) for the Marshal Service. He lost his life during the apprehension of a Neo-Nazi running illegal guns.

Keeping my focus at this time was difficult, but as soon as I could walk, I was out there with broken bones, torn rotator cuff, nerve damage and all. The walk eventually turned into a jog and then into a run. Maybe, I should not have been running with all these ailments, but it kept me "together." It was the toughest marathon training I ever did.

They changed the Rhode Island Marathon route for November 1, 1992 to finish in downtown Providence. I focused my efforts on the fact that the finish line was in Providence because my Dad was born, had been raised and buried there. If I could finish in 3:20 or less it would qualify me for next year's Boston Marathon. It gave me something on which to concentrate that was positive and something to hope for in this time of heartache. I was 43 years old in 1992, but felt much older that summer.

My shoulder would hurt so much from just swinging my arms back and forth while running that I learned if I held my arm out in front of me or straight out to the side every 2 miles or so it eased the pain. My running friends, who did not know the whole story, kept asking me if I was trying to fly like a bird. Whatever I did, it helped. My plan was to try to qualify for the Boston Marathon and then end the day over at Swan Point Cemetery in Providence to place flowers on Dad's grave. It would be a very emotional day and something I will always cherish, even the pain. I missed finishing under 3:20 with a time of 3:20:47. I missed by 47 seconds, but found out later that day that the Boston Athletic Association does not "count" the seconds for qualification. I had qualified for Boston. It certainly was not the fastest of all the marathons I ran, but it was by far the most gratifying.

People often ask me at the YMCA and at other places where I work out how I stay so motivated. I tell them to forget the scales, forget about how you look in the mirror and forget all thoughts of strutting, posturing machismo. I answer the question by saying, "It's all about having goals and dreams." Be a dreamer, dream big dreams and understand it does not really matter if they all come true or not. What matters is that you have them. Some have come true for me, some not, and some I am still working on to this day. Chase that carrot and do not beat yourself with a stick because having the carrot to chase is a means to your happiness. Never give up and do the best you can with the hand you have been dealt. The main thing is to never quit and to hang on to the belief that there is a better day coming.

That early morning bike crash back in June had landed me in the emergency room. There I was introduced to a Sports Medicine Orthopedist. "Look, he's grimacing in pain," he stated as I was clenching down with my teeth as the nerves were firing lightning bolts to my brain. All he figured out that morning was I had a fractured clavicle. I believe a veterinarian or a child would have been able to come up with this diagnosis given that the break was in the middle of the bone, and it was sticking out from my upper chest. After "treating" just that injury, he gave Karen his business card and told me to call the office and make an appointment.

Before they would release me, I was required to give a urine sample. I could not urinate and sat in a room alone with my wife with the gallon of water I had finally been given. I drank almost three quarts of water before some urine dribbled out. I was not in my correct state of mind; later I realized I had also downed a quart of water before hopping on my bike, and the accident happened within the first mile of my home. I now had a gallon of water in me and could not seem to give a urine sample. I did not urinate properly for the next seventy-two hours and thought I had done damage to my urinary tract. Someone later explained I was retaining water because I was in shock and that I owed my survival in large part due to my excellent condition as I was in training for my first 1/2 Ironman.

All I wanted to do was to go home and crawl into a hole. I tried to find a comfortable position, but could not, and would not find one for months. Karen drove me back to the hospital the next day for a tetanus injection because of the blood and "road rash." My left arm had been trembling out of control since the crash, and I brought it to the attention of the doctor on duty.

"My arm hurts so much, especially my biceps area, like someone is stabbing me with a knife, and look at my arm shaking. I think, there's something wrong with the nerves connecting to my skeletal muscles," I stated with a feeling of panic.

"Listen, you took quite a jolt to your body with that accident; we don't cast a broken clavicle or rib, and I know they can be very painful," was the doctor's reply. Once again I was sent home in pain.

Karen drove me down to see the Sports Medicine Orthopedist a few days later, and he went through his examination sending me home again, this time with a script for Tylenol with codeine to help with the pain. Each night my wife and kids would go to bed upstairs, and I would sit on the couch surrounded by pillows and attempt to dose off only to be jolted awake by pain. After not sleeping for weeks, I could not wait any longer for my scheduled appointment and ended up going back to the Sports Medicine Orthopedist's office.

As calmly as possible I stated, "I need to see the doctor."

"What time is your appointment?" I was asked.

"Not for another few weeks, but I can't wait. I'm in too much pain," I stated in near delirium.

"Well, you'll have to come back for your scheduled appointment then," she returned.

"No, you don't understand, I can't sleep and can't do anything with this pain, please let me see the doctor," I begged with tears of pain in my eyes.

"Okay, sit down and maybe you can see him, but as you can see, he's very busy," she said as I looked at a full waiting room.

"I'll wait, but I can't sit still in here and will be outside in the hall walking around. I'll pop into the waiting room every once and a while," I stated. After three hours of pacing in the hallway. I was told to come inside. After another long wait alone in the examining cubical in a sleep deprived state of painful delirium, the doctor finally came into the room alone and shut the door.

"Listen you can't just come in here and expect to see me without an appointment," he scolded.

"Doctor, I can't take it anymore. I'm in so much pain, I can't sleep, I can't think, I can't do anything. I'm right handed and can live without my left arm. Please just cut it off and get rid of this pain," I begged in delirium.

"You have a frozen shoulder. Now stand over here against the wall."

The doctor then lifted his leg up, leaned against me and took my left arm in his hand. He began forcing my arm from my side lifting it to a parallel position to the floor as I screamed. Once he let my arm drop to my side I tried to catch my breath.

He shouted out as he exited the room, "I'll be right back."

What's this guy doing to me, I thought, standing alone clutching my shoulder and clenching my teeth in excruciating pain.

He again returned and handed me another script for Tylenol/codeine and said, "Now take this to help you with the pain you're in, and I'll see you soon."

I went home and called my primary care physician to get a referral to see another doctor I had researched in Boston for a second opinion, but my doctor was as confused as I about receiving care from outside my HMO's network. After almost a month, the Sports Medicine Orthopedist finally recognized I had done serious damage and physical therapy started at his facility. More importantly, he referred me to a neurologist.

Finally on September 7, 1992, some two and a half months after the crash, I had my consultation with the neurologist. It proved to be enlightening, and I would begin to have some hope.

"Before we begin, I have to ask you a few questions," he said leaning forward in his chair from behind his desk. "When did this accident happen again?" he asked as he looked over the paper work in my file.

"June 23rd," I answered.

"You must have been in incredible pain in July," he stated.

No one had ever really addressed the subject of pain, and it set a spark in me answering, "Thanks for asking, doctor. I couldn't sleep and sat in an upright position on the couch with pillows my wife would help pack around me. At times, I'd dose off but the pain was so great I would pace downstairs alone while my wife and kids slept upstairs. I flushed the third script of Tylenol/codeine because I was afraid it would cause another problem with me, addiction. I started to self medicate with ibuprofen always taking it with food and one day counted 30 tablets. It scared me to think of what I was doing to my liver and began weaning my way down."

"On a pain scale of 1 to 10, where are you now?" he asked.

Laughing, I answered, "It's nothing now compared to then, probably about a 4."

"What's been going on with you?" he asked

"I can't seem to work it out with my HMO to see a doctor in Boston. My primary care physician and I can't seem to find out how to get treatment out of the network," I replied. My HMO had twice rejected my request to get treatment from specialists in Boston.

"The EMG nerve testing showed you have some serious damage to your brachial plexus nerve, and I will deal with your HMO. I want you to see a neurosurgeon and orthopedic surgeon in Boston," he told me.

"Thank you, doctor." I sighed in relief. "I do triathlons and need to swim freestyle again," I stated.

"I'm sorry, but it won't happen. You will probably be able to do the breast stroke or the dog paddle, but with the damage to your arm, forget trying to do the crawl," he stated.

"You don't understand. I have to do the crawl," I returned.

"You sound like one of those pitchers, who are old and their arm is gone. Don't frustrate yourself," he returned.

"No you don't understand. I'll find a way," ending the conversation.

I finally got into Boston in November and saw both doctors. I had made the decision to refuse any surgery believing there was a chance for more damage from any such procedures. But once I walked into the office of Dr. Anthony Schepsis, I realized I was finally in the presence of the right doctor. This appointment was nearly five months after the crash.

"Dr. Schepsis, my HMO is only allowing me one visit and I think I may have another problem," I stated after shaking hands.

"What's that?" he asked.

"I've been reading Gray's Anatomy and am having pain in my shoulder right where the rotator cuff is. I think it's torn," I stated.

Chuckling, he said, "Well let's do an examination and see what's going on."

I had an exam like I had never had before using all kinds of instruments to measure my range of motion and doing other evaluations.

We returned to his desk and upon sitting down he stated, "I think, you're correct about the rotator cuff. I hate to do this to you seeing you have already had a MRI for that brachial plexus nerve, but would like you to have another MRI to confirm that rotator cuff tear," he said.

"Doctor, I want to swim again and if you told me I had to crawl backwards on my hands and knees all the way home I'd do it to get my shoulder back," I said with emotion.

Doctor Schepsis picked up the phone asking, "Where did you have your other MRI?"

"Weymouth," I replied. He put his hand over the phone after calling them in front of me.

"You can't get in there for an appointment during their regular hours for quite some time, but they said for me, they will squeeze you in first thing tomorrow morning, if you arrive at 5:30 AM. Can you make it tomorrow morning?" he asked.

"I'll be there," I stated.

The MRI confirmed the tear. I decided to send off a letter to Tom Harrington, a physical therapist I knew and respected, telling him that I needed to do the crawl again and asked for his help to make this happen. He assigned me his best therapist, a guy name Bruno, and we began our challenging work. We had a great patient-therapist relationship and a bond which grew as we worked. "You're such a pleasure to work with because you work so hard with me to get better. Most of the people that come in here don't really want to improve. So many are on some type of workman's comp and just want to sit on the couch and have a reason not to go to work," Bruno said to me in frustration.

Bruno told me to continue doing my thirty-six laps or more of the dog paddle at the pool, and to never try to do the crawl until he said it was okay. I finally brought in a video camera, and we went to the pool together to film my attempt at doing the crawl. He understood, after we viewed the film in slow motion, that he would be able to devise a treatment plan for my arm to make it happen. I eventually combined a crawl with a side stroke. In one phase of the stroke I would do the flutter kick and the second phase the scissor kick. It is difficult to explain how it works with my arms, but I could finally swim the crawl required for a triathlon. A year later I was covering a mile swim just three minutes slower than before the crash. Fourteen months after this bike crash, I made it to the starting line of that 1/2 Ironman triathlon. Upon crossing the finish line, I continued running away from the crowds and into the woods. Alone with tears streaming down my face, I celebrated with laughter and joy.

After almost a year of physical therapy, I was left with permanent nerve damage to the brachial plexus nerve, which runs out of my fifth vertebra behind my left shoulder, down my left arm through my biceps, into the radial part of my arm, and into my index finger and thumb. The result of this permanent damage was I could no longer carry a heavy pack. I thought my dream of hiking the Trail was over. The damages from this horrific accident could have been far worse, putting me in a wheel chair or bed for the rest of my life. To continue hiking at all, I finally realized I had to adapt.

If you have a desire to reach a dream there is not much that will stop you. I had to accept that there would always be some pain in my fifth vertebra and behind my left shoulder. It became necessary to make the pain manageable, or the hike would never happen. I needed to lighten the load. Feeling at home in the woods would allow me to carry less. My hiking technique became more Spartan, and I worked to hike with just the basics. Adjusting the weight of the pack to lie on my lower back and more on my right shoulder was a challenge, but it would be necessary to carry even a light pack.

There was a return policy at the hiking store. After working with the staff trying out five different packs, I realized nothing worked. I knew the only hope was to leave stuff behind and go without. I started traveling with no sleeping bag, no rain gear, no cooking. I would go "dry." I knew what to eat for energy being a marathon runner and nutrition teacher.

Where there's a will, there's a way and I was determined to find it. Nothing was going to stop me from my dream, plus these kids in the anti-gang program believed in me just like I believed in them and their crazy dreams. The challenge and purpose of my dream had now become greater. I had a great personal desire to hike the Trail, but now it became necessary to do the thru-hike from Georgia to Maine, whether I wanted to or not. As I said before, these kids had enough people who had let them down, and I was not going to be just another over promising phony.

Chapter 20
I Reveal My Dream to "Hankshwa"

"Go confidently in the direction of your dreams.
Live the life you have imagined." – *Henry David Thoreau*

As I mentioned earlier, from the time he was very young Tom had entered my thoughts when it came to my dream to thru-hike the Trail. In my mind, the thought that he might be part of the adventure began in the back woods down at Forge Pond when he was just two years old and would come to fruition when he graduated from high school. It would be the same year in which I planned to retire. If he shared my desire, we could do it together before he went off to college and a career.

As the years passed, I had spoken to a few father/son and father/daughter combinations whom I had met on my section hiking of the Trail in New England. Some advised me not to attempt it. I realized it would be much tougher to thru-hike the Trail with "Hankshwa" than it would be to go it alone. However, I also believed, it would be an amazing adventure that we would never forget. Granted this was my dream, but I would bring him along if he wanted to be part of it. He would only come with me if he was 100% sure he wanted to go. There is nothing worse on a hike (and this would be a long one) than being with someone who does not want to be there. Whether "Hankshwa" would be with me or not was something only time would tell.

Over the next fifteen years, Tom and I would hike the mountains and canoe the lakes and rivers of northern New England. My son would develop a love of the outdoors and nature that would last a lifetime. It would be something I felt sure he would share with his own children some day. Then one cold Saturday in January 2007 during his last year of high school, I asked him to take a ride with me. We ended up in the deserted parking lot of Duxbury Beach and told him I needed to talk to him about something very important. I made him promise he would not speak to anyone about our conversation.

"What is it Dad?" he asked, as the cold wind shook the only vehicle in the beach parking lot, on that cold winter day.

"I want to tell you about something I have been dreaming about for a long time, but you must promise to keep this between you and me," I demanded.

"Okay, Dad, if that is what you want," he said.

"Tom, just hear me out," I said.

I went on to tell him about my dream to hike the Trail; I was revealing it for the first time to anyone besides those kids in my anti-gang program. I explained how I had met someone when I was 26 and going nowhere in life and how this encounter had changed everything. I went on to tell Tom that this man was one of the first to ever take the adventurous journey from Georgia to Maine. I shared everything with Tom just as I have laid it out in this book. I focused on the fact that the dream had started when Christina was just 18 months old, and how I had always known I would have to wait to fulfill my dream. I told Tom that the dream of hiking the Trail was the fuel behind my becoming a hiker, marathon runner and triathlete. I related how it had impacted my decision to go back to school and become a health educator and track coach. Then I told Tom that when he came along after sixteen years of marriage, he had entered my dream.

"Ever since I first put you in that backyard tent when you were two years old, I've thought that when you graduated from high school I would retire, and we could do the Trail together. But I do not want you to become part of my dream and come along unless you are 100% sure you want to do this hike. Don't tell me how you feel now. I want you to think about it for a long time," I explained.

"How long have you been thinking about this?" he asked with confusion.

"Thirty-two years!" I told him.

"Old Buzzard, do you really think you can do this? I mean you're kind of old aren't you?" he asked calling me by the hiking nickname he had dubbed me several years earlier.

"You mean physically?" I asked.

"Yes," Tom stated.

"Tom, this is more of a mental challenge than a physical one, and I'm not worried about me, as much as I'm concerned with you," I said.

"What do you mean by that?" he asked.

"Listen, I'm a lot stronger than you mentally. All those years of marathon running and hiking have made me headstrong. Don't think I want you to come along for me. It will be a lot tougher to take you along than to hike the Trail by myself," I explained.

"Why is that?" he inquired.

"If you sprain an ankle, then I will have to contend with you. If I go it alone, the only one I have to take care of is me. I can hike as many miles as I want, take a rest when I want, and get up when I want. If you do this with me, it will be harder; some mornings I'll tell you to hike alone, and we'll meet up somewhere later on because being on top of each other every day and every night will wear on both of us. At times we'll need our own space," I explained.

I then went on to say that if he came along, I had figured we would go southbound from Maine to Georgia, taking off right after he graduated and I retired in June. I had based this start time in consideration that the bugs are bad and the rivers are raging in late May and early June in Maine. I told Tom that if we took off at the end of June we would be home in time for Thanksgiving dinner, if things went well, if they did not, we would at least be home by Christmas. I explained that he could start college in January or work until the next September before starting school.

"Like I said when we started this conversation, just think about all this and give it time to sink in. I don't want you to tell me whether you want to come along now. Please don't feel you have to do this for me. Your decision should be based solely on whether or not you truly want to go. This is my dream, but if you want to enter it you're welcome," I again explained.

"What's Mom going to think?" he asked.

"I don't know, but I'm hoping she realizes how important this is to me. I have saved up enough to get her an RV, and she can invite her girlfriends along for company, if she wants to do it this way. I just need to do this. It has been my dream for all these years and hope she'll understand," I answered.

"How long do you figure this will take?" Tom asked.

"I know myself as a hiker and have section hiked most of the Trail from Rutland, Vermont through to the Bigelow Mountain Range in

Maine. So I have planned on it taking five months to do the entire thru-hike, but it's hard to say, as so many things can happen or go wrong. I have saved the Trail north of the Bigelows on purpose for this thru-hike. I have always wanted to hike the "100 Mile Wilderness" portion of the Trail in the Great North Woods of Maine, but kept it for this adventure," I replied.

Tom's head, I could tell, was spinning during the drive home from the beach parking lot. I had let out a bombshell, and it was a lot to comprehend all at once. He had just received early acceptance and a scholarship at the University of New England in Maine less than a month ago. I know he had his heart set on going to college in the fall, but I wanted to let him know now what I was planning, in case he wanted to delay starting college.

This would be an experience that most 18-year-olds would never have, and it would benefit him in many ways. I did not want to spell it out in those terms or attempt in any way to sway or bribe him into hiking the Trail. If Tom wanted to come along fine, and if he didn't want to be part of my dream, well that would be fine too.

Tom graduated and I retired in June 2007, and he had never come to speak to me. I knew his heart and soul were not into my dream, so I went ahead to make my own plans to thru-hike the Trail northbound from Georgia to Maine in the following Spring of 2008. It was time to prepare and let the rest of the family know. The only way I would go to Georgia and finally realize my dream was with a 100% commitment from Karen and my kids to support me; otherwise, it was not going to happen.

Chapter 21

I Break Thirty-Two Years of Silence
with My Family

"I have spread my dreams under your feet; Tread softly, because you tread on my dreams." – *William Butler Yeats*

They say the toughest mile of the whole Trail is Mahoosuc Notch. So I decided in late August 2007 after retiring in June to hike the one section I had not done between Rutland and the Bigelows in Maine to see if my heart and soul were 100% a go. I figured, if I still enjoyed hiking after the section from Gorham, New Hampshire to Grafton Notch, it would be time to reveal my dream to Karen and my daughters, Christina and Samantha, both of whom were now grown and married. The Mahoosuc Range is rugged, and the hiking had been slow and cautious. A smile was still on my face when I came out of the woods. It was time to go back to our home in Maine to organize my thoughts in order to communicate my dream to the rest of the family after thirty-two years.

Karen and I had put our home in Massachusetts up for sale with the game plan to build an in-law apartment attached to my daughter Samantha's home in Kingston, Massachusetts. My wife did not want to spend all winter in the sub freezing isolation of Maine. Both Christina and Samantha and their husbands had settled into their own homes in Kingston along with our grandchildren. So Karen and I planned to head south from Maine to spend winters in Massachusetts and then to head back to Maine in the spring each year. Of course, I would still venture north during the winters from time to time to be in those mountains. I would use the "closed for the winter" house in Maine as my outpost.

I had to figure out how I would tell Karen and my daughters about a dream I had harbored in silence for over thirty years. Busy as everyone always seemed to be, it was never easy to get everyone to sit down together without a lot of advanced notice. I certainly wasn't about to break the news around the Thanksgiving table or the Christmas tree. So I made the decision to divulge my plans on paper and made copies for Karen and my daughters. I summed up the last thirty years in a six-page handwritten letter explaining how this dream originated, grew and changed my life for the positive.

On September 10, 2007 I sat down with Karen and asked her to read something very important to me. She read a little, put the paper down, stared, read some more and finally asked,

"Why didn't you tell me about your dream over the last thirty-two years? What are you trying to do to me? This is a total shock!"

"It started slowly as a distant dream and grew over years. I wasn't sure it would ever materialize and didn't want to bring it up until I knew. I just finished section hiking the toughest part of the whole Trail, and I still want more. I know now how much I want to do this thru-hike. If you read the section about coming along with me..." I started to say.

"I can't hike with my knees, and I wouldn't do this even if I could. What are you talking about?" she interrupted.

She looked at the section explaining how I had saved money to buy her an RV allowing her to follow me along the Trail, and how I could stay with her most nights. It included how she could ask her friends to come along for periods of time for company, and they could shop 'til they dropped. I felt that there had to be a way to make it work for her. Well, she's not the adventurous type.

"I don't want to drive one of those things around the country following you. I just can't believe you waited all this time to drop this bomb on me. Can you understand why I'm a little taken aback by all this?" she asked.

"I'm sorry, but I wasn't sure it would happen and have always thought that a person should keep his or her dreams close to the vest until it is truly possible. People thought I was crazy when I started running marathons. I figured if I started telling everyone that I wanted to hike from Georgia to Maine when I was around 60, they would duct tape me to a chair and send me to a home. I felt it would be better to stay silent until I was prepared and knew I could do it. So please think about coming along. This could be quite an adventure together," I replied.

I like to surprise people, but this was too much. I had my daughters in tears. They finally understood their father... why I ran all those marathons, triathlons, and why I was so damn cheap. They said they would hate to see me go, but thought it was a wonderful dream. My son Tom said it was the greatest thing he had ever heard, and he urged me to fulfill my dream. Karen, on the other hand, had a reason to be upset, specifically for not sharing my dream with her for over three decades. My family is close and the only way I'd do this was with their approval. My three kids were all on board, and I gave Karen the next three days to think about it all and change her mind about coming along. For the next three days she gave me long looks with her piercing icy blue eyes and slammed a lot of doors.

She finally came to me, the good girl she is, and said, "I can see your whole life is wrapped up in this dream, and you won't be fulfilled until you do this hike from Georgia to Maine. I don't want to keep you from reaching this crazy dream of yours. I just can't believe you waited all this time to drop this on me. Can you understand why I'm so upset? So if you really want to do this go ahead, hike the stupid Trail. Get it done and get back to us safe, but there's no way I'm following you around the country in a stupid bus!"

Realizing I would no longer need all the money I had saved and wanting to get my wife settled in the new in-law apartment by spring, I lowered the price of our Massachusetts home and sold it exactly eleven days later. We settled the sale on September 21st, which coincidently was the date I had first kissed this girl some thirty-eight years earlier.

With my dream "a go" I felt elated. I hiked to the summit of Mt. Adams alone one day in mid-week. I found myself standing on the top of this mountain screaming at the heavens and thanking God for this chance in life. Tears streamed down my cheeks because I understood how lucky I was to have this opportunity to make my dream come true.

Once more people found out about my plans, I got a call from Captain Sargo of the Brockton Police Department. He said he knew people in the city and wondered if I would be willing to blog my adventure from Georgia to Maine in the city newspaper, the Brockton Enterprise, so my students and others could virtually accompany the "Old Buzzard" making his dream a reality at long last. There was just one minor hitch. I did not even know how to turn on a computer, as I had lived a different life. Point at a tree, hand me an axe, and I'll drop it where you want it, but a computer...forget it! I have enough trouble with telephones. Technology and the Old Buzzard are not simpatico. But I got a crash course from Samantha, my graphic designer daughter, who agreed to coordinate with Ken Johnson at the newspaper.

I bought the first cell phone of my life and was instructed on how to take pictures to send back home to be inserted into the blog as I journeyed north. I got a phone you could drop on a rock, plunk underwater and it would still operate fine. The newspaper put out the word that I would be blogging as I hiked the Trail. I started getting emails from students I had not heard from in over twenty years, as far off as Taiwan. It was wonderfully exciting.

The in-law apartment was completed, and Karen settled in to be with Samantha, who was expecting her first child on March 25th. This became a little bit of a problem seeing as how most thru-hikers are already heading north from Georgia by this time. It was also a blessing, as Karen loves babies, and this would keep her occupied and content in my absence. Springtime came, and my daughter told me to leave. I told her Grand-Daddies stick around for their grand babies to be born. So I delayed my flight to Georgia planning to be at Springer and begin my first steps northward on April 8th. I was a little concerned with the late start, but figured I would have time to make it to Maine by the fall. I had been blessed with another grandson and spent the first two weeks of his life with him before hitting the Trail.

Chapter 22
My Time Had Come

"Each man should frame his life so that at some future hour fact and his dreaming meet." – *Victor Hugo*

I had made a visit to the Boys & Girls Club in Brockton just a few weeks before my departure and presented a slide show of some of my hikes in the "Whites." I shared with the kids the minimal supplies that I would carry on the Trail. I explained how having this dream to hike the Trail had made all the difference in my life. The kids would be following my adventure from Georgia to Maine by reading my blog on the computers at the Club. I thought of all my students in the anti-gang program who had known before anyone else about my dream. Those kids knew and believed in me, just as I believed in them. It remained my hope that these kids would look at themselves and realize their own personal dreams were up to them and no one else. I thought if they followed my blog and saw their former old teacher hike that trail from Georgia to Maine, who had told them about it so many years ago, that it would spur them on to follow their own dreams.

Karen, my understanding and loving wife, drove me to the bus terminal in Plymouth the morning of my departure. This would be our longest separation since we met nearly forty years earlier. I realize it would not be easy for her to let me go. But our love is so strong, and she wanted me to fulfill the dream I had carried inside for so long.

As the airport bus pulled up to the curb, I hugged and kissed Karen good-bye and the last thing I teased was, "You won't even know I'm gone. You love babies, and I don't know what to do with them until they're at least four years old."

It was difficult to believe this was really happening, and I kept thinking that I was still just dreaming. As I rode from Plymouth to Logan Airport in Boston, I sat in the back of the bus listening to inspirational music related to goals and dreams. Tom had compiled a playlist for me on an iPod that all my kids had given to me. The plan was to fly to Atlanta, Georgia and from there take the local MARTA train to the last stop, where I would wait to be picked up by a shuttle van which would take me to Josh and Lee's Hiker Hostel for the evening. I would sit on the porch and gaze in the distance at Springer Mountain, where I would begin my journey the next day. I would hike more than 2000 miles up and over hundreds of mountains, through fourteen states and then finish on the summit of Mt. Katahdin (Mt. K) in Maine, the northern terminus of the famous Appalachian Trail.

Karen and the kids had been nervous about me and worried I would some how screw up the flight plan to Atlanta. I had only been on a plane a few times in my life, and I had to change planes in New York City. They treated me like a little kid traveling solo, but their fears were justified, as I do much better in the woods than I do with crowds and schedules. So I paid attention to all the directions, made my Atlanta connection, and hoped I would make it to the shuttle van to the Hiker Hostel by late afternoon. I wanted the time to sit on that porch in a rocker and take in the view of Springer.

When they ticketed my backpack in Boston, I watched it leave my sight, and I felt nervous that I might never see it again. I finally found the baggage claim area in Atlanta and was so relieved to see it on the carousel belt. My pack and I would soon become one, like another appendage of my body. It would never leave my sight again during the next five months. Many hikers will put their packs in the trunk of a car when they hitch a ride or leave it outside a store when resupplying, but not me. My plan was to sit with my pack on my lap or wheel it around a store in a shopping cart. Everything I owned for my journey was in that pack, and I intended to guard it with my life. I had told myself that I would only give it up to a bear. If a bear wanted it, all I would have to do is unclip my chest and waist straps, lay it down on the ground, and walk quietly away. This was my plan, and I stuck by it.

After retrieving my pack at the baggage claim area of Atlanta Airport, I asked an attendant where I could board the MARTA train. I felt independent and carefree as I took the long walk through one of the largest airports in America to the train. Just a two-dollar fare and I was through the turnstile on my way to the MARTA train platform. As the train pulled up and the doors opened, I entered noticing a young man sitting alone with an old, very large, external frame pack in front of him. I walked slowly towards him with my small, interior framed pack, noticing his tattoos, earrings and a pink guitar he had attached to his pack.

"You hiking the Trail?" I asked.

"Yeah, you?" he responded.

"Yes. Where you from?" I inquired.

"Caribou, Maine, once upon a time," was his answer.

"Caribou Joe" or later "Guitar Joe" would be the first thru-hiker I would meet of the eventual hundreds I would come across. I had thought this hike would be a time of solitude, but it turned out to be totally the opposite. The socialization of the sub-culture of hikers was something I had not prepared for, and it would be one of the biggest surprises of the entire adventure. They come from every state in America and from all over the world to experience this adventure. I met hikers from Europe, Asia, New Zealand, and Australia. Over 3000 would attempt to make the entire journey in that spring of 2008, but just over 500 of us would stand on the summit of Mt. K close to six months later.

Joe and I would hike together in the early days of the Trail in Georgia, and he would tell me his story. He was an adventurer in the truest sense of the word. He left the far reaches of northern Maine known as Aroostook County (hereafter the County) in his early twenties and had never looked back. Joe had finished two years of college in electrical engineering. He intended to eventually finish this education, but the open road and adventure was calling first. He had seen a lot in his short life and had experienced much hardship. He spoke of a close girlfriend back in the County who had strung him along for years and about the games she played. The final blow came when he discovered she had not been straight with him about her rehabilitation from drug use. He had finally walked out when he discovered her further addiction to heroin and the "tracks" in obscure parts of her body. He had a strong aversion to conviction against drug use and had seen the destruction of many lives and futures in the County. Joe had then hit the road with his pack and pink guitar. He had been in almost every state in the continental United States. He had been living out of his old car for most of the last few years, taking odd jobs including working on a ranch in Texas, in factories, bar rooms, and even playing that pink guitar now and then for money. Everything he owned was in that old pack.

"Are you taking the shuttle to the 'Hiker Hostel' to stay the night?" I asked, as we got off the train.

"What shuttle?" he asked. Joe's plan was the same as usual, no plan. He figured he would somehow get to Springer Mt. by "hitching" or by whatever means were available. I explained that for $69.00, I would be shuttled, stay the night at this nice log cabin owned by former thru-hikers, have breakfast in the morning and after be driven to the trailhead to begin the hike.

"Forget it. I'm not paying any 69 bucks," Joe replied.

"Well, maybe there will be room in the shuttle and they can get you close to the trailhead for a few bucks," I explained.

As we waited for the shuttle, Joe lifted his pack saying, "I got to get rid of some weight. This thing must weigh ninety pounds."

I went to lift it, laughing, "I couldn't carry that thing across the parking lot. What do you have in there?" I asked. Joe started emptying his pack, throwing assorted items into the nearest trash barrel. What came out of his pack put me in a fit of laughter: an old blanket, textbooks, notebooks, gardening tools, and a tarp. I loved this kid. He was a bright, carefree character, living life to the fullest; this kid from the County had a passion for experiencing the open road and adventure.

"Is this where I pick up the shuttle?" a voice from the parking lot asked.

"This is the place," I yelled back.

He introduced himself as Barney, a dentist from Tucson, Arizona. He had never hiked in his life. But I would soon discover he was one of the many I would meet in the beginning of this adventure. There were countless individuals I would come across in the first few weeks who had read some book about the AT and fantasized about hiking it. I could not understand why there were so many who came to make an attempt to hike more than 2000 miles over rugged terrain with little or no knowledge of hiking and the outdoors. Barney and others had invested thousands of dollars in state-of-the art hiking equipment to come to Georgia to hike the Trail. For so many it would remain just a fantasy. They were unprepared both physically and mentally, but even with no real preparation or hiking experience, they came.

I had known from the beginning there would be many obstacles against my reaching Mt. K. This hike was more a mental challenge than a physical one. I had prepared for the hike for some thirty-three years. But even with all my research and years of work to prepare both physically and mentally, I still understood that the chances of completing the thru-hike would not be in my favor. Bad luck in the form of injuries, falls, unexpected problems at home, sickness, insect bites, missing my family and other unforeseen circumstances could keep me from making it.

But as I have said many times before, whether or not I made it all the way to Maine was not the most important thing. It was having the dream of doing so that had transformed my life from one of misery to one of happiness. Finishing the thru-hike of the Trail would be just the frosting on the cake for me. It would be the culmination of my entire life in this journey of hope. I prayed that luck would be on my side, and fully understood that with one false step it could be over.

My final preparations would involve hiking daily with my pack filled with soda cans wrapped in towels. Many experienced sources had told me that if a hiker is still on the Trail after 500 miles, that hiker is in AT shape and from a physical condition perspective is likely to make it the whole way. Whether you are in hiking shape from the start is not as important as making the 500-mile mark. After the 500 miles, the only thing that will stop you now is what I already mentioned, bad luck.

I had waited so long to hike the Trail there was no way I wanted to struggle getting into hiking shape those first 500 miles. I wanted to improve my odds by showing up in good hiking condition, so I could enjoy the whole journey. I had waited most of my adult life for this and wanted to enjoy the experience from the very beginning. So in the months immediately prior to my departure for Georgia I would drive forty minutes each morning to Blue Hills. With my twenty-five to thirty pound pack I would hike up and down "Skyline Trail," a one and a half mile "climb" with an elevation gain of 600 feet. I would fly up and down this trail for a 3-mile loop two or three times each day, as long as it was free of frozen snow and ice.

Although I had retired from my position as a health educator in Brockton, I had still coached winter track before hitting the Trail in Georgia. So after hiking in Blue Hills, I would make the short twenty minute drive to the school track where I could work out and take a shower at the field house before anyone else showed up. Once the snow and ice set in, I also used the facilities of the local YMCA. With my pack on my back, I would hit the treadmill for an hour or so cranking at 2.8 to 3 miles an hour at a 13-15 incline (15 is the max level). After this I would hit the weights, concentrating on my core, legs and back. My YMCA regimen and afternoon coaching at Brockton High kept me busy until it was time to head south.

On the day of my arrival in Georgia, as I crawled into the back seat of the van to the hostel, I looked around at the other hopefuls. Many of my fellow passengers were not in optimum condition. They spoke of being overweight, and as I listened intently to their conversations, I concluded that most had little or no hiking experience. Some of them even spoke of hiking the Trail as a way to lose weight and to get into shape. So although I was surrounded by these others, most of whom were less than half my age, I felt confident and mentally ready for tomorrow.

As I revealed earlier, Old Buzzard, my hiking name, was graciously given to me by my son, Tom, back in 2003 while hiking with him in the Whites that summer. Every 15-year-old views his old man as some ancient old buzzard. As my nose is rather prominent and I am somewhat round shouldered from sclerosis, Old Buzzard seemed fitting and has stuck with me ever since that fateful day. It was the name bestowed upon me with love from a wonderful son with whom I had been hiking since he was 4 years of age. For twenty years prior to Tom christening me Old Buzzard, I had gone by the hiking name "Tonto." But the Lone Ranger had passed away, and a new name seemed more appropriate. I could not completely shake off this former label and would start signing the AT registers as Old Buzzard-Tonto.

From my vantage point sitting in the back seat of that large transport van on the way to Josh and Lee's "Hiker Hostel," I evaluated the group and silently thought to myself that the only one making it to Mt. K besides this Old Buzzard would be the kid from Connecticut with the hiker name "Fred." His tall lanky frame and experience hiking in the Whites of New Hampshire gave him the advantage over the rest of the passengers in the van. I did not know it at the time, but Fred and I would become very close and hike many miles together. Eric Fredricksen had given himself his hiking name Fred to prevent others from placing a label on him he would not enjoy. It was not long before I would change it.

Fred was 27 and had his MBA and a good job back home. His boss granted him the time off to hike the Trail and with his job waiting for him upon his return. He also told me his story of having a girlfriend for the last 10 years, that some day he was going to propose to and get married. He should have never displayed all this information to an old curmudgeon like me. With this knowledge it didn't take long to label him with a new hiker handle. When hikers meet, someone usually gets around to asking you your hiking name.

"No his name isn't just Fred. The kid has his MBA and a great job back home, which he walked out on. He also has some girlfriend he's been stringin' along for the last decade telling the girl he's going to marry her some day. Ya right, the guy's totally noncommittal to the workforce and to this poor girl. He's out here freeloading and tries telling everyone his name is just Fred. His full name is Freddy the Freeloader. The kid's a bum!"

To this day I never knew what Fred thought of this ribbing. His poker face never showed how he felt about my speaking out like this. I guess it didn't irritate him too much, as we are still friends and on occasion hike together. He went back to that job he had and that girl he was supposed to marry some day was long gone. Freeloader crossed paths one evening with a SOBO (southbounder) sweetheart named "Sled Dog Kristen" (SDK), and a year later Karen and I were honored to attend their wedding. They now have 3 kids and counting.

The owners of the hostel, Lee and Josh, had thru-hiked the Trail back in the late 1990's, and after their adventure decided to look for a piece of land near Springer Mt. to build this beautiful log cabin with a view of the mountain from their back porch. They are a wonderful, caring couple who service hikers either starting or ending their hike.

As we pulled our gear out of the back of the van, I noticed a young lady in her late twenties who had come all the way from Michigan with her overweight husband, she was struggling to carry her 6000-cubic inch pack up the stairs of the cabin. Again, I wondered what people were thinking, and what could possibly be so necessary to have a pack that size. I would not have carried a pack that size even without my cervical spinal problem. I would be amazed at the people and personalities I would come across during the initial stages of hiking the Trail.

I took a moment alone just before sunset to sit in an old rocker on that back porch and to stare at the summit of Springer Mt., where it would all begin the next morning. I had a feeling of great comfort and happiness. I had made it after thirty-three years of wishing, hoping, and preparing for this day. The journey had been all worth it, a journey which changed my entire existence for the better. I was filled with excitement and barely slept that night. I found myself lying awake in a bottom bunk, sharing a room with three other hopefuls.

After a killer breakfast where I stuffed in one last pancake, we all piled into the van with Josh and headed to the trailhead. As we headed up the winding dirt road, Josh talked about his own thru-hike experience. He explained he had taken thirty days off trail and told us to enjoy the adventure and hike our own hike.

Sitting next to Josh on the passenger side was a 2006 former thru-hiker, whom I had just met that morning. He had a three-week window of opportunity before he had to report for his National Guard duty. His fellow guardsmen thought he was crazy for wanting to come back to the Trail to sleep on the ground and "rough it." It was something they were all required to do as part their duty, so they could not understand why anyone would want to do this as some kind of R & R. As I sat in the back of the van, I listened intently as he spoke. His love and respect for this Trail rang loud and clear. He would not be the only former thru-hiker I would meet along the way who had returned for more. He spoke with an almost spiritual reverence about the Trail. To him it was so much more than a path through the woods.

His plan was to "section hike" from Springer Mt. to Hot Springs, North Carolina before reporting for duty. I decided, as we pulled our gear out of the van, that I would tag along with this experienced thru-hiker. I figured he knew the Trail, and I was eager to learn whatever bits of wisdom he would share with me. "Grizzly Bear" or "Grizz," as he was known, kind of looked like a bear. I wondered how anyone of his size and girth could hike, but discovered early on he was as strong as a bear too. We headed to the summit of Springer and signed the register to begin the journey north. Now there was just 2176 miles to reach my dream of a lifetime.

I paused to take a few pictures at the cloud covered summit after "Grizz" and the others had set out. I got on my knees next to the plaque in the rock signifying the southern terminus and the beginning of the Trail; I thanked God for the last 33 years of my altered life and for the journey that had brought me to this path in the wilderness. My prayer was one of thanks for the journey that had changed my life, saved my life, and got me here to the trailhead. I knew I owed my life to my beautiful wife, Karen, my "Sugar Babes," to that stranger I had encountered around the campfire in the New Hampshire woods so many years ago, and to the dream of hiking the Appalachian Trail.

In decades past only 10% of those who attempted to thru-hike would make it all the way to the summit of Mt. Katahdin, "The Holy Grail." The odds are better now with so many helpful people catering to the hikers in the little hamlets along the corridor of the Trail. The success rate in 2008 was up to 15%. As I spoke to God that first morning, I again realized that making it all the way was not the most important thing; the fact that my journey had brought me to this spiritual path in the woods was what mattered.

I then pulled out the letter Tom had written and left on the front seat of my truck less than four months before on Christmas Day. Still on my knees I read it again. Tom had never spoken to me about whether or not he wanted to come along since our discussion that cold and windy day sitting in the beach parking lot over a year ago. With his permission, I share his letter:

"Follow Your Dreams"
(December 25, 2007)
Dear Dad,

I've been thinking about this for awhile now and I really wanted to give you something special for Christmas this year. That's why I have waited to write this to you. Follow your dreams.

Last winter when you shared your dream with me about hiking the AT so many things were racing through my mind. How long has he been thinking about this? Is he capable of doing it? What is the rest of the family going to think? Most importantly though my number one thought was "Go for it!" "Just do it," as Nike says. I thought it was the greatest thing I had ever heard. It made so much sense to me about you after you had told me about it.

Some of the greatest advice I ever came across I received this past summer from a close friend. She told me when you want to do something or are thinking about doing something you have to "just jump." She explained how she went bungi jumping with her brother and mother and was naturally afraid to jump. Her brother and mother took two hours to finally go, but she told me that she just said screw it and jumped. She explained how it was the best feeling in the world. Not the bungi jump in itself but the way she "just jumped." That is what you have to do, Dad. Don't be her mother and brother up on the ledge second guessing things. It's just something you just have to "jump" for. You don't know where you're going to land, but how will you ever know if you don't jump? I am a big believer of "What if it all ends tomorrow" because think about it... what if there was no tomorrow? Tomorrow is never guaranteed and each day of life is a gift. These are things that were not only self-taught by me but taught by you as well and I know you believe the same. There are some great proverbs from Poor Richard's Almanac that describe these types of things that I read this past semester.

"Work while it is called for today for you know not how much you may be hindered tomorrow." "Have you something to do tomorrow? Do it today."

I know you are ready for this challenge now and ready to fulfill your dream. I am astounded that you want to include others dreams in your own and there are no words to explain that. I hope everything follows through to get that part rolling, but even if it doesn't just know that this is your dream that you are chasing.

There is more that you already know but that I would like to touch upon. "A dream unsought is a dream never dreamt." I didn't find that one anywhere I just made it up, but the meaning is to go after your dream and strive to do everything you can to accomplish it. If you make it the whole distance or not doesn't matter. What matters is the journey not the outcome. Shoot for the stars because if you fall you will land in the clouds.

Sometimes I think about how you never sleep. I always think to myself that you were not meant to sleep and that's the reason for it. You can sleep in the grave, why waste time? "The busy man has few idle visitors; to the boiling pot the flies come not." No flies are going to come to your pot, Dad, because you are boiling far too hot. Keep doing all you can to prepare yourself for this.

"For age and against want, save while you may; no morning sun lasts a whole day." I'm telling you Dad you weren't meant to sleep, "The sleeping fox catches no poultry." Take it as a gift.

There will be challenges but each little one is a rung on the ladder. Everything in life comes at us for a reason and it is crucial to our development. Treat your challenge and life as a blueprint to a house. Small things may have to be changed to the blueprint such as measurements and whatnot, but in the end the house always gets built. Even if for some reason your house (Dream) doesn't get built, at least you did everything you could to build it. As

Michael Jordan said, "I can accept failure, but I can't accept not trying." My personal favorite also from Michael is, "If you're trying to achieve, there will be roadblocks. I've had them, everybody has had them. But obstacles don't have to stop you. If you run into a wall, don't turn around and give up. Figure out how to climb it, go through it, or work around it."

I am so happy that you are going to do this and I am appreciative of the fact that you wanted to include me in all of this. Dad, I love hiking and in fact it is the number one thing I want to do right now over playing basketball and going skiing, but I don't love it enough to hike the whole AT with you. This is your dream and I wouldn't want to hinder you in any way by going. This doesn't mean I wouldn't like to go because I want to meet you once you hopefully hit the New England area. There's nothing I would love more than to hike this area on your journey with you. You will have all the knowledge and experience that I would like to hear at the end of the trip. I know my knees are able to meet the challenge as well. I haven't felt this good in a very long time. I actually wish I had known that my school's basketball team would only have 9 players because if I had trained all summer I probably would have made it. However, I am not questioning it because I know everything happens for a reason and God has a plan for me and I am following it. My dream was to play as long as I could and make it as far as I could. When I was younger I thought I was going to be in the NBA or something. I was a dreamer, but it's good to be a dreamer because it made me who I am today. That is the good thing about dreams, Dad, because they bring a lot more than meets the eye.

I couldn't be any more behind you about this. Go for it, jump, just do it. Dream on... Dream until your dream comes true. Let the Dream take you where it's supposed to and wake up when it's over!

I love you, Dad... You've taught me so much.

Love, Tom

Tom is a deep thinker. For eleven months he had thought about my dream and about what I had said before placing this letter on the seat of my truck. He was off to college in September on a scholarship to further his studies in psychology. My plan was to carry this all the way to Mt. K with me and read it during those tough times ahead.

As it turned out, Tom would go down on the parquet floor of a basketball court one more time, three weeks before I headed off to Georgia. This time he would require a complete reconstruction of his knee including having to undergo an ACL surgery. So joining me for any part of this thru-hike would not happen. We had both accepted it.

It seemed strange to be finally here. The adrenaline was coursing through my veins and I could feel my heart pounding in my chest with excitement. My breathing was becoming erratic so I invoked my old mantra, "calm... calm... calm." It was time to take my first steps northward, catch up to Grizz from South Carolina and continue this journey.

Chapter 23
Trail Lessons

"Hike Your Own Hike" – *Mantra of the Appalachian Trail*

A s much as I had built up my dream to thru-hike the Trail in my mind, it turned out to be a far greater experience than I could have ever imagined. The natural beauty of this walk in the wilderness, the hundreds of mountains I went up and over, the change in vegetation and animals as I moved north, the little hamlets along the Trail and the people with whom I crossed paths all would bring me tears of joy along the way. Each state I walked through had a unique flavor all its own for me to savor.

Experiencing the wilderness of the Trail in solitude must have been common back when that pioneer with whom I had shared a camp fire in New Hampshire first thru-hiked it in the early 1970s. The Trail has since become internationally known and is now on the "bucket lists" of many hikers from all parts of the world. Most days I would hike for ten hours. While there were days when I never saw another person, those days were relatively rare.

But the biggest and best surprise of the hike was the amazing diversity of personalities I met along the way. The strong spirited and adventurous cast of characters I discovered on this path in the woods has left me with a lifetime of joyful memories. The culture of the Trail is unique, and its personality uplifting. The camaraderie and bonding I enjoyed with my fellow hikers would remind me at times of my running club back home. But I found being part of a "family" of fellow thru-hikers to be even more emotionally intense; we became a band of brothers and sisters. Our friendships will last forever.

Feeding off others enthusiasm and encouragement on those tough days pushes a hiker northward. It isn't just your fellow hikers who are a positive influence but the people along the whole length of the Trail. These people kept our spirits up that summer of 2008, even over a 23-day stretch of nearly daily rain. Total strangers in the little villages adjacent to the Trail were so amazingly helpful, kind, and so giving from deep within their hearts. The trusting, down to earth individuals I came across during my thru-hike in the little towns and crossroads rekindled my hope for America. The inhabitants of these places from Georgia to Maine are the true heart and soul of this country; they retain what so many others have lost in the past half century.

The old American spirit of neighbor helping neighbor is still alive and strong on the Trail. All of the "Trail Magic" (gestures of kindness) that I was lucky enough to receive during this walk in the woods was greatly appreciated. I vowed that in the years to come, I would return Trail Magic to other hikers struggling to make it to Mt. Katahdin.

As we go through our daily lives and observe acts of unkindness and as the media bears witness to the evils some people perpetrate on others, it is all too easy to become jaded and mistrustful of the world. Too many people hide behind the protective walls of their homes with complicated alarm systems and, for some, even a gun at the ready. I never feel this way in the wilderness of the mountains.

There are a lot of wonderful people out here willing their fellow humans forward along their journeys toward their dreams. This path through the woods from Georgia to Maine, often described as "The Green Tunnel," is a mystical place in that it somehow manages to be both an escape from reality and the ultimate reality. The Trail is a literal and figurative breath of fresh air in a struggling world. Through my experience I was able to validate that the heart of America is still alive and well.

"Hike Your Own Hike" is an expression you hear a lot out on the Trail. During the initial stages of the hike some of the older hikers reminded me of this as I moved along with Freddy the Freeloader and a dozen other "20-somethings." They would say, "Old Buzzard, you're not hiking your own hike. You're hiking their hike."

"Where are you kids hoping to get to today?" I'd ask before breaking camp each morning. They would offer up a destination about 20 miles or so north and ask,

"You gonna make it Old Buzzard?"

It sounded like some type of challenge and at the end of each day, an hour or so after these young whipper snappers had already settled in for the evening, I would haul my tired, old, wreck of a body into camp. "Hike My Own Hike." I thought about this each day in the beginning, but finally realized I was hiking my own hike. It's hard to describe the feeling of being 59-years-old moving through these woods with its tough terrain and challenges with 23-year-olds. I had a feeling of life and renewed energy that most people wouldn't understand except for those my age, who have done something similar. I had the time of my life with these wonderful young people. Guitar Joe, Freeloader, and Grizz were just the beginning. Later there would be "Moccasin," from Detroit, "Space Dots," from Richmond, Virginia and his side-kick, "Wildflower" hailing from somewhere in New Jersey.

Then there were the three kids from Ohio State University, I had labeled the "O.S.U. Boys," and they had two other young characters tagging along with them; "10 O'clock" from New Hampshire and "Pre" hailed from Houston. "Daisy" was an international young character from the "Land Down Under" with whom I would have so much fun comparing accents.

"Hey, Buzzard, say 'Park your car at Fenway Park' again." The young guy from Australia loved my combination of the Boston/Maine accents, and I cherished his dialect from another far off part of the world.

In Virginia, I would meet up with a wonderful young couple from Georgia, "Meatbag" and "Doxie," and later on with "Catfish," the 23-year-old farm boy also from Georgia. The politeness of the kids from the South was well appreciated and welcomed. I came to love the young people from the South, especially Georgia. They are so respectful and thoughtful of others. It seems they know how to raise their "youngins" down there. Here is my initial exchange with Catfish:

"Catfish, I know it's customary to address an older guy like me as sir, but you can call me Old Buzzard like everyone else."

"I'm sorry sir, but I can't do that."

"Why not? Everyone else does."

"It's disrespectful, sir."

After further discussion Catfish finally compromised by dropping the Old and addressing me as just Buzzard. So Catfish and Buzzard would be connected one day in Vermont being both adamant "Purists." There are all kinds of hikers on the Trail. Purists walk every inch of the Trail passing by each white blaze (the 2"x 6" white painted markers on the

AT), whereas "Blue Blazers" take cut off portions of the Trail to shorten the distance or take an easier route from time to time. Lastly there are those on the Trail called "Yellow Blazers" who will take rides along the way to avoid certain difficult mountains. I discovered a few "wannabee" thru-hikers telling people they hiked the entire 2176 miles when in reality they did not. I could not understand this group and their disrespect of the Trail, not so much because they did not hike the Trail as a Purist, but because they lied about it.

A bunch of older hikers like me discussed the character of the wonderful young people we met on this walk. We opined that doing something as challenging and difficult as hiking the Trail should be a prerequisite for being a politician or other government official in this country. These kids had what it takes to be leaders. Those that continued through the rain, snow, humidity, heat, cold, bugs, mud, sicknesses, injuries and the Trail's daily tough ups and downs had the discipline, determination, dedication and desire to overcome most any obstacle. It would be great to have leaders with these qualities.

Some hikers can be ornery, while others can take themselves and the experience too seriously. When hiking along side so many diverse personalities and age groups, it helps to have a warped sense of humor and to be thick-skinned. It is best to bear in mind that the kidding and pranks are in jest, and even part of the Trail's culture and camaraderie. The creativeness and imagination of many of the young thru-hikers were constantly evident as they established nicknames for greenhorns and other hikers on the Trail. They hung new "handles" on people based upon some observation of their behaviors or aspect of their personalities. I would find great pleasure and humor with this bunch of young hikers. We have remained friends, and I have since been honored to attend the weddings of four of them.

I hiked the Trail differently than almost anyone else I came across. I really had no choice given the forementioned damage to my cervical vertebra. Georgia started out very tame, but quickly became tougher. The terrain reminded me of the mountains up north. Although this first state only encompasses 75 miles of the Trail, hiking day after day started wearing on my brachial plexus nerve and hence my left shoulder. At times I wondered if I'd even make it to the North Carolina border given the pain I was experiencing. I had to adapt by making changes to lessen the agony.

After struggling one day, an idea went on in my head like a light bulb. I unclipped my sternum strap extending it as far as possible, slipped off my left shoulder strap and then I clipped the sternum strap under my left armpit. A hiker wants most of the weight on the hips, and I would now carry my pack with a tight hip belt and tight right shoulder with no weight on my bad shoulder. This was certainly an unorthodox way to carry a pack, and some of the young bucks I was moving down the Trail with found it amusing, but the Old Buzzard needed to do what was necessary to continue on the Trail.

Carrying the pack tipped side ways across my back was working. After two hours or so with the pack in this position my pain was alleviated. I would now switch back and forth—lugging the pack for the next two hours in a more conventional upright position, but still with the weight on my hips and right shoulder, leaving the strap over my left shoulder to hang loose. The rest of the way I would only tighten the left shoulder strap when going up steep grades because, as any hiker knows, the pack should hug close to your body for safety reasons during these times.

I hit the Virginia border in less than five weeks and understood with the warming temperatures that I would be able to get down to the barest necessities to lighten my pack to less than ten pounds. I was now traveling down the Trail with no sleeping bag, and no rain gear. Each night I would change into light-weight running tights and a tight long sleeve running shirt. I would put on a pair of biking socks I kept dry in a zip lock bag and put on a light-weight stocking cap that I bought for 99 cents. You lose much of your body heat through your head and feet, so you want to keep them warm. I slept in a light-weight sleeping bag liner up off the ground on my air filled sleeping mattress. I utilized the 3-sided shelters spaced out along the Trail a lot during the hike, and if it was a cold evening I would enclose myself in my 24-ounce tent for extra warmth. Being from New England, my ability to adapt to the cold is different from someone from the Southern or even Mid-Atlantic States. I was comfortable with no sleeping bag or windbreaker for over 1200 miles of the hike.

I had purchased an 8-ounce hiking umbrella shortly before the trek. I figured it would come in handy if I had to crawl out in the middle of the night in a rainstorm to take care of bodily functions. I had taken it along, but told Karen that I might not need it and would probably end up mailing it home. The young bucks found my hiking umbrella unconventional and started calling me "Mary Poppins." That is they did until a horrific day of hiking in Tennessee during a tornado watch.

We hiked most of the day in deep woods in the wind, rain and clapping thunder. It became a little frightening when my peripheral vision caught sight of a lightning bolt smashing a tree to the ground. I experienced the smell of the burning ozone for the first time in my life and hope it will be the last. I hiked the entire day in my shorts and wicking t-shirt with that open umbrella attached to my pack freeing my hands to use my trekking poles.

Looking at the others sweating in their rain gear with water running down their pants into their shoes made me realize how vital this little hiking umbrella was for my comfort. I was not overheated like the rest of the crew, and I also realized that it gave me another advantage over wearing rain gear. When hiking in rain over wet slippery granite, your stride length naturally shortens, and I began to notice my feet were drier as the umbrella was keeping the rain from running down into my shoes.

"Hey, Old Buzzard, aren't you cold?" one of the young bucks inquired with the temperature hovering around 45 degrees.

"Where you from?" I asked.

"Georgia."

"No, as long as I keep moving I'm comfortable and not cold at all. In New England where I come from this is tropical. If I had on that gear you're hiking with I'd be swimming in my own sweat." They all witnessed the magic of my little hiking umbrella, and the hysteria began when some of them started buying conventional cheap umbrellas in town. I'd be laughing as their generic versions ripped up in the wind. Only Fred, whom I had met that first day in Georgia, sent away for a hiking umbrella and used it the rest of the way.

I'm also different than most when it comes to eating on the Trail. I heard of some others "going dry" as I did, but never ran into another hiker who didn't cook at all. In all my hiking years, even in winter, I have never cooked anything. One evening in the Great Smokies while everyone else was busy firing up their little stoves, cooking, cleaning up pots and utensils, I found myself finally explaining to the group why I never cooked.

"It has finally dawned on me why I never cook when I'm hiking. I'm married to an Italian-American girl, and she prepares some of the greatest meals I've ever come across in my lifetime. She had a grandmother who came over to America from Italy and taught her mother how to master a kitchen, and in turn she taught her daughter, my wife, the same dishes. Some of these recipes are over a hundred years old and have become a family tradition. This wonderful woman cooks for me, serves me, asks if I want seconds, and when I am done, I just deliver my plate to the counter, end of story. I have been spoiled! Watching you all cooking and cleaning up looks like a lot of work, and I want no part of it."

It is commonly said that a thru-hiker making decent time burns 4000 to 6000 calories a day out on the Trail. One of the greatest challenges is carrying all those calories on your back. The rest of America was counting calories to keep their weight down, and we were doing the total opposite. The most important food item for me on the Trail was olive oil because it has 120 calories per tablespoon. You can't get a bigger caloric return for the weight you carry than this precious oil. I carried a 4 oz. plastic bottle of this energy packed fluid and would ask to have it filled in the local diner or luncheonette invariably found in every town I hit along the corridor of the Trail. Only once when I was refused, did I pull out the almighty dollar bill.

The kids I was moving north with laughed when I came out of a store during a resupply with a one pound loaf of 100% whole wheat bread.

"Buzzard, what are you doing with that loaf of bread? It's going to take up half of your food bag and weighs a whole pound."

I stuffed it in my empty food bag and stomped on it to condense the loaf. I answered, "Do you know how much vitamin B is in that one pound and how water and bread fill up your gut? Vitamin B is packed with energy. You guys would be better off eating the cardboard box than that crap you're cooking up for dinner when it comes to nutritional value."

Someone asked me once as I stuffed a half piece of whole grain bread in my mouth taking a swig of olive oil, "What you're doing is kind of like dipping your bread in a plate of olive oil at a restaurant. Why don't you get a little plate?"

"I don't even have a spoon and am going as light as I can, so forget any plate."

We were out in the wilderness and eating with proper etiquette was not a priority. What was a priority was maintaining a diet high in nutritious energy foods to keep the motor running in top gear. My day would start with a 31-gram protein bar followed by two granola and fiber bars and a good liter or two of water. If I wanted to get going early in the morning I would chomp on the bars as I walked along warming up for the day. I would eat every two hours to keep my energy levels up and would also stretch during this ten minute break.

This every two-hour eat and stretch would continue day after day. It worked for me and I never lacked the energy necessary to keep up with this group of young, wild, fun loving kids. So I lived on bread and olive oil, protein and granola bars, and a few handfuls from my gorp bag. My gorp consisted of dried fruits, nuts of all kinds, seeds, dry oatmeal, M&Ms for flavor and anything else I could find in the "hiker boxes" at the hostels I stayed in along the Trail.

On the AT, people put their unwanted items in hiker boxes and anyone can take what they need from them. Many people had supply boxes from home filled with food sent to them periodically as they moved north. I found plenty of supplies in the hiker boxes along the way, and many were overflowing with perfectly good food. I often found full bags of nuts and other calorie dense food items in these boxes. It seemed at times that it maybe possible to hike the entire Trail feeding solely out of hiker boxes.

Dinner was always a 7 oz. pack of either salmon or tuna eaten with some bread. I would open the pack of fish and clean off a small stick with my 1" razor sharp knife. This was the only tool I carried as it only weighed a couple of ounces. This would be followed by more gorp, high fat cheese or what I found as a great hiker food, potato chips. Chips are lightweight, filled with fat, calories and salt, a hiker's dream food. I'd leave every town with the biggest bag of fat filled chips I could find. A pound of chips supplies you with over 2500 calories!

As a teacher of nutrition and a distance runner I had learned the value of fat and salt when exerting oneself for the long haul. Fat weighs in at 9 calories per gram whereas protein and carbohydrates only give you 4. It makes sense to eat a diet high in fat when the challenge is to carry as many calories on your back to feed a 6000 caloric need per day. Calories are the energy source that fuels you, and high fat foods will give you the biggest bang for your buck per ounce of weight carried.

I love ice cream, and the first thing I would search for when hitting a town was some type of chocolate-chunk-walnut-fudge-swirl deluxe. I can't tell you how many ½ gallons of chocolate something I ate along the way. Ice cream was my incentive to keep going in order to make it to the next little hamlet. I'd come into town after town drooling and fantasizing about what kind of chocolate supreme deluxe ice cream I was about to find.

"Buzzard, you're not going to continue eating this way when you get home are you?" asked Tom during a phone call home.

"No, I'd die of a heart attack in no time. I need the energy from fat right now, and it's keeping my weight up."

Of everything needed by the body there is nothing as crucially important as water. The problem with carrying water is that it's heavy.

One liter equals 2 pounds, so early on I decided not to carry any water. I was overly concerned at the beginning of the hike as some days in Georgia it hit 80 degrees, and I was coming from cold New England in early April. However, after a week or so, I was acclimated and figured out that I could hike about ten miles on one liter of water. I started hiking from one stream to the next where I could treat water with a few drops of Aquamira, which are two little plastic bottles of chemicals weighing next to nothing. I had conditioned my body to "camel up" over decades of time and could take down as much as two liters of water in a sitting and hold it with ease if necessary.

The stretch through New York and New Jersey is the only place where it's necessary to carry water because it is dry on the Trail in these states. I carried a little container of sea salt and sprinkled some into all those liters as I refreshed my body. The water was pretty much the consistency of the ocean and salt retains fluids, so this would reduce my hydration needs. I never once got one of those nasty painful muscle spasms even on the hottest days.

My "Sugar Babes" had fought through a bout with cancer a decade earlier, and I knew she would be having one of her periodic check ups while I was hiking in the south. I prayed Karen would be clear of the dreaded cancer; otherwise, I would be headed for the nearest airport. One phone call about any major problem back home, and my journey would be over. Thankfully during my thru-hike, Karen's check-ups indicated she was all clear.

I struggled with aches and pains mostly from injuries and the foolish mistakes I had made over the past three decades. The daily aches and pains were numerous and my cervical spinal area wasn't the only part of my old body barking at me. I had also damaged my lumbar spine and left sacroiliac joint back in my 30's while unloading 18 wheelers to make money during an 11-month layoff from teaching. It was a continuous battle with my ankles, knees and feet. I lost seven toenails, suffered from the dreaded plantar fasciitis at times and had continuous forefoot pain. But I kept inching closer to my home in Maine changing and adjusting the padding in my trail shoes.

I had close encounters with bears, rattlesnakes, poisonous spiders and other animals, but what I feared was the most dangerous animal in the wooded mountains, the deer tick. This tiny parasite can stop the strongest hiker in his tracks, and numerous times in the past I had found them on my body. The trick is to find these tiny insects quickly before they do their debilitating harm. I was constantly searching my body for these horrible creatures, but I missed one in a hidden spot on my back side.

I ended up having to come off the Trail in Massachusetts and landed back home in bed. I suffered with fevers of 103 degrees, was nauseous, dizzy and had debilitating aches and pains in my joints. I was also exhausted and had no desire for food. Karen couldn't believe how each night I would sweat through all three of the beach towels with which I had covered the sheets. I had worked hard at keeping my weight up and only lost ten pounds from Georgia to Massachusetts, but lost another seven pounds in just nine days lying in bed. I was on doxycycline for three weeks. Then, against doctor's orders, I got back on the Trail exactly where I'd left it. In a somewhat weakened condition I continued my journey to pursue my adventure.

Dr. Cody, my primary care physician, had informed me that the doxycycline would make me very sensitive to the sun. I told him that I had to get back on the Trail and would be wearing my safari hat, a long sleeved white wicking shirt, and would use sun block to prevent sunburn. He tried to talk me into also wearing white gloves, but I didn't want to do so. As it turned out, on my second day back on the Trail I entered Vermont and heard a clap of thunder in the distance. It rained most days for the next three weeks.

"Hang in there!" the crowds would scream during the last miles of the countless marathons, triathlons and other endurance events I participated in over the last 30 plus years. This torn and batted warrior heard those screams from the past now beckoning him on to Mt. Katahdin with the amazing youngsters who were still on the Trail.

"You're almost there," I told myself upon entering Maine. I stopped and had some one take a picture next to the little board nailed to a tree in the rugged Mahoosuc Range. This part of Maine, I believe, is the toughest stretch of the entire 2176 miles. Remember, this had been my last section-hike before I made my final decision to say "All systems go," and inform the family of my secret dream to thru-hike the entire Trail.

"Hey, Buzzard, don't tell me the whole state of Maine is like this?" one of the kids asked in a depressed, frustrated tone.

"The next 15 miles or so are the toughest. Maine is the best! There won't be much cruising the rest of the way, so slow down and enjoy what I call Maine's rustic beauty. It's all roots, rocks, dense forest and steep ups and downs. You'll be flying along a stretch, and all of a sudden there will be an ancient boulder the size of a truck left in your path by the Ice Age. So don't attempt to move at any cruising speed like you have been doing in the past. You'll just frustrate yourself slamming on the brakes and then restarting the engine. There's also a good possibility of breaking bones or ripping up a knee joint. Many have done just that after coming all this way and it certainly isn't worth it. I've heard of people who made it all the way to Baxter State Park and in the last 5.2 miles up from 'the Birches' broke a leg. So kick back and enjoy Maine... "the way life should be," was my response.

It would happen climbing a steep section of the Trail. You'd think after coming all this way I'd be doing things right. I got up in the morning after a night at a hostel. I had just met a young hiker from Maryland, and we hitched together back to the Trail to continue our journey north. I had packed my bag in haste after a resupply, and it was now top heavy with food. I wanted to catch up with the O.S.U. Boys as they were just 3 days ahead of me now. I hadn't seen these characters since Damascus, Virginia, and I still hoped to summit Mt. Katahdin with them.

All these factors would contribute to the fall. We had hit a hand-over-hand section about 4 miles into the day's hike, and the Maryland kid, I had just met the night before at the hostel, was moving fast. I wanted to keep up with him hoping to cover a lot of ground to close in on the crew from Ohio. I mentioned before that when I went up steep grades I would pull that loose left shoulder strap taut to secure my pack tight to my body. Well, I forgot! While reaching up with my left hand for an exposed root to use as a handhold, my loose pack sprang back. I would come within inches of grasping that life saving root, but instead the momentum of my top heavy pack launched me backward and into the air.

As I flew into space for a second or two it flashed through my mind that this could be the end of my hike and maybe the end of my life. Then came the sickening sound of the top of my skull hitting a boulder of ancient granite. I was out cold and 4 miles away from any road with that young hiker from Maryland. The closest hospital was a good 50 miles away.

Did I get up? Did I pull myself out of the hospital and continue chasing my dream of 33 years? Did I reach the sign on the summit of Mt. Katahdin? At the very outset, I told you that the purpose of sharing my story was centered on two themes neither of which was whether or not I reached the destination of a hike from Georgia to Maine.

No, the first purpose of this story was to convey how the healing power of nature can help children cope with childhood trauma and the importance of exposing children to the natural world in general. The spirituality and therapeutic healing of nature can put a child's world in context and help them feel that they have a place in the universe. The second purpose was to illustrate how the power of having a dream can transform a life and in so doing save that life. The power of having a dream comes from the journey of pursuing that dream.

You will recall that it was Captain Sargo of the Brockton Police Department, who had called me two months before I went off to Springer to begin my hike. He was the person who encouraged me to blog about my journey in real time in the local newspaper. Our conversation that day went as follows:

"I could speak to people at the city newspaper, and they may be able to journal your hike, if you would be willing to do something like that." The Captain said.

"Thanks, Captain Sargo, that would be a wonderful way to communicate with the young people of Brockton. I want these kids to see the importance of believing in the power of having a dream and a vision of hope as we had discussed in class. If they see an old guy like me following his dream, hopefully they will ask themselves what excuse they have for not pursuing their own goals and dreams."

"But are you sure you want to put this in the paper? I mean what if you don't finish? We had a couple of officers a few years ago that were doing a charity bike ride across America. One of the officers had a problem with his knee and didn't make it. People hassled him about quitting when he got home."

"This is what I'm trying to show people."

"What's that?"

"That the value in having a dream is about the journey, not the destination."

As it so happened, we were having this conversation in February of 2008 a week after the Super Bowl. So I brought up the example of the New England Patriots. The Pats had just gone 16-0, a perfect season, and then played a perfect post season right up to the waning moments of the Super Bowl when they lost the game to the New York Giants.

I went on to say to the Captain, "Does this mean the whole wonderful ride of the perfect season was for nothing? Did all those victories, the training, the fellowship and closeness of the team members, the excitement and joy that carried so many fans through the season mean nothing? Was everything the Pats had accomplished worthless because they did not win the Super Bowl? Of course not! The crowds that greeted the team at Logan Airport in the middle of night after that game let them know what we all need to know, especially our young people. It's no cliché; what's important are the journeys and not the destinations in life. Don't worry, Capt. Sargo, I'll finish. Cut off both feet and I'll finish because if I don't no one will listen to me."

I realized there were many that believed in me. I could not let them down. Too many of these kids had been let down before. I had to get back on that path and finish up. I walked back in the woods alone after I got patched up at the hospital and took some time off. I stopped at the granite boulder with the dried blood on it and shivered with fright. I paused to say a prayer for my safety. The day after the fall I discovered I also had pain behind my shoulder, which obviously took some of the impact off my skull. This small fact probably saved my life. I was lucky to be walking at all. My skull to this day has a bump on it. I moved north alone and was very uneasy going up or down steep sections of trail. I could not get that fall out of my head.

I walked into the town of Scranton a few days later to resupply, hit a restaurant, wash my clothes and take a hot shower.

"Hey, Buzzard are you okay," a voice rang out.

"Catfish, you're a sight for sore tired eyes. Ya, I'm doing okay," I returned.

"I heard about your accident and saw some of the bloody pictures the hikers took of you. You're lucky you're doing okay."

I took care of what I had to do in town and realized that wonderful kid from the South had slowed his pace hoping this old goat from the North would show up in some sort of hiking condition. Catfish and I headed out of town together up to the beautiful and challenging Bigelow Range. We stayed overnight at the Horns Pond Lean-to and hiked together over the next few days.

As we rested sitting and snacking in the sun the following day, I said, "Catfish, it's nice having you with me. I have been scared hiking up and down steep areas and can not get that fall out of my head."

"Buzzard, I know how much this hike means to you, so I'll be with you the rest of the way to make sure you make it."

"Thanks, Catfish."

It was great being with this slow and easy polite mannered Georgian boy. We were total opposites in many ways. He was young, and I was old. Catfish was from the southern terminus and I the northern. He had that laid back deep southern manner and I the high driving northerner. I planned this adventure for 33 years, and the kid decided to hike it a month before. I prepared for months physically hiking and working out at the gym. Catfish, I found out, prepared by eating at Wendy's. But we both loved the rustic wilds of Maine and enjoyed each other's company.

We decided to take an extra day off in Monson, the last trail town. We both enjoyed the pleasant little village and wanted to rest up before entering the "100 Mile Wilderness." Catfish seemed in a hurry now to finish the hike up and wanted to skip thru this 100 mile stretch in just 4 days. We decided we could lighten our packs with just 4 days of food. I told him it would be fine with me seeing I could sneak out my back door in Maine and do it as many times as I wanted with my son and others in my family in the future. We were both hiking machines after coming the 2000 miles from Georgia. Seeing the terrain in the Wilderness was not challenging, it was doable.

One drizzling cloudy day we decided to give each other some space and meet up at the end of the day at one of the shelters. It was one of the most memorable days on the Trail. I didn't see another hiker all day and felt like the only person on earth in the wilds of the Great North Woods. It was such a peaceful tranquil day in nature, an experience I will hold dear to my heart forever.

We stepped out of the Wilderness and stood on Abol Bridge now in bright sunshine and blue skies seeing the monster in front of us for the first time. Catfish and I stood in awe of the "Great Mountain" for the next 15 minutes. Mt. Katahdin was always socked in with clouds and we never saw her until this moment. We both agreed it was fitting to never see this amazing mountain until this very moment and were glad it happened this way. There was now only 15 miles of trail left. It was now time to hit the general store and feed our faces before heading to the last shelter, "The Birches," for the night. If the weather held tomorrow, it would be our summit day.

With many different emotions I sat around the campfire that night at "The Birches," a thru-hiker only lean-to, just 5.2 miles from the summit. I was happy and excited that the adventure and dream was almost complete, but also sad that my journey was to end. I had put so much time and effort into this dream; it was hard to see it coming to pass.

We both slept little, and at the first crack of dawn were packing up to summit. It was a spectacular sunny day. We were lucky.

"Catfish, I'll be right out. I just got to hit the privy," I said, as we headed out of camp.

As I stepped out of the privy, I noticed Catfish was no where to be found. I thought it odd and wondered where he was. Shortly after hiking up the Trail I stopped to sign the register and noticed Catfish had signed it just ten minutes before me. He went on alone, I guess.

Mt. Katahdin is no easy climb and has the greatest vertical of the whole Trail. There was a good mile and a half of very steep climbing, and I inched my way along hoping I would make it without another fall. It was an exciting challenging climb, but I was so close and felt uneasy. The cold wind picked up, and my hands became somewhat numb; gripping rocks became a chore. I finally, in the increasing blowing wind, was relieved to reach the "table top," as it's known. The walking was now flat and easy. I saw a sign, "1 mile to go." I slowed my pace. I didn't want it to end. I thought about 1975 and went over in my mind each of the 33 years to get to this point in my life. I looked around and saw I was alone. I broke into tears of joy and laughter. Did anyone hear me? I let my emotions go. What will I do now? I was afraid to finish. Where will my journey lead me from here? What will I do? Will there be another dream? What will life now be? It's time to finish this and get home to my family, life.

It's hard to describe all the mixed emotions of that moment. I could see in the distance the sign on the summit signifying the end of the Trail and Catfish standing there. As I approached him, I could see a concerned look on his face as he yelled out, "I hope you didn't mind me taking off on you, but I thought you might want to be alone with your thoughts."

Laughing, I yelled back, "It's good you weren't with me. I was laughing and crying and talking to myself. If anyone heard me, they probably would have thrown a net over me."

Again, the Georgian boy amazed me with his thoughtfulness and consideration. He understood how important this moment was to me and granted me that space and time.

We both bathed in the moment and the overwhelming feeling of completing such a momentous challenge. I had a feeling of fulfillment that I cannot describe. I labored over half of my life for this moment in time. Many of my dreams and challenges in life had come true, but never before something of this magnitude. This Trail had made all the difference in my life.

As we made our way back down the mountain, I just hoped my path continued in a positive vein in the days and years ahead. I had a powerful feeling of happiness and completion I had never known. Before we made it back to the campsite the idea entered the dream section of my brain that I was now moving south on the Trail heading back to Georgia. Maybe, just maybe some day...

Chapter 24
The 3 Essentials to Happiness

"Don't put the key to your happiness in someone else's pocket." – *Unknown*

People have to live their lives and not let their lives just happen. They have to figure out what makes them happy and find the time and wherewithal to pursue happiness. When I was in my late 30's, my teaching involved conveying the importance of self-esteem to adolescents. One day when preparing my lesson plans, I came across some readings on happiness. They included the "3 Essentials to Happiness" passed down to us through the centuries by some of the greatest thinkers and philosophers the world has ever known. It was like someone threw a pail of water in my face that day. The realization hit me through trial and error that I had come to live my life with a focus on these three essentials. Moreover, I realized that those times in my life when I had found myself feeling discontented coincided with the times I lost my concentration on these essentials, and I quickly refocused. Happiness doesn't just happen. You have to work these "3 Essentials" every day and build your life around them to understand and reach your own utopia.

After retiring from the classroom, I started banging on the doors of lock-up facilities and alternative high schools, places where troubled kids had been pushed out of the main stream of society. My intention was to spread the word of happiness. It did not take me long to realize these kids had no clue of what true happiness, according to the great philosophers, was all about. I had also started doing presentations to adults and found that these paths to true happiness had eluded them as well.

It quickly became apparent to me why so many people are having difficulties with life, especially our teens and young adult populations. My dream in life now is to assist people, especially our youth, find happiness and fulfillment in life. With the assistance of my daughter Samantha, a graphic designer, I developed the website, "traildreams.com." Through it, I hope to spread the word of happiness and its essential needs which, for so many people, have been lost in our fast-paced, and technology-oriented modern society. I am dedicated to helping people understand that happiness is not some tangible entity. It is something that can be found in each and every one of us; people need to know that they have the capacity to be happy.

So what are the "3 Essentials to Happiness?" Look back at my story from misery to happiness, and you will discover each one of them.

Someone to Love: "Love conquers all" …"all you need is love." Well, not exactly, but it is one third of the equation. True love is not all about how you feel about another person; rather it is about how that person makes you feel about yourself. Like all kids, my kids asked me as they were growing up why I had married their Mom. Half kiddingly, I replied, "Your Mother was the only woman in my life who didn't run away from me. I couldn't scare her off. She took the time to get to know me and to make me feel worthy of love." I went on to explain that their Mom has the qualities everyone is looking for in a partner: someone who offers good advice, cares, understands, listens, and can be trusted. In addition to all of this, I told my kids that their Mom made me feel good about myself and was the first person to do so. I told them that if they were ever lucky enough to find all of these qualities in one person to hold on to that person.

Examining the life of Edgar Allan Poe will certainly clarify the importance of love as an "Essential Need to Happiness." Poe, "the father of horror," is an extreme example of what happens when a life is void of love. Take the time to read his life story.

Also understand that love does not always have to come from another human being. I lived by the water much of the time, and had a 7-year-old son who wanted a dog. That is when "Luke," a purebred English Bench Labrador Retriever, entered my life. This dog was amazing, the easiest animal I have ever had to train. He ran in the woods with me and climbed mountains; even in snowstorms, he was at my side. I taught him to lie down in the bow of the canoe for balance when I was paddling in the stern. He'd sleep with his head on the gunnel as I paddled the rivers of Maine. I loved that dog, and he loved me.

After thirteen glorious years old Luke was suffering, and I knew what I had to do. I held my friend in my arms as they injected him. I watched and felt the last breath of life leave his body. I was saddened. What would I ever do with out him? I asked myself over and over. Well, it didn't take long to figure out the obvious. That is when "Otisfield of Thompson Lake," or as we call him Otis, came to us. He's related to old Luke and is another male black lab. Certainly not Luke, Otis has tipped the canoe over more than once, but he is getting better. Although he is harder to train and to deal with than Luke, the love and bond we have is growing and will continue to grow between us. I have come to value this young dog's natural exuberance and boundless joy. Every day rain or shine, winter or summer, we start our day the same, a walk in the woods alone for an hour or two each morning. When we hike the mountains, Otis may run ahead. But he will only go so far before he waits for me to catch up, and if I take too long, he comes back to check on me.

So understand that love doesn't always have to come solely from another person. We use therapy animals with troubled kids to teach empathy, caring, compassion, and love. Understand that to be happy in life you need love. Once you find it, hold on to it, and never let it go. Cherish and nurture it. Never take it for granted.

Something to Do - A Passion: According to the philosophers, the second essentials to happiness is simply finding something to do. Personal fulfillment and happiness involve discovering your true passions. Whether it is playing the guitar, writing, painting, running, photography, basketball, or making furniture does not matter. The list of possibilities is endless. Moreover, it is not important how proficient you become in pursuing your passions. What is important is that you regularly engage in doing things you love. I become very concerned with the person who has no constructive passions or puts everything they have into just one. Be diverse and "spread your wings." Whether they are indoor or outdoor activities, understand where you feel most at home and happy within your own skin.

Most people I have encountered in my life don't really understand themselves because they have never given themselves the chance to know their true self. That, in and of itself, can make it difficult to identify your true passions. So often you meet people who seem to have everything, yet they are still not happy. Conversely, you encounter people with very few material things who seem very happy. Constant exposure to some "norm" presented by conventional society and the media has caused too many people to define themselves by those external influences. Invest the energy to understand who you really are, and allow your children to do the same. You will learn what makes you one of a kind, unique, and special if you give yourself the time to know yourself.

I cannot over emphasize the importance of hobbies to your happiness. This second essential need to happiness also means that you have to manage your life to carve out and protect the time needed to pursue your passions. Absent conscious planning, the everyday responsibilities and tribulations of life will become all consuming. You hear it all the time from people everywhere, "I don't have the time to do what I would really like to do. I have too many responsibilities and am too busy." Well, you better make the time. Your quality of life and happiness depend on it! For most of us, it is not a matter of not having the time, but mismanagement of the time we are given on this earth.

It's amazing how much extra time you will have in your life to pursue your hobbies and passions once you shut-off your electronic devices. If you want to live your life and immerse yourself in what really excites you, turn off your television, phone, computer, tablet, and video games for a period of time each day. Dedicate that time to discovering and engaging in your life's passions.

If you really want to find that zest for life and spend your short existence on this planet enjoying your time, base your goals and dreams around those you love and what you love to do. Find your niche, and you will feel that you were meant to be here; your life will have meaning. Let me tell about two people who have figured it out, Jim and Charlie.

Jim: I was in my 30's when I first ran into Jim. He was about 20 years my elder. I could tell in an instant that he was a very interesting character, a deep thinker and not the "run of the mill" guy you meet along the way. I discovered after some time, he was a woodcarver of birds, and my wife loves the birds.

I had given Karen the nickname "Bird Lady" as she was always filling the feeders, watching and studying the birds. During snowstorms in New England her first duty in the morning was to throw on some old boots of mine, a jacket over her nightgown, and some type of hat. Then with shovel or broom in hand, she would carve out some type of crude path so she could tromp through the snow to fill those feeders of hers. It was always a hysterical scene with her flowing nightie flying in all directions in the blowing, snow-filled air. She loves all the animals, not just the birds, and she reasoned that if she put enough seed on the ground for the squirrels they would leave the feeders alone for the birds. One day I arrived home looking for a bag of walnuts I had bought a few days earlier. I found the contents of the entire bag on the ground to keep the squirrels away from the feeders. This was the Bird Lady's logic about the whole thing. I teased her that she should have put out signs explaining the walnuts were for the squirrels and the feeders were solely for the birds. Maybe then things would have worked out better between the birds and the squirrels; I was not sure. This was the world of the Bird Lady.

I think our yard had more squirrels per acre than any other place in New England. The word must have gotten out to the squirrels that the Bird Lady's house was an easy hit. I would constantly buy bird seed by the 50-pound bag trying to keep up with the demand. I'd pull into the driveway, drop the tailgate of the old pickup, hoist the 50 pounder over my shoulder, ring the doorbell and announce another delivery for Bird Lady.

I was always trying to think of what to get Karen for her birthday, Christmas, Valentine's Day, etc. I talked to Jim about purchasing one of his birds. We discussed the options and came to terms on the carving of a mother robin feeding her chicks. Perfect! After a few months, he delivered it to our house for her birthday. The Bird Lady couldn't have been more surprised and pleased with Jim's work. Everything including the worm in the mother bird's mouth was made from basswood. She was perched on the side of the nest with the worm while three chicks waited in the nest with open mouths. Jim had carved it out of the top of a cedar fencepost placing a real, abandoned, fumigated robin's nest inside the hollowed section of the post. It is a magnificent piece of art work. Jim has made shopping for Karen, the Bird Lady, much easier over these past decades.

As the years passed it became a tradition to show up unannounced at Jim's place on December 24th. He'd answer the door with a smile, saying, "I figured I'd see you some time today." Jim would put out a half dozen or more birds he was willing to part with and we'd come to terms. Every year it was the same. He often worked on as many as forty birds at the same time. Some would be in the beginning stages from that block of basswood he always bought in Kingston, Massachusetts; others were the product of many more hours and had some definition to them; still others were in the painting stage, close to the finished product.

I would often see a bird he had not put out for me to choose and ask about its purchase. He would explain to me how it had been a blue ribbon winner at some art contest in years past, and that it wasn't for sale.

But as our conversation continued, he would often give in and tell me it was about time he let that one go. Jim spent so many hours with his birds they became an extension of himself. I could feel his passion and to let one of them go was difficult for him. But he had so many and would say, "I've had that one for 9 years and it's about time to let her go." Carving was Jim's passion, and a bit of his soul dwelled in each bird. I bought his birds for decades; sometimes more than a year passed between purchases, but I would always return to buy another bird to surprise Karen.

Jim went on a cruise to Greenland for the sole purpose of viewing the puffin in its natural habitat. This was Jim. He had fourteen bird feeders at his home, most equipped with one way mirrors. These feeders were adhered to the windows, so he could view the birds from just inches away. His passionate approach to capturing each bird required studying them up close and personal.

His art studio was in an ordinary unfinished basement. It was always an experience to climb down those old cellar stairs into Jim's world. There were maybe as many as forty birds of all types being worked on at the same time. Jim kept meticulous records of the time he spent laboring with each bird, filling notebooks on his progress. A sparrow, cardinal, woodpecker, nuthatch, chickadee, red-tailed hawk, blue jay, and purple finch would all be there, being worked on with love and care. The walls of the room were filled with photographs and drawings of birds. Feathers were scattered about, bird magazines were piled high, wood shavings covered the floor, paint brushes soaked in cans and jars, and different lighting areas mimicked the four seasons and various times of day. His precious carving tools were spread on a well-worn work bench. This was a creative and gifted artist at work in his domain. It was always a pleasure to see this incredible man down in that cellar. Jim was a man who understood his passion and the happiness it gave him.

I found Jim to be a caring and likable guy, and, as previously mentioned, one of the most interesting individuals with whom I have crossed paths during my life's journey. This was a man who had found his niche in life, knew what made his life worth living, and managed his time so he could spend a part of each day to pursue what he truly loved. You have to understand, Jim had a full time job, and it wasn't carving birds.

One night I came across a segment on the nationally televised program "Nightline," featuring Jim, the woodcarver. The next time I was in his studio, I asked him,

"Why not just quit your job and carve? I mean it, Jim, you're famous."

"It wouldn't be a hobby anymore; it would be a job," was Jim's simple, low-key answer. Jim understood, as I did, the importance of a hobby for your happiness.

Charlie: Then there is Charlie. He is an avid outdoorsman who enjoys hunting, fishing, and camping in the woods. He has built himself a crude cabin on the more than 100-acre parcel of land he owns in the backwoods of Pennsylvania. His official residence is in Massachusetts, but every chance he gets he takes that 6-hour ride to Pennsylvania to his cabin. When this 80-year-old backwoodsman isn't hunting or fishing, he is painting scenes of the woods.

The first time I met this man, so full of life, he invited me to his art gallery. I was surprised on my first visit to learn that his art gallery was an old garage. Paintings were displayed everywhere on easels and walls. Invited into this man's domain, I realized immediately I had stepped into Charlie's private slice of heaven. The excitement sparkled in his eyes as he explained each wilderness scene. This man was so happy and full of life. He had found his niche and every day was another adventure in his private world.

"Charlie, these paintings are beautiful. My mind is racing, and I can think of so many photos I have taken of mountains, rivers and other wilderness scenes that I'd love you to paint for me." I stated.

"Bring 'em down and we'll see what we can do." he replied.

One day I said to Charlie, "If you didn't make a dime on these paintings I bet you'd continue to be out here slapping that acrylic on canvas because you love what you're doing and can't stop."

Laughing, Charlie answered, "You're probably right. I love it."

Our friendship was cemented, and eventually I asked this talented artist if I could take some of his art to gift shops and galleries in Maine. I'm not a professional evaluator, but was pleased to find many experienced appraisers who recognized Charlie's talent.

Jim and Charlie had figured it out. They had found their passions and had made the time to pursue them. They fully realized the importance of making the time to do what they loved a priority and not just an "if I get around to it" afterthought.

So find your passions and build your dreams and life around them. Your greatest wish will be to find more time to indulge in these passions. Be someone who takes action and moves closer every day to fulfillment and happiness. Don't get caught up in the fast paced "rat race" of society. Break away and discover how wonderful life can be once you discover your passions and incorporate them into your life.

Something to Hope for in Life...A Dream or a Goal: The third essential to happiness is having something to hope for in life. This translates into having dreams and goals that you hope to pursue over the course of your life. A dream gives your life direction and purpose; it's a reason to get out of bed each morning. It keeps your focus moving toward a positive outcome, and anything good is worth hoping for over the long haul. Life will inevitably bring tough times, and when it does, having hopes and dreams is what helps get you through those obstacles and emotional land mines.

I keep reiterating that it is all about the journey and not the destination because so many people don't see life that way. We have become a nation only concerned with the outcome, not the adventure and the wonders experienced during the journey. We must savor our journeys as we pursue our dreams. You never know what your journey will bring, the places you'll go, the things you'll do, the people you'll meet and all the wonderful events along the way. Don't let winning and all of its misplaced glory become your all consuming motivation as you pursue your hopes and dreams.

Stop being afraid to fail. The only real failure is not having a dream at all or quitting on your dreams. Everyone falls on their face at some time or another. History is rife with the stories of great individuals who fell many times as they pursued success and happiness. The true champions are the ones that get up and keep going. As Winston Churchill is famous for saying, "Never, never, never quit!" Look upon your mistakes as learning experiences, not as failures. There will be many hurdles and barriers in life to overcome on the journey to reach your dreams. Understand that you will eventually find a way forward, if you hang on to that dream long enough. So give yourself a chance! Keep tweaking and improving your approach and routines. Give it your best shot, learn from your "goofs," and do not overly concern yourself today with the eventual outcome. Just keep putting one foot in front of the other.

Don't be afraid to seek out others willing to help you master the skills necessary to chase your dream. Realize there are people willing to mentor you as you hone those skills and build your knowledge base. These people usually ask for little, if anything, in return for their advice and wisdom. Remember those "brain picking" conversations I had with thru-hikers in the mountains of New England while they ate the apples I offered to them before my own thru-hike? Don't pass up such opportunities for free information. Let's face it; what do you have to lose? There are many people, who enjoy sharing their knowledge. It makes them feel good to help someone find their own personal happiness.

You can also feed off those around you in a competitive atmosphere, whether it be in sport, your occupation, or in general living. But do so as positive motivation to spur you on and not to compare yourself to others. Don't set yourself up to "lose." Recognize that there will always be someone better than you are at a given endeavor, and you will run into them somewhere at some time. So don't compare your performance to others' achievements. This is a big reason why millions walk around feeling bad about themselves and eventually quit. Instead use others to better yourself and bring you closer to your dream.

Dreams are personal and private, so be careful with whom you share them. Stay away from the whiners and those for whom "the glass is 1/2 empty." You know who they are and you don't need them criticizing you, discouraging you, or laughing at you. If the people you surround yourself with are a negative force in your life, you may have to walk away from them. If I had not stopped hanging out with drinkers and substance abusers, I would have continued with a life of misery and would not be the person I am today.

Never look too far down the road in life. Just focus on what's immediately in front of you. Deal with each little step and you'll be surprised how they lead to your dream. Most people look too far down the road and after awhile begin to worry about the distance to the end. They become overwhelmed and eventually give up. They quit. So don't look for the end of the road. Focus on that small space immediately before you. Tell yourself you can do it, and it will happen. Surprise yourself and be more than you ever imagined you could be. Understand you are a lot better and tougher than you are, giving yourself the credit you deserve. Training your mind to see yourself succeeding and having this positive vision will make your hopes reality. Take a few moments every day to quietly sit alone in an quiet space and visualize your journey to your dream. The more you concentrate on this vision the more real it will become.

When I hear people say how they "coulda, woulda, shoulda," I think, "Then why didn't ya?" You need to resist blaming others and making excuses for yourself. Don't let your past dictate your future. Stop spending all your time and energy looking in your life's rearview mirror. It's destructive and can hold you back on your journey to happiness. Believe that you deserve more in life. Live a life with no regrets.

Too many people wait too long to define and pursue their hopes and dreams until they have "all the answers." By the time they have it all worked out, they are too old or too tired to make it happen. I stepped out the door to pursue a distant star on February 1, 1976 without a well-thought out plan. Instead, I just stepped into my dream. There was no organized plan in '76, '86 or even by '96. There was just my vision of a dream to someday hike the Trail. Step into your dream today, and let the planning take care of itself as you move along chasing that far-off star.

So many people today have no concept of delayed gratification; they want what they want, and they want it right now. The work, sacrifice, and discipline exerted over time often lead to the greatest satisfaction and fulfillment. The feelings of success and happiness do not come easily. Don't be afraid to work, because without the sacrifice and effort you will never realize your full potential for happiness. Cut your own path based upon your values, passions, beliefs and goals to fulfill your dreams. You can just "go through the motions in life," as my Dad would say, or you can create your own life of excitement, meaning, and adventure as you design a wonderful future for yourself.

Write down your personal "Top 10" list of what is most important to you. Your list may include people, places, things, ideas, activities, beliefs, or values; etc. This exercise is something I would do with my students the first day of class. It would tell me so much about the hundreds of personalities I would work with each semester. Once you complete your list, rank your choices in order of importance, and there can be no ties. This task will clarify what's important to you, will make you aware of your passions, and will help you to decide the direction to take as you pursue your goals and dreams.

So have a dream or, better still, many dreams to follow, and happiness will surround you. Be a dreamer and dream big dreams. It doesn't really matter if you reach every destination and fulfill every dream. Think about it. What would you do when you do achieve a dream? Do you rejoice, throw a party, crack open that bottle of champagne and have a parade? After all that celebrating, what would you do next? Hopefully, you will pursue another dream based around your passions and pursue another journey.

Time management becomes crucial. You have to be disciplined to set aside the time to do what is necessary for your happiness. Even if you can only find small blocks of time in the beginning, you will eventually discover more and more time along the way. Your life's happiness is at stake. So fight for those minutes to pursue your dreams. Single-minded, strong-willed and focused people can sometimes frighten other people and be labeled "fanatics." But just as often, the happiness you exude as you journey on your quest is contagious. Just like that stranger in the woods of New Hampshire I encountered in the summer of 1975 lit a fire deep in my soul; your duty is to pass this power of motivation on to your own children and assist others in reaching their own dreams, happiness and fulfillment.

So realize that you may play a very important role as an example to others. You can talk to kids and the people most important to you all you want, but your actions are what really resonate with them. Show them the way to happiness and fulfillment in life. Be the spark that lights a fire in another person's soul, changes a life, and saves a life. This is our greatest responsibility as humans on this earth, the planet we all share.

Chapter 25
Look to Others for Inspiration

"Dare to reach out your hand into the darkness,
to pull another hand into the light." – *Unknown*

The trail to your dreams does not have to be a solitary, lonely road. Look for people who are positive and who "roll with the punches." So often you will find that the people who have found fulfillment in life are not those who have had an easy road. Some of the most inspirational people I have ever met were not happy and successful because of what came their way, but rather in spite of it. Modeling yourself after these people can help you move forward with your head up through those "bad patches" in life. This is when you find yourself looking to them for inspiration. Their very existence can give you the hope you need to get out of bed, to keep putting one foot in front of the other and to move forward despite your circumstances.

There have been dozens of such people in my own journey through life. These are people who figuratively picked me up when I stumbled. What's more, many of these people do not have any idea what they did for me. There are amazing individuals with whom you have crossed paths during your journey. Let their example inspire you. Feed off their determination.

I was always a lone wolf and ran alone, mostly off road in the woods, for my first four years of training. I experienced the "loneliness of the long distance runner." It was therapeutic and mind cleansing at times, but some of those 20 mile training runs became more work than I asked for from a mental perspective. I wanted company.

The *Marshfield Road Runners:* After moving to Kingston, Massachusetts, I discovered there was a running club 10 miles away in the town of Marshfield that met each Sunday at 8:45 AM for anyone wanting to run long distances together. It didn't make any sense to me to drive 10 miles to run 20 and than drive that 10 miles back home, so I continued to run those long training runs alone for another two years.

The drudgery finally got to me one cold, rainy day and I decided to join the group the next Sunday. But instead of driving my beat up Chevette, it made more sense to me to ride my old ten speed bike over to Marshfield and back. I figured this would be a good work out in addition to the run. The biking only lasted the first two Sunday mornings, before I bit the bullet and drove over to meet the group in the Martinson Junior High School parking lot. I learned quickly that if you weren't there by 8:45 AM, you'd be standing in the parking lot alone. This tough group of crazy, competitive, individuals waited for no one. The clock visible through a classroom window determined the official starting time.

During the winter months there were always big crowds on those Sundays preparing to run "Boston." At times the training conditions were difficult as we battled the elements of another New England winter. At times the running was slow, and we had to be cautious on those slick, ice covered roads. One slip could mean months of hard training down the drain due to a torn muscle, ligament, tendon or a broken bone.

Twenty milers and beyond became easier when you paced yourself within a group that was compatible with your training style. There were more than fifty wild guys to choose from at times. It was like a bakery filled with 52 varieties of donuts of every flavor and consistency. Some of them became my sources of inspiration.

Herbie Baker: Herbie is considered the guru of the Marshfield Road Runners. This oldest curmudgeon was a joke a minute for the entire long run. He told it like it was, and he would razz people to get a laugh and a rise out of everyone. You better have thick skin and be able to laugh at yourself with this old goat on your case. He'd show up wearing the craziest winter hats and uniforms for his run. It became difficult at times to keep a serious pace next to this fun loving, full of life guy. Herb would be telling another one of his stories and I'd be listening, laughing, hyperventilating, practically breaking a rib as I attempted to run and breathe. I always marveled that this old guy, 18 years my elder, could stay with me on those long runs.

Dr. Bob Hillman: Bob is an oceanographer. He is a reserved, soft spoken, kind man. He was also one of the toughest road runners. One Sunday in the dead of winter he was with the mass of "Boston" hopefuls pushing into heavy wind on a road covered with solid ice for the first half mile straight away. We conversed as I ran along side him.

"Bob, this footing is insane. It's all black ice. Whatever you do, don't slip and go to the pavement." I said.

"Yes, I hope the roads aren't this bad the whole way." he replied. "How old are you Bob?" I asked.

"Sixty-seven."

"I can't believe you're out here today in this sub-zero cold and wind with these road conditions. I hope I'll be here when I'm your age." "You're crazy enough, and you'll still be out here too when you're my age."

I took it as a compliment. I had the utmost respect for this guy. Bob had run countless marathons all over the world, and he ran his favorite "Boston" more than twenty times. He's still jogging down those roads at 81 years of age.

Gene Spriggs: Gene is another story of inspiration. When we first met, this 5'8", 197-pound little fat man would waddle down the road with the group in the back of the pack. In one year's time, he was running marathon after marathon at his fighting weight of 143 pounds. Gene had designed a regime of training more structured than the rest of us. He was a student of the sport, reading and studying diverse coaching methods. In less than 2 years time, he popped out a 2:38 marathon. Gene established goals to break the 33-minute barrier for a 10K and to run a sub 5-minute mile. Through hard work and by following his personally developed speed training, he accomplished his goals.

Roger Welch: There was one Marshfield Road Runner who stood out among all the rest, especially to me with my dream of hiking the "Trail." I called him "The Martian" and asked him on more than one occasion to see a cardiologist to have his blood, heart, lungs, and blood vessels analyzed. This guy wasn't human, and I always wanted to see his blood, as it must have been green.

Roger, one of the founders of the club in 1970, was a Marshfield resident. He worked for a nationally known company in a supervisory position, and was financially comfortable, living in a nice home on Rexhame Beach. But none of this seemed to matter to him. He showed up on Sunday mornings pulling in at the last moment, climbed out of his old pickup, and finished his second cup of coffee. While the rest of us were stretching out, getting that last gulp of water, and making last minute preparations, Roger would be ready to do his thing. When it was time to go, he would just take off with us down the road. I started to also notice this guy never stopped at the watering holes on the way or chomped on an energy bar like the rest of us did as the miles piled up.

"I'll do a circle through the neighborhood and catch up to you guys after your water stop," he'd say, as I'd stand there with the other runners swallowing down cups of water to replenish the body.

No stretching before or after his runs, no water, no energy packets of goo, no scientifically advertised exercise formulas, no structured running regimen and no coaches. He just ran. This 5'10", 145-pound flamingo with no muscle tone and feet that went out to the side like a duck didn't want any of it, but he could outrun us all. Not the fastest over 6, 12, or 26 miles, but he could outrun anyone. Run Roger Run. We'd all make it back to the school parking lot, and Roger would just keep going. He was into the long run. Roger was interested in numbers. "The Martian" was an ultra-marathoner, which is anything over the traditional 26.2 mile distance.

Given that some day I wanted to hike over hundreds of mountains through fourteen states and cover some 2200 miles from Georgia to Maine, Roger Welch was my guy. I watched, listened and studied him.

"Hey, Roger what did you eat before you came to run this morning?" I asked one Sunday.

"Well, let's see this morning I threw a 1/2 pound of bacon between a couple of slices of toast, three cups of coffee, and four or five chocolate chip cookies. Oh, I almost forgot. I had some juice."

"Are you serious? All that bacon? I'd be throwing up all over the road!"

"You have to understand I need that fat to fuel me for these runs," he replied. I soon understood his diet and would use it for long distance hikes. My diet would change during these hikes, and I would pack in the cheese, nuts, seeds, olive oil, and what I thought was the best hiker food possible, potato chips.

During the summer months of 1993 training in the heat and humidity for my first 1/2 Ironman Triathlon, my calf muscles constantly cramped up when I hopped off the bike after a hard 35 miles and transitioned into the 10-mile run. It always seemed to happen during the second part of "the brick" (bike/run training) in the run phase of training. I experimented with my diet and nothing seemed to help. I was confused and frustrated, and then one Sunday spoke to Roger about it.

"Roger, I'm taking in all the foods high in potassium, magnesium, calcium and other necessary nutrients and can't understand why this keeps happening." After discussing my intake of foods and fluids in detail, Roger finally asked,

"What about sodium? You haven't mentioned this at all."

"Heart disease and stroke genetically runs in my family, and the first thing they told my father to cut out was salt. I should be getting enough salt as anything that grows in the earth is a source of sodium. I try to stay away from that salt shaker."

Laughing, Roger asked, "Do you know how much you are sweating biking and running in this heat?" Start salting your food, and I think the muscle spasms will end."

I had found out that Roger would go through a salt shaker a day during heavy training in the heat, and before his ultras would remove his rings due to the swelling of his fingers from the increased salt intake before these major events. My cramps were gone in two weeks and have never returned. When hiking in the summer my water tastes like that of the ocean, and I never suffer from those painful spasms. "The Martian" taught me much of what I needed to know for the hike of my life.

I was amazed at his feats of endurance. He would run a 26.2 mile marathon on Saturday. Then on Sunday, when most of us were crawling around the house putting our legs up on the recliner to relax and watch some football on TV, Roger would drive to some other location in New England early in the morning and compete in another 26.2 miler. I witnessed this autumn tradition of his for five years in a row when he was well into his forties. The most remarkable tidbit was he would run the first marathon on Saturday at a comfortable 7:00 minute per mile pace and the one on Sunday faster at 6:25 per mile. "I find Saturday's marathon kind of warms me up for Sunday," he said to me one day when asked about his dual marathon events.

Once the traditional amateur "Boston Marathon" changed to "an all about money" professional event like the rest of the corporate world, the entry fee skyrocketed. This caused Roger to lose interest. He wasn't about to shell out all those beans to run 26.2 miles. He ran marathons all the time and couldn't see paying all the money for a publicity circus. The club would rent a bus for us to ride to the start in Hopkinton early on "Marathon Day," and sitting across from Roger one time, he explained he wasn't paying the big bucks. Instead he would jump in as an unofficial "Boston Bandit" and use it as a training run for a race he was keying on six days later in Connecticut. This yearly event would involve him running lap after lap around Lake Waramaug at under a 7 minute per mile pace for 100K.

Then there was the Border to Border, a little more than 60 miles, starting in the hamlet of Guilford, Vermont. "The Martian" would fly down Route 5 south to pick up Route 202 in Connecticut. Roger would clip off mile after mile at a steady sub 7 minute pace again, which was comfortable to him. The average 16-year-old in America today couldn't do this for one mile, never mind for 60.

Roger Welch was a bonafide superhuman. There he was in the national "Runner's World" magazine with his shades on, running around the Waltham High School track in Massachusetts. He was competing and clocking more miles on the track in a 12-hour contest than anyone else. The simple idea was to see how many times you could run around that 1/4 mile oval. This Forest Gump type event that would drive most people mad was "The Martian's" contest. Roger closed out the 12-hour merry-go round circling the oval track 288 times. He had run some 72 miles.

Probably the most amazing feat of endurance I have ever witnessed was when Roger drove himself to New York, a good 4-hour drive, to compete in a 24-hour run. The strategy was as simple as before, except this time you ran an entire day, not just 12 hours. This time it was the U.S. 24 Hour Championship at a park in New York City over a measured mile course. Around and around the runners go like a carnival carousel that never shuts off, with the infield supporting an ambulance, cot beds, porta-potties and tables to set up your personal food and drink. Roger's favorite was bread layered with greasy, fatty "Spam" covered with salt. Roger understood his body needed enormous amounts of calories to run, and fat calories were his best fuel for the long runs.

That day saw some 200 endurance athletes toe the starting line with the then 49-year-old Roger. After 23 hours he was so far ahead of the pack and given that his calf muscles were screaming at him; he decided to walk the last 4 miles to finish up the day. "The Martian" covered more territory than anyone, finishing with some 138 miles. He did not hang around for the awards ceremony and declined the trip to Switzerland to compete in the world championship, explaining to the officials that he had to get going. He had a long drive back to Massachusetts. So he gulped down a few cups of coffee and headed home after changing into dry clothes. He was at work the next morning.

This super human being would be brought back to earth by the tiniest of creatures every endurance athlete and long distance hiker fears. Roger probably just thought it was the normal aches and pains in his joints he had experienced over the last 40 some odd years, so he ran on. The parasite was doing its destructive work after sucking the blood from this amazing athlete's body. It can cause a multitude of health issues destroying joints, tissue, and the valves of the heart, along with memory problems and many additional maladies. By the time Roger arrived at the doctor's office the Lyme disease from a deer tick had slowed him down and his ability to train. This would hamper the incredible feats of the one time New England 100K Champion.

I would see Roger now and then down at the coffee shop sipping on a hot coffee, laughing with the other guys about the old times. He was now a mortal, human. The alien was gone. He had become overweight and out of condition from sitting on the shelf for years.

But he would climb into his space ship one more time, taking one more ride into space. He strung together two months of somewhat healthy training during a period of remission from his Lyme disease. He entered the "Twilight Zone" again for 12 hours covering 52 miles of ground at age 70. I often think he somehow came to us from Mars or some other planet, and wonder what galaxy or distant planet he would be venturing to, if it weren't for that damn little deer tick.

Roger, I thank you for all you taught me for the long hike. You made it possible for me to climb up and over those mountains day after day with some comfort and understanding of dietary needs. You are my inspiration when covering long distances, whether on the roads or the trail to that distant mountain I see on the horizon.

Joe Gaughan: Approaching forty years of running and hiking, I've met some amazing people. They were unique, positive individuals, full of life, who demonstrated incredible courage and never say die attitudes. Then there was Joe Gaughan. Joe is easy to describe in one simple word, guts. Never in my life have I witnessed the strength of a man like Joe. When I think of a powerful man and one with intestinal fortitude, it always comes up Joe. He battled cancer on the road.

"Joe, everyone is worried about you. Do you think you should be running and training to run the Boston Marathon, while you're going through the chemo?" I asked one Sunday morning jogging out the first mile with him and some fifty other "Boston" hopefuls in training.

"Either I'm going to kill the cancer, or the cancer's gonna kill me. My plan is to run it into the ground," was Joe's reply.

He was battling an aggressive form of prostate cancer, as well as a cold head wind that January morning in New England, but this was Joe Gaughan. Physically, he was a hairless scarecrow and shell of the man I once ran and trained with, but "Guts" would never quit. They say distance runners never die, they just fade away, and Joe Gaughan was fading, but still he ran. He had more courage than ten men. For me Joe was "The Man," and I admired him in his fight for life.

I had gotten to know Joe both from working in the city of Brockton where he was the First Assistant District Attorney of Plymouth County for 20 years, trying many high profile criminal cases, and as a Marshfield Road Runner. Many Sundays in years past, I found myself running beside Joe. Whether I planned it or not, he was there beside me, as we seemed to train at the same 7-minute plus pace on those Sunday 20-milers.

Some of the young people I knew in my classroom would later be found in Joe's court room. We had some interesting and all too often depressing conversations over the years about some of these lost, rebellious kids.

He was a quiet guy and took his running seriously. Like me, running for him was an outlet to deal with a stress filled job that required him at times to work with "the bowels of society," impacting people's lives and future. Joe told it the way it was; he never pulled his punches and was a product of hard work both on the roads and in his successful career. He was the son of Irish immigrants, one of nine children, raised in the projects of South Boston. A "Southie" kid, he got his work ethic, his resilience and moral compass from his family. He worked from the time he was 12 years old. Everything he accomplished in life was from his efforts. Nothing was given to him. That was how he wanted it. He was a self-made man and a self-made marathoner.

Joe had graduated from Northeastern University in Boston and worked for five years as an electrical engineer before he decided to change his career and go to law school at night after working all day. He had four brothers who were police officers in Boston. They inspired Joe to study criminal law, and he landed in the District Attorney's Office in Boston. He incorporated his science background in the study of DNA, prosecuting the first case in Massachusetts where DNA was admitted as evidence, which led to a conviction. In 1997 he received the Prosecutor of the Year Award from the Massachusetts DA's Association.

Like me Joe didn't come from a running background as a kid, but in the early 1980s to deal with weight and stress management, he got to know runners at the Brockton YMCA. He read a book on distance running, followed a marathon training program, ran his first "Boston" unofficially, and he was hooked. Joe then ran marathons all over the country and the world. He clocked his personal best, a 2:58, at the NYC Marathon at the ripe old age of 51. He celebrated his 58th birthday running a 1/2 marathon on Cape Cod in 1999 at a fast 7:08 pace for someone his age. Two months later Joe was diagnosed with advanced inoperable prostate cancer.

Joe went through six months of torturous, aggressive chemotherapy in the first half of 2000, and in August, the doctors felt the disease was confined enough to do surgery removing the gland. Joe was back out pounding the pavement every day just three months later in November. His 10K time had dropped now to a 7:50 pace, but he worked to get stronger.

Joe was struggling, but never gave in to that struggle. He wanted to make his favorite "Boston" for the 105th running in April. Joe trained throughout that winter, despite being a physical shell of his old self. I grabbed the paper the day after the Marathon to see how he did. "Guts" had always finished. As I looked through the thousands of names in the paper, I finally found his time of 4:16. Tears welled up in my eyes and ran down my face realizing how much he must have endured to cross that finish line. There was no way to stop this monster of a Man. In June he announced, "I'm coming back."

He ran a 1/2 marathon in September and in November ran the Philadelphia Marathon for his second anniversary of being diagnosed with cancer. He finished 2001 running the Yuletide Stride in December at a 7:38 pace stating, "It's a good day to be alive and running."

Joe continued to run daily and more than one marathon a year until the summer of 2005. The cancer was progressing again, and he required two months of radiation. This knocked "Guts" to the pavement, but again he got up and back to running. That is, until 2007, when it was clear that the cancer had continued its aggressive, murderous course, advancing to his lungs and bones.

Each Sunday he showed up to run with the doctors telling him he couldn't train and run the Boston Marathon that April, but Joe wouldn't hear any of it. He was a marathon runner and "Boston" doesn't wait for anyone. You either put in the work and effort or you don't make it from Hopkinton to Boston. Joe would do whatever it took to make that annual spring journey through the hamlets and to Boston's city streets. There was no way to stop him. He was running on nothing but pure guts. There was nothing else left to him, but for Joe Gaughan there was enough to cross that finish line on Boylston Street.

Holding back from the rest of the group a mile into one of our cold Sunday morning runs, I spoke to Joe alone. "It won't be long, and you'll be back up with us running strong again," I tried to say encouragingly.

"What difference does it make anymore, as long as I'm running? Hey, don't let the group get too far ahead. You better go catch up with the guys," Joe urged. I respected him and moved on ahead knowing he would not want me to hang back with him.

How Joe ever made it to the finish line for the 111th running of the Boston Marathon, I still can't understand. Breathing like some emphysemic three-pack-a-day smoker and riddled with cancer, Joe crawled across the line collapsing with fatigue. His clocking of 5 hours and 26 minutes certainly wasn't his personal best, but by far the greatest run of his amazing life.

Joe continued to run until August of 2007 when he was so symptomatic the doctors at Dana Farber recommended another round of chemo. He had weekly therapy sessions and blood transfusions until June 2008.

On June 11, 2008, I was on the Trail hiking in the Shenandoah Mountains unaware that Joe had died this day. Once I found out he was gone, I went back and looked at what I had done that day in my hiking log. It was strange to see I'd hiked 26.4 miles that 11th of June. I wish I had known, as I would have pitched my tent in the woods .2 short of where I did. It would have seemed fitting to honor him by stopping instead at the 26.2 mile mark for the bravest marathoner I have ever known.

Whenever things get tough I think of Joe. During the last leg of a triathlon when I'm struggling after the swim and bike I focus on him. How can I slow or quit when I think of "Guts?" What this man endured is hard to comprehend. I never once heard him complain or question his fate. He just ran. He ran alone and every step was one of agony as he fought for life, but still he ran on with courage and hope. Hiking during the winter months above the tree line in the Northern Presidentials of New Hampshire, as I push through hurricane force winds trying to steady myself with my crampons and hiking poles to summit Adams, Jefferson or Madison, I concentrate on Joe. He inspires me and gives me the strength to power through the challenges in life.

I can still feel him running beside me at times or pushing me from behind through the wind. He will always be with me during those struggles and hard times. Joe's toughness and "surrender is not an option" attitude are with me forever and will carry me to the summit of many mountains in life. I miss my friend, as do all Marshfield Road Runners. We still feel him with us on those Sunday morning runs. He will always be out there running. I still hear his footsteps.

George Rose: One day as I stepped out of the car in the parking lot, I noticed a distant figure running like a deer around and around the oval track. Stepping closer, where I would be joining in with the neighboring South Shore Striders summer track workout, I got a better look at this solitary runner.

"Who is that?" I asked one of the guys.

"Oh, George Rose."

"Boy that kid can run!"

"He was the high school two-mile state champ in 1977."

"Really."

George was there alone, flying around his old high school track that hot, humid, summer evening in July of 1984, banging out 24 quarter miles at some unbelievable pace. He was 24 and I was 34 at the time. All he had on was a pair of running shorts and his New Balance sneakers. I figured he must have weighed in at around 125 pounds and stood about 5' 9". There was nothing but skin, bone and sinew to this runner.

Later, in my late 40's, I would end up running with George almost every day for four years in the woods and bogs. He lived just two miles away. George was a wonderful cross-country and track coach at the high school where he taught history, and his kids won state championship after state championship. As I got to know him, I discovered he was a wonderful person. He was also deeply religious, having done missionary work with his father in Kenya. George cared more about his passion for running than winning. It was all about the movement and flow of the activity that gave him that twinkle in his eye.

He told me the same story at least a dozen times over the years we ran together about the greatest run of his life. It wasn't about the two times he missed making the Olympic Trials by less than a minute or all those marathons, road race victories or some college race he won. It was that solitary 33-mile run through the paths in the woods and dirt roads. He practically drooled when he talked about it. It was all about the norepinophrines, the beta-endorphins, the surges of adrenaline and the "runners high" he experienced. This was the run of his life, alone in the wilds running free. His eyes would be on fire telling me this tale of his most beloved, running adventure. "Boy George" wasn't about the glory and recognition of winning and being the champ. No, it was about his passion of moving through nature like an animal chasing rabbits.

He had driven his coach, Billy Squires, crazy with his undisciplined approach to training. He was an emotional runner who wanted to run unleashed and free in the woods. He couldn't follow any type of structured regime and schedule designed by this legendary coach. Squires had coached the best marathoners in the Boston area and four-time

Boston Marathon champion, Billy Rodgers. George had the potential to be one of the best, but this child just wanted to go out and play.

"George, is it worth running with me?" I asked one day.

"I have a great aerobic base," he answered in the middle of one of his fascinating running stories. It was so much fun and entertaining to run with this guy, as he told this slower, older me tales of some of the top runners in the world he shared the roads with.

As the years past, I would see the pattern of this unleashed talent and told him he was a great coach, but he needed a coach. I tried to convince him to strength train to protect his frail body. I offered to coach him, but he just laughed. This guy needed to run free, and for years, he would come banging on my door asking if I could come out and play. Never did I meet someone who had so much running talent but cared so little about the victory. George burned for that momentary second in the running phase when a runner is off the ground floating through space. It was the passion and love of the activity, not being on the victory stand that inspired him.

We should all take note of his message in this over-structured, competitive world of drudgery. So many of us become wrapped up in reaching that destination and never take the time to enjoy the journey we are on in life. George Rose is a living breathing Peter Pan.

Joe Lemar: Joe was a student in my health class in 1986. He was a quiet, polite, young kid with decent grades. He wasn't someone who stood out from the rest, and I didn't know a great deal about him. One day after class he waited until everyone left the room and approached to ask shyly, "Aren't you the track coach?"

"Yes," I replied.

"I was thinking about trying out for track."

"That would be great. We'd love to have you out there."

Joe was having difficulty finding the words to tell me something, and I became confused with our conversation. He went on to explain, with what seemed to be embarrassment, that he was missing the toe next to his big toe.

"Really, how did that happen?" I asked.

"I had a growth on it, and they had to take it off," he explained.

"It would be good to give it a try and just see what you can do," I replied.

As Joe left the room I was taken aback and realized it would be difficult running without that important body part. The big toe and the next two are extremely important during the push off phase of running.

It turns out that was just about the time I took a hiatus from coaching after seven years of being on the track. I wanted to spend more time with my young daughters, and so I missed out on coaching this amazing young man. The tumor would progress and he would have additional operations on his foot, cutting piece after piece away. I kept in contact with his running, officiating during home meets at the Brockton track. I witnessed the heart of a lion through his high school career, as the tumor progressed and the doctors kept removing sections of his foot.

In October of his senior year, during the cross-country season, he got the news that his foot and lower leg would have to be removed to save his life as the malignancy was now aggressively moving up his leg.

"Mr. Cook, they want to cut off my foot," he stated one afternoon to me, as we spoke out at the track.

"I'm sorry, Joe. What's happened for the doctors to make this decision?"

"The cancer is moving up my leg, and they tell me it has to be done, but I can't let them do this!"

"Well, what if they don't?"

"They told me I'll die."

"It doesn't sound like you have much choice here."

"Yeah, but I can't let them do it because I won't be able to run. Sorry, Mr. Cook, but I gotta catch up to my friends. We have a big meet today, and I gotta start warming up."

Joe took off to meet his teammates for the meet that afternoon, and I realized this 17-year-old man was going through the normal stages of denial, anger, and depression associated with the inevitable. He hadn't come to accepting his fate and would continue to run like the hungry, joyous creature he was. The courage this young champion would display is hard for me to put into words.

During the winter indoor track season, he would put his heart and soul into every painful step he took, as they cut more of his foot away. With little more than a half a foot he would go on that season to place first in the Massachusetts Division 1 Finals. A week later he would finish 3rd in the Massachusetts State Finals and the next weekend go on to win the New England Finals at Brown University in Rhode Island, all in the miracle mile. The very next day he would drive to Syracuse University to run in the high school National Meet in the Carrier Dome. With most of his foot gone, he would place 11th, running the 800 meters against the best in all of America. Just three weeks after this national event, on April

4, 1990, Joe would lose his leg. He had spit at the pain of every step he took to run with the very best. How he ever did this is beyond me. He ran those steps with his leg wobbling in pain like it was the last race of his life. He was a young man running with pure guts and emotion.

New England Medical at Tufts University in Boston made a deal with Joe. The doctors told him he could leave after the amputation as soon as he could master the crutches on one foot. He was out the next day and showed up at the track meet to see his teammates compete against their rival, Cambridge Rindge & Latin.

I officiated that afternoon and watched this gutsy, young man sitting in the stands laughing with his friends. His attitude was beyond belief. Joe wasn't "looking in the rear view mirror"; he was moving on with the hand he was dealt.

One month later, in May, while I was warming up to run a 10K road race in Rockland, a good distance from Brockton I would see Joe again. He had ridden his 10 speed bicycle over from Brockton to watch the race. "They're making me a prosthesis, Mr. Cook, so I can start running again. I figure, I can keep in half way decent shape riding this bike until I get it fitted." Joe would ride mile after mile on his bike waiting for that prosthesis. Six weeks after losing his leg below the knee, Joe received his "every day" prosthesis, and against doctor's orders, went for a jog the same day he got it. This lion hearted kid needed to run. He combined hundreds of bike miles with his slow progression back to running.

Joe would eventually re-connect with his old Brockton High track coach, Billy Jennings, and get into some serious training. His goal now was the Paralympic Games. He did his road work, track work and strength training in the weight room over the next year and a half. Joe ended up in Barcelona, Spain winning the Gold Medal in 1992 in the 400 meter event.

Joe wasn't finished. He would compete in the Paralympics Revival Meet the next year and was now coaching high school runners in the neighboring town of Stoughton. He would coach his runners on his bike during their road work. In 1994 he was hit by a car while doing so. He went down to the pavement damaging his prosthesis, knee and splitting the helmet.

After years of physical therapy and hard work he came back in 1997 to win National Titles and in 1998 would compete in the 800 meters in Birmingham, England at the World Championship. By 1999, "The Lion" was back in form and would again return to Barcelona to place first in the 800, second in the 400, and second in the 4x400 Relay.

Joe would wrap up his own competitive running career placing third in the 800 at the Paralympics in Sydney, Australia in 2000.

He is at present coaching and inspiring cross-country, indoor and outdoor track and field athletes at Durfee High School in Fall River, Massachusetts. He is also training young amputee athletes, some in preparation to represent America in the next Paralympics.

Such people are all around you. Let them push you along through the wind and tough times in your life. It makes the journey so much more pleasurable and meaningful when you are inspired by the amazing and dynamic individuals you meet along the way. So join a group or a club with similar interests and dreams. It will make your journey all the better.

These incredible men, young and old, have been my inspiration in life. How could I ever lose hope or give up on my dreams and happiness when I thought of them. But I owed them more than gratitude for keeping my dream alive. I owed them my life when I could have given up on myself.

Offering my gratitude to those who inspired, supported and believed in me is not enough. I feel I owe them so much more – I have to pay it forward.

Chapter 26
The Healing Power of Nature

"Everybody needs beauty as well as bread, places to play in and pray in, where nature may heal and give strength to body and soul." – *John Muir*

The Trail was completed in 1937 by volunteer members of hiking clubs from the fourteen states it passes through and by participants of the Civil Conservation Corps, a federal program founded during the Great Depression to provide young people the opportunity to work. At the time, no one conceived hiking the entire Trail in one season until Earl Shaffer did it in 1948.

Earl Shaffer was born in 1918 in rural Pennsylvania near the Trail, and it was where he always made his home. Earl enlisted in the army in 1941, and he served in the Army Signal Corps in the South Pacific during World War II. After the end of the war, this avid outdoorsman returned home and made the decision to hike the entire Trail. Earl, "The Original Crazy One," said he was hiking the Trail to "walk the army out of his system." Earl understood the transformative solace of nature, and that it is the journey that can heal life's "wounds" not the destination or outcome.

In 1965, Earl thru-hiked the Trail for a second time, this time becoming the first to hike it southbound starting in Maine and ending in Georgia. To celebrate his 50th anniversary of his original first thru-hike, he again hiked the Trail at age 79. Hiking the Trail was Earl's healing journey throughout his entire life. This pioneer of the Appalachian Trail understood the value of nature, and this gift given to us, the Appalachian Trail.

Not much has changed in the almost 70 years since Earl's first thru-hike. Many have undertaken the journey to hike this Trail over the decades to heal and understand its spirituality and the positive therapy that nature offers. Currently the Appalachian Trail Conservancy has coordinated efforts with the "Wounded Warrior Project" bringing many veterans suffering from PTSD to the Trail to be soothed by its magic.

I have met and talked with many vets on the Trail during my thru-hike northward from Georgia, through my trail maintenance work, while section hiking, and by feeding hungry hikers on the shores of Black Brook in Maine each year. These military casualties are finding, as Earl did, the wonders of the Trail in adjusting back to civilian life and in dealing with the pain and trauma of war.

The soldier that stands out in my mind more than all others was a Captain in the U.S. Army. He was a West Point grad, who after 14 years and four tours in Iraq and Afghanistan got out before he lost all sanity. I met him during my thru-hike at a hostel where we both took a day off. Unlike me, he was hiking south and hadn't been on the Trail all that long. He sat in a chair most of the day, drinking one beer after another, and talking to anyone who would listen to his raging rant of anger. I sat and listened to this man, who I felt deeply for and respected. I also learned that despite having just six more years to serve to receive a military pension for life, he opted to get out.

Most of his heart-felt conversation was about the men who served under him and how their lives were ripped apart over years of time serving tour after tour away from their wives and children. He spoke of the "Dear John" letters many of his men received, how wives were carrying a child who wasn't theirs, and how these men missed seeing their children grow up. He spoke of the many suicides, the alcohol and drug use, and the depression of his men. The anguish and suffering of these men was too much for him to witness any longer. It was gut wrenching to sit hour after hour listening as he pounded down beer after beer. I hadn't seen anyone drink like this since my own days of alcohol abuse. I went to a restaurant in town with him that evening for dinner.

Before I left in the morning, I took the time to talk to him alone outside at the edge of the woods. I knew he might not like what I had to say to him, but I respected and cared about him too much to stay silent. So I said, "I understand you have been torn apart and understand why you felt you had to leave the military, but drinking the way you did yesterday is not the answer. Please keep talking about it. Find the right professional to counsel you, and by all means, stay on this Trail.

There is magic out here in these woods on this path to Georgia you are walking. As you hike it, smell the scent of balsam, marvel at the views on the summit of every mountain you reach, listen to the hoot of that owl when you're tucked in your bag, and taste the purity of that natural spring bubbling from the earth. Lastly, when you are struggling to climb hand-over-hand, hold on to the billion-year-old granite, feel its strength and let its strength come into you. The Trail is like a living breathing organism. Take it all in and let it reach to your core, your soul. It has a way of healing wounds. Let it heal you." He shed a tear and thanked me as he hiked south and I headed north. I pray he found some peace on the Trail just as Earl and many other soldiers of war and horror have done for almost 70 years.

Just like Earl Shaffer and soldiers of war we all need a connection with the natural world. Although our own personal battles and stresses in life may not compare to the trauma to these battle warriors, nature is a necessity for all of us. For so many in their hectic life it has become distant and may be a piece of the puzzle missing in our technologically advanced society today. Every time I turn on the news it seems the world keeps getting a little crazier. May part of this be due to the world we have created by segregating ourselves from nature?

Nature has a tremendous psychological, therapeutic importance to one's mental being and overall health. A bond with the natural setting is powerful and brings an understanding of man's place in his surroundings and the world. Nature has a calming and soothing effect on a person's soul. It's important for all men to have this connection for stable emotional health.

This statement and observation of mine is supported with countless research and studies. This book is a study of one. If you would like to read the research start with the book written by Richard Louv, "Last Child In The Woods." His book is filled with research and studies on the subject from all parts of the world, with a concentration on America. It is an amazing piece of work and is a wonderful place to start your study, if this is what you are looking for. I don't need all the studies and research to convince me of what I already lived and know. We have created a world separated from the natural world. We now have a world of asphalt, concrete, buildings, skyscrapers, motorized vehicles, jet airplanes, subway stations, trains, and advanced technology in the name of progress.

We have come to understand that for so many acres of asphalt, concrete and buildings it's necessary for the sanity of the occupants to have "green spaces," a place to escape from the man-made environment.

Without some type of connection to the natural world man moves toward psychological imbalance. There is a psychological, spiritual effect from nature upon the human spirit. We know this today, and there is no question or debate to the contrary.

I sit on the shores of a beautiful lake in the woods of Maine and watch people come roaring down the dirt road from their towns and cities in southern New England, New York and New Jersey. It would be the same in any other natural area of the country. To reset their inner selves, people continue to escape suburban and urban areas that lack the peace and tranquility of nature.

I walk along with Otis, my dog, each morning in the woods and rarely see anyone. I listen to the silence, watch a hawk soaring in the sky above me, stand in silence studying wildlife, am soothed by the sound of the stream I walk next to. This replenishes my soul to start each day I am on this earth. I take the time to slow down. I listen to the sound of my feet walking across the floor of the forest. There are few man-made sounds or sights to interrupt the spirituality of these morning saunters. It's just the dog and me, and the natural world right out my door. I feel like a child still at play, enjoying the place I belong, not in a world of concrete and buildings.

The earth is inhabited by plants and animals. We are classified as an animal, more specifically as mammals, but many of us seem to have forgotten this simple fact. A great number of us have forgotten our place on this earth and where we fit in. It's not "natural" to live the way most of us are living. We belong back in the natural world. I'm not saying we have to live the way I want to live in the woods of Maine. What I'm saying is we have separated ourselves so far from where we belong; it is causing us great mental, emotional and physical distress. We have even created man-made diseases that were foreign just a short time ago. We are over stressed, overweight, over-medicated, drink too much, drug dependent, depressed, angry and going "nuts." It may have something to do with our disconnection with the natural world.

Our children, in particular, are having a difficult time. Research and studies are making this very clear. What are our children doing, if not playing and enjoying the adventures of the natural world? How are they spending their time, if not living the life of a child as it was just a short time ago? Our children are sitting, sitting, sitting staring at screens, the television screen, movie theater screen, computer screen, laptop screen, iPad screen, Blackberry screen, texting screen, tablets, kindles, and video game screen. If not sitting staring at some type of screen, they are wired in their ears. This is the norm today: how the great majority of our kids spend much of their time.

No longer can they hear the silence of the woods, the mysterious whispering wind in the trees, the soothing, rhythmic sound of the water running over the rocks, or the sweet melody of the songbirds in their ears. How many will witness that first deer stepping out of the protective covering of the forest and bolting across an open meadow or the hawk soaring in that crystal clear, sunlit, blue sky and then suddenly swooping down, grabbing something off the forest floor and shooting back up in the sky like a rocket?

The first time I became aware of this childhood disconnection with nature was in January of 1983. The dirt roads and paths in the bogs were covered with snow and ice, so I was restricted to running down a country road. As I turned the corner of a gradual downhill stretch of pavement, I looked down over my left shoulder at a bog pond a good hundred yards in the distance. It was covered with a perfect sheet of ice. It must have frozen after the dumping of deep snow we had last week. That ice covered pond was just right for skating or a good pond hockey game. The day was clear, filled with bright sunshine, and the temperature was probably in the high 20s with no wind. It was a perfect day to be having fun on that pond, but there was not a child to be seen that Saturday afternoon. I was perplexed that day to see not one kid out there.

When I was young that pond under those perfect conditions would have been covered with youngsters having a great time in an extremely healthy environment on the edge of those woods. This was my first dawning that things had changed radically in this country. Where were these children? Were they playing hockey at an indoor facility in a structured program, organized and run by adults? Where were the rest of our children? Were they sitting around the house watching TV after sitting at a desk in school all week? What were our kids doing? It was a day I will always remember.

It was the beginning of my serious interest in this disconnection of our kids with nature and the outdoor environment. Rarely, over the next 30 years did I notice that pond or any other outdoor environment being used as a playground for our children. I also started noticing other adventurous activities dying. I haven't seen one kid climbing a tree in decades. Playgrounds are being taken down all over America in the recess yards of our schools, and some schools are developing structured "games and activities" chosen and controlled by adults during recess time. Many schools have rules at recess preventing our children from simply running or playing a simple game of tag. Our children are being constantly watched, hovered over, with their time structured. There seems to be also a great fear that a child would get hurt, bringing on the possibility of litigation.

The imagination, creativity, sense of adventure, wonder and natural childhood fun have been taken from many of their lives. We now have built very expensive playgrounds for our children in parks, thinking we are doing them a service. Many parents have decided it's better for our children if we structure and organize all their events. In 2011 I started noticing signs at the gym advertising "Instructional Lacrosse" for boys and girls starting at age 3 along with structured wrestling programs, indoor T-Ball, floor hockey. And the list goes on.

In 1990 I was in the exercise room looking out over the gymnasium. The gym was filled with many children, maybe 20 or more with one adult in the middle. I stood there for a few minutes watching and trying to figure out what was going on. I finally called one of the regulars at the gym I had known a couple of years over to watch with me. We both stood there in amazement until I finally said, "I can't believe it, I think that guy out there in the middle of the gymnasium is teaching these 3- and 4-year-olds "how to play." We both noticed many parents, grandparents, and guardians sitting around the perimeter of the gym watching.

My friend answered, "I think you're right. Why don't they leave these kids alone? No one had to teach us how to play!" I stood there thinking of how our society was changing. What I was seeing every day in my health classes in public school confirmed my thoughts of the direction America was headed. Many kids now have structured play time set up by an appointment called a "play date" by their parents.

The next year in 1991 I would be assigned another title, "Violence Prevention Educator." It all made simple sense to me. In past generations there wasn't all this structure and organization for our children. Past generations of children learned and functioned without all this adult interference. Working things out on your own and learning from hard knock experience has value. The small lessons learned, as a child experiments by trial and error, are invaluable to becoming a functional independent adult.

We'd go down to the field, buck up sides, and play the game with no adult supervision, no organization, no umpire or referee, no limed boundaries on a manicured fertilized field, no new shoes and uniforms, no water jug and oranges sliced up for us, no score board, no public address system, no parents to interfere with our game of fun and no over-zealous, competitive father or mother putting undo pressure on us to "win" the game! If someone was called out and someone thought he/she was safe we worked it out somehow. No one was there to help us figure out the problem. We had to discover and learn the process on our own. We had to think and not have all the thinking done for us. We learned how to communicate, negotiate, compromise and settle it on our own. We were learning important lessons in life, moving toward mature independence.

I was a public school educator for 35 years of my life with three certifications. This range of teaching knowledge afforded me the opportunity to be a classroom teacher in our elementary, junior high and senior high schools. My teaching career took me to rural America, suburban America and urban America. Witnessing on a daily basis the lost art of being able to communicate, negotiate and solve problems made me realize we are setting our kids up to lose. Being certified in Elementary Education, with an undergraduate degree in Social Sciences (the study of people, places and society) and my graduate degree in Health Education blessed me with the background to spend most of my career in the classroom as a health educator discussing adolescent social issues related to health. The majority of my time as an educator was spent assisting teenagers with the overwhelming social issues they were facing every day.

What I have witnessed in my lifetime working with children from all levels, different socio-economic and ethnic groups, has afforded me an understanding of children and their society. We as a nation are in deep trouble, and the future of America is in great jeopardy, if things continue in this vein.

Part of being a child or adolescent is to explore, create and discover as I have been saying. It's a time to make some errors. The experience that comes from making these small mistakes can be great learning experiences and often life saving later, especially for teenagers. Parents believe they are doing the right thing for their children by protecting them from harm, but in reality, they are doing them a tremendous disservice. It is one reason that violence has increased in our youth.

Our children reach an age when they are now left on their own to deal with life and life's problems, and they have no clue how to do this. Childhood is a time to discover and learn, and the adults are prohibiting this discovery. Let children be children; don't protect them so much from getting their hands dirty. I see advertisement after advertisement warning us about germs. This further encourages parents to keep their children indoors in a sterile environment to protect them from what lurks outside their scrubbed interior. The illusion again is that the woods and outdoor world is something to be feared.

In August of 2011 I read in a Boston newspaper that the incoming college freshman were the first class in America to grow up entirely in the internet world. In just one generation the lives of our youth have been drastically changed. Contact with the outdoor world and nature for many has become almost nonexistent, the process of separation began much earlier.

I remember that the innocence in American society ended when someone put poison in those Tylenol capsules, resulting in the death of 7 people, one a 12-year-old child. The murderer has never been discovered. Terrorism and fear entered our world—the birth of all the fear and paranoia that is still being escalated by the media. This was the beginning, as I remember it. The year was 1982, and America would never be the same. Our society and world became different in a hurry during the '80s. Fear causes great changes and will destroy everything—freedom, childhood, playtime, fun and life itself. We have become a nation of people trapped in our own homes, prisoners. It was reported on national news during the early fall of 2016 that the average child in America spends less than 7 minutes a day outside. This doesn't mean in nature, just outside.

Entertainment for many has become sitting staring at some type of screen. This lifestyle change for our young has been reported incessantly on the national news. One out of every three children under age 18 is now suffering from obesity, and Type 2 Diabetes is now the fastest growing disease in America. There are countless programs in place to combat this health epidemic, including the federal "Let's Move" program and the NFL's "Play 60 Challenge."

If anyone told this health educator back in 1989 that Type 2 Diabetes would be the fastest growing disease in America and this generation would be the first generation in American history to live a shorter life span than their parents, I wouldn't have believed it. Ten years later I could see it all coming, especially from reading the research and studies available to a health educator and track coach.

The focus of these studies concentrates on the physical problems that technology and fear of the outdoors have created for our children, but the problem is so much more than just this. This unwarranted separation from nature is also causing tremendous mental and emotional difficulties for our young people. Psychological problems and learning difficulties are growing. Our children are not as creative, imaginative, or adventurous as they were just a generation ago. Children used to go out into the woods and create their own games using their minds and imagination. This disconnect with nature and all its lessons is inhibiting their natural childhood development.

Millions of children are now being medicated in an attempt to control their hyperactivity, depression and ability to think. It was reported on the national news in February 2011 that more than 5,000,000 of our children are now prescribed drugs to deal with their hyperactivity. Anti-depressants for our children have become common and suicide is on the rise in our teenage population. Does any of this have anything to do with being controlled and deprived the natural world? If I had been separated from nature and the woods as a child, I know I wouldn't be alive today.

Christina, our first child, was born in 1974 and grew up in a more trusting world. It was a world where she could still be a child. A time when a young girl could still walk, run, ride her bicycle around the neighborhood, or play down at the brook in the woods adjacent to our home out of her parents' sight. A child still had some freedom to be a child in the late 1970s, but the life of a carefree child in America was soon to end. It was not a world as trusting and free, as the one I was lucky enough to grow up in, but it was still a better and freer world, than just a few years later.

Samantha, our second child, was born four years later in 1978 and there was a difference when she was four years old in 1982. American society had changed. If my daughter wanted to play with her friends, my wife or I would walk her down to their home under our watchful eye. When it was time to return home, one of us would walk back down to the neighbors and escort her back to the house. Things were changing quickly in these United States of America.

Many also thought it cruel and unusual punishment to institutionalize certain individuals with psychological problems. It didn't take long before the abductions of little, innocent children and other horrific acts increased and the hysteria grew. Overnight it seemed children were not able to roam freely. Nature and the great outdoors were suddenly off limits to an entire generation of kids.

The backwoods would no longer be their playground. All the lessons once learned were taken from their developing lives. This generation will never have that vital connection with their environment and world around them. They will only be able to make a confused, messy connection to the world of animals, plants and other cultures continuing to live in their sterile, protected, organized, competitive, technologically advanced world.

When I ended my career as a health educator for children in grades 2-6, part of the curriculum that I was required to instruct was on the subject of "Stranger Danger." My job was to teach kids to be untrusting and fearful. I certainly understood the dangers in our sick society, but also understood that the woods and the wilds of the natural world are safer than any street in America.

In our discussions, eight-year-olds would explain the restrictions on them. I clearly remember some of these sad encounters with the youngsters. It was a subject they were well attuned to, and participation by them was never lacking.

"Mr. Cook, Mr. Cook, my mother told me I can no longer go out and play in my own yard because there's a child molester living next door. Do you think it's fair that I can't even play in my own yard?"

How do you respond to this pathetically sad question asked by an eight-year-old?

Every week my school mailbox, during the last years of my long career, contained a colored picture and information on another Level "whatever" child molester. It gave specific instructions to notify the principal if the individual was sighted around the school perimeter. Is this fair to our children to be prisoners in their own homes? If it's this bad in a city of less than 100,000, what must it be like for a child living in New York City, Chicago, Los Angeles, Detroit or any other America city?

I wore many hats as a health educator working with a curriculum dealing with societal health issues. There was little time for the teaching of health issues not seen daily on the news that threaten our youth. One of the hats I was required to wear I mentioned was that of the "violence prevention educator." A subject I took numerous workshops on as our American society became more troublesome for our young people.

What a horrible society we have created for our kids. No longer do they have the freedom and rights of past generations. It's sad to realize that our children are not safe and in danger on any street in America. No longer is America a free country. It's just an illusion, and anyone saying it is must be living in some kind of fantasy, a dream world of denial.

I would introduce the topic of violence, each year with the teens I taught, by giving the class a scenario.

"Pretend you're a Mom or Dad with a 10-year-old son, who comes to you on a Saturday morning explaining he plans to ride his bike 4 miles out of town to an undeveloped 400 acre wooded area to play in the woods for the day alone or with some of his friends. He asks you what time he should be home for dinner. Would you grant your 10-year-old permission to do this? How would you respond or what would you say?" I asked.

Almost every hand in the classroom would be flying in the air. The kids all wanted to respond. The media, their parents, teachers and other organizations in our paranoid society had taught them well to be untrusting and fearful. I would listen to their responses with such sadness for them and realized these poor kids could no longer be children. The natural world and all its lessons had been taken from them. These young people had no connection with the world around them.

They would be telling me with such excitement, demand and forcefulness why they would never let their son do such a thing. The "Dangerous Stranger" was out there waiting to pounce on that 10-year-old kid. Their paranoia was overwhelming.

I would finish this discussion sadly explaining to them, that this was exactly what I had done on many Saturdays. I would be out of my parents' sight in those woods two towns away for some eight hours or more. They would sit there in disbelief, as I would end this discussion explaining I had had something they would never have or understand. Yes, it was gut wrenching, but honest. I also wanted these kids to understand from the outset that violence had affected all of us. It didn't matter if you lived in the "hood" or in a rich suburb, you were affected and no longer lived in a free country. We have become prisoners in our own homes, just like that little girl, who can no longer play in her own yard. Freedom in America is just a word now, and we must change things.

I have hiked with young people as old as 17 with organized programs that attempt to bring our youth back to nature. Many of these young people have told me they have never ventured into the woods in their entire life, and many thanked me for taking them for the greatest day of their lives. It's both a sad and happy occasion when a kid tells me he or she never knew how beautiful this foreign world was, and thanked me for taking them there. While not surprising to me, it was extremely depressing. It gave me a clearer understanding of why so many of our young people are having such a difficult time coping.

In an attempt to bring the therapeutic powers of the natural world into our children's lives, Wilderness Therapy Camps have been growing in popularity. Parents of depressed, drug dependent, rebellious, suicidal teens are paying as much as $500 a day in an attempt to save their child. I have nothing against these programs, but have to ask, if our children had the opportunity to have that connection with nature and all its spiritual, therapeutic benefits as young children, would it be necessary to send your seventeen-year-old off to one of these camps? I also wonder if someone can be rehabilitated or saved with a 3 to 6 month connection with nature, after having been deprived of the natural world for 17 years.

Children do not have a voice. Children have no rights, no vote, and no control over their vulnerable lives. Parents direct their children down a certain path in life. They help them choose the activities and are there to assist and encourage their interests. These same parents should be responsible for introducing them to nature and fostering this crucial development. Disregarding this we clearly understand, will result in physical, mental and emotional problems.

A parent under the age of forty who grew up in the 1980s has been indoctrinated with this fear of the woods. Many see the value of nature, but are themselves understandingly fearful of venturing into those mysterious wilds, never mind taking their children. The need to take these two generations back to where they belong have become necessary and have resulted in the development of nature based youth programs. Outdoor organizations and outdoor schools are exploring ways to make both parents and children comfortable in the woods, helping our youth to reestablish this connection. Many grandparents, like myself, who grew up with nature, understand the tragedy of this separation and are also working hard to bring our youth back.

The medical field is now beginning to prescribe time spent outdoors for our youth rather then filling that prescription at the drugstore. It's becoming a national movement. Doctors, witnessing the damage being done to our youth, are asking parents to involve their children in nature based organizations. It's about time we looked for a better solution than drugs for our suffering kids.

Early in my story I told you that when I was a child, I had access to several natural venues within a bike ride from my house.

One such place was the Rocky Woods Reservation with its hiking trails, lakes for fishing and boating, ponds for hockey, hills for sledding and skiing, and a lookout tower to climb. This was a place that became critical to my happiness and ability to cope. As it happened, I was visiting my mother as an adult in my early 30's on a beautiful day in the spring of 1981.

I said, "Mom, I think I'll head up to Rocky Woods and climb the tower with Chrissy." My oldest daughter Chrissy was 7 years old at the time and at the right age to really enjoy this experience.

"The tower's gone," my Mom explained.

"What are you talking about? I was just up there a couple of summers ago. The tower's fine," I returned.

"No, last year Bob and Pete went up there with 4-wheel drive jeeps and heavy rope and pulled it to the ground." Bob was the warden of the property and Pete was his part-timer. I had known them since I was a kid.

"That's crazy! Why did they do that?" I asked.

"There's no more skating, sledding, downhill skiing, and the boats are all gone."

"Am I hearing things? What are you talking about?" I interrupted.

"I'm not sure, but I think everything is ending up there, and it is not going to be the way it was anymore." she stated.

So it was that I did not take that trip to "The Woods" with Chrissy back in 1981. I didn't want to see the changes that were happening at the time. I did return a quarter of a century later one day in January 2008. For hours I walked my old trails and visited some of my private caves and the special spots I had loved as a child. I scrambled to the highest spot on the reservation to find nothing left of the tower but the four cement foundation blocks. There was no downhill skiing or tower climbs for the generations after mine. Tears of nostalgia filled my eyes and flowed down my old, weathered, face as I walked by a now deserted, snow-covered Chickering Lake. The last to go was the "Clubhouse." No longer is there a wood stove or beautiful stone hearth to sit by, sipping on a cup of hot chocolate from the snack bar after a good healthy skate on the lake.

The perimeters of the Rocky Woods Reservation are now surrounded by expensive homes and upscale neighborhoods. This wooded land trust, which was never to be built upon, now offers limited "active recreation" compared to the Rocky Woods of the 1950's and 1960's. I spent some time with Richard Desroiser, the town historian, who explained the gory details of what happened to my childhood wonderland. He told me he's so upset with what's happened he has never gone back, as he wants to remember Rocky Woods as it once was. He went on to explain that there are many others in the community of Medfield who feel the same sadness and never ventured into those woods again. Like me and so many others in the community of Medfield, he remembers Rocky Woods as it was "back in the day."

Here is an article written by Richard, which appeared in the local Hometown Weekly newspaper on January 26, 2011.

This Old Town: Rocky Woods

As the January snows fall across the meadows, fields and lawns of Medfield; as the winter cold thickens the ice along Vine Brook and throughout Kingsbury Pond, those who lived here in Medfield before 1980 will have their memory drift back and once again think of Rocky Woods.

Here in the 100s of wooded acres, bought up over the years by Dr. Joel Goldthwait, once stood one of the greatest recreational areas in Massachusetts. To get a membership at Rocky Woods was a prized holding, almost like season tickets to Fenway Park, the waiting list was years into the future.

During the winter months the skating on Chickering Pond was without a doubt some of the best anywhere. Here the families came during the weekends, and weekdays, here the teenagers came during the Friday and Saturday nights to skate under the lights that lit the pond in an orange glow.

The pond was hosed down each morning leaving a crystal clear sheen of ice. During the snowstorms the snow blowers and jeeps with plows created an attacking army that overcame even the fiercest blizzards. During the coldest nights, skaters of all ages could retreat into the log cabin clubhouse to get warmed by the roaring fire, drink hot chocolate or order a hamburger or hot dog.

For the kids growing up in Medfield it was the social place to be. It was checked for safety, it was chaperoned, it was plowed and scraped, it was lit at night and it contained a warm clubhouse for shelter. Fun was had, romances were made down at the far dark end of the pond, skating lessons were taken... it was special and it was Medfield.

Next to Chickering Pond was the hockey pond. Here pick-up hockey games, with players of all ages and abilities, took place. Goals were scored, passes were connected and missed and a recreational outlet was made available for many a youth in Medfield, Westwood, Dover and other area towns.

For those into skiing, there was even a rope tow to a small skiing hill. Before the trips to the White or Green Mountains, many a Medfield youth learned to ski first at Rocky Woods. There was also, of course, cross-country skiing through the bending pines and sturdy oaks and along the miles of snow covered trails.

In the autumn, a hike through Rocky Woods rivaled the best foliage trips into New Hampshire or Vermont. One could hike through the trails and on up to the tower. After climbing the tower, one could see the skyline of Boston, the Blue Hills and looking west; see miles of gold, red and orange trees and the hills of central Massachusetts. Families packed lunches, ate in the famous granite caves along the trail or ate at the top of the tower.

During the summer months, families and picnic baskets invaded the many wooden tables that dotted the leafy land-scape along the pond. There were boats to rent by the half hour. The pond was filled with people in a sea of paddleboats and rowboats. There was a sandy wading area where young children and parents found relief from the scorching summer sun.

Dr. Goldthwait, a Boston surgeon who moved from the city out to Medfield, believed in active recreation. After buying up all the area now known as Rocky Woods, he created a recreation program and turned the facility over to the Trustees of Reservations. A local Medfield Committee was formed and names like Pederzini, Allen, Bassset, Meaney, Kreager, Kinsman, Sweeney and so many others volunteered more time than we will ever know to keep Rocky Woods alive. Dr. Goldthwait set aside a trust fund to keep the program running whenever bills exceeded receipts.

Then came 1980, with Dr. Goldthwait now dead, the Trustees of Reservations made the decision that Rocky Woods would no longer have active recreation. The local Medfield committee was disbanded and all decisions and trust money was transferred to a central committee, under the control of trustees from far away locations. The snowplowing equipment was sold off, skating ended, the paddleboats were sold, the tower was dismantled, and even the ducks that the little kids used to feed were taken away. The Town of Medfield tried to lease the pond from the Trustees, with the town taking over all skating expenses, but the Trustees said "no." Seven years ago the clubhouse, the last remaining hold-out of the skating years, was demolished and a field of flowers planted in its place.

During these cold winter night the reservation is dark and silent...the sounds of skaters, children and families are now only distant memories. Rocky Woods still serves the town as *invaluable open space, but ice skating, hockey, downhill skiing, paddle boats, rowboats, fishing, towers to hike to...Don't ever say one person doesn't make a difference. Dr. Goldthwait is gone, Mario Pederzini is gone and Rocky Woods as an active recreational facility now lives only in the memories of those in Medfield fortunate enough to have experienced it.*

As an advocate for children spending time outdoors, I fully acknowledge that the Rocky Woods Reservation remains a very important resource for the families that live nearby, and the time spent there is valuable for exposure to nature and green space. There are 6.5 miles of marked trails and former woods roads available for hiking, horseback riding, mountain biking, catch and release fishing from a dedicated platform, cross country skiing and picnicking. But Rocky Woods now closes at sunset and children are expected to be accompanied by an adult. There are no longer swimming, boating, ice skating, pond hockey games, sledding, downhill skiing or a tower to climb. For those of us lucky enough to have known it back in the 1950's and 1960's, our Rocky Woods has changed and we cannot help but feel a bit nostalgic.

Some of us are working very hard making an effort to bring our kids back to nature. There are pockets of revival in all parts of this country, if we look hard enough for them. This grass roots effort continues for this young generation. There are parents who are becoming overwhelmed and fed up with our youth's addiction to technology, and are attempting to do something about it.

But while I feel nostalgia for my old Rocky Woods, I recognize how much such a place would mean to many communities. I have hope too. Many people are working very hard to bring our kids back to nature and nature back for our kids. Across the country, pockets of rural revival are being created, providing opportunities for this and future generations to turn off their electronic devices in favor of physical activity in natural environments. There are many example, but let me give you just one in Walpole, Massachusetts, Turner Pond.

The Turner family lived on this small pond. Roger Turner, Sr. was an Olympic figure skater back in the '60's. He and other Olympic hopefuls would use this pond in the winter months to practice their routines. It became a bustling place for them and others to skate over the years, so a small cabin was built and used as a warming hut on the water's edge. A Swedish skating organization, "The Skridsco Club," was created that provided a joyous annual winter carnival on the pond in the dead of winter.

As things changed in America, the skating and use of the cabin faded into the past. After a quarter of a century of disuse, a group of concerned parents and others in the town brought it back from the grave. It's now maintained by a committee of volunteers parents, mostly in their 30's and 40's.

I have visited this place on occasion in the winter and spent time talking to the volunteers, parents and children. It's like going back in time; it brings a smile to my face and warmth to my heart. It's growing in popularity in the town and in the surrounding communities. Parents are valuing this time spent outdoors with their children, and the kids are having healthy, unstructured fun in a natural environment. There are now more than 400 families involved, and a waiting list of others hoping to join. The cabin has been revitalized with a wood stove and old furniture, and it is a place to gather for other family events. During the summer months, young people are fishing and canoeing and exploring the pond's shoreline. These parents are to be congratulated for providing their children with the opportunity to engage in activities out in nature for their health and happiness.

Many hiking clubs, canoeing clubs and other nature based organizations are aware of the urgent need to bring this generation back to nature and are making a concerted effort to do so. It's a movement that is gaining traction. The goal is to introduce the wonders of nature to children at a young age so they will love it for a lifetime and value it for future generations.

By the time Tom, my son, was born in 1988, a child was constantly under the watchful eye of a parent. Our society had now become too dangerous to let our children run free. Sitting around that campfire in the wilds of Maine, he has asked me in the last few years if I knew what I was doing when I put him in a tent for the first time when he was just 2 in the backyard. This question of his has come up and been discussed several times.

"Tom, I loved to camp, hike, canoe and be in the woods, and I thought it was something I could maybe do with my son. It was also an activity with no interruptions, no phones ringing, television, video games, radio and certainly later that computer. I gathered this might be a way to bond with you and hopefully teach you about nature and its lessons of life, all it has to offer and a way to also appreciate and respect it," I answered.

"Dad, I want to thank you for all you did. It was the greatest thing you could've ever done for me. I'm the person I am today because of it. Now everything makes sense to me and I can understand why so many people and past friends are having a difficult time in life," Tom said.

Tom now works for the state of Maine in the Department of Protective Services for Children. The horrific happenings he witnesses daily is gut wrenching. His visits to "heroin dens" and the chaos, turmoil and danger these kids live in is beyond belief. He and others in our society work for the protection of these trapped kids, who are innocent victims living with insanity. He's good at this work and has been commended by his supervisors and the Attorney General.

He has commented more than once saying, "What these kids really need is to go hiking, canoeing, camping and getting out in the woods. They need to get away from the stress and craziness they didn't ask for. They would find great solace in nature, Dad." Tom's love and respect for those mountains, rivers, woods and the sea will last a lifetime. My son and Kryssi were married just over 2 years ago and both look forward to sharing their love of nature with the children they hope to have some day. Kryssi grew up in Vermont, just 3 miles off the Appalachian Trail, and like my son, has a great appreciation for nature. This life long love and respect for the natural world starts in youth, and the younger the better. I've seen this in my own life, my son's and others. Like anything else it's best to plant the seed early.

It is important for parents to create opportunities for their children to spend time with them outside in the natural environment. Let them see, hear, smell and touch nature. This means designing outside time around what works best for your child and not necessarily for you. These first outings should be kept simple and of relatively short duration. Do your groundwork and find a safe easy path for a short hike, and be willing to go at the child's pace.

Again, simplicity is the key. Watch for signs of animals, identify local birds or just admire the views. During that first night you sleep outside in a tent, even if it is in the backyard, show your child the North Star and the Big Dipper in the sky. Make sure that your child is comfortable and feels safe. Have favorite treats at the ready. Make your child feel that there is no one else with whom you would rather be with during these times.

For me it's the woods and the lakes, rivers, streams, trees, mountains, and the fauna and flora found there. Walking in the woods alone with the smell of the pines, the spruces, the scent of the decaying foliage underfoot, with the mixture of the blossoming flowers, mosses and underbrush signals I am in safe haven and in a world I can identify with. The smells are constantly changing with the seasons, temperature variations, after a rainstorm or the falling of snow covering the floor of the forest, the heat of the scorching sun or the cold, winter wind. The combination of all these scents in my nostrils makes me realize I'm back home.

For other people, walking alone on a deserted stretch of sandy beach, their senses may be awakened by the sound of the waves slowly breaking on the shoreline and then receding back to the sea. You smell the salt air, you feel the light wind on your face, the oozing wet sand coming between your toes, the taste of the salt on your tongue. As you look toward the horizon, you see the glistening sunlight shimmering off the surface of the water. Such magical memories of nature that will open your soul.

Standing on a mountain summit and seeing mountain tops as far as the eye can see, strolling through the forest during a light rain, walking across a frozen pond watching an eagle soar above in the updrafts, or sitting by a bubbling brook touches you like no street corner in America. There may be nothing more wild and soul awakening in nature than the distant, mysterious, howling of a wolf in the wilderness or the cry of the loon coming out of the darkness as you camp on the shoreline of a crystal clear lake.

If you just slow down and open your senses you will feel all the beauty and wonders of the woods. A snake moving almost silently through the dead leaves or what is almost impossible to hear, the owl in flight, but if you open up, you will hear it. The squirrels chattering, the pecking of the woodpecker searching for insects deep in that tree, the croaking of the bullfrog, the painted turtle plunking into the water from that fallen tree stretching out across the pond, or the beautiful sound of a cardinal in early Spring are just some of the many wonderful sounds of life around you. Listen and awaken to the forest.

I recall the cold night in November when Tom and I were camped on the banks of a river in Maine. We were lying in the comforts of our sleeping bags being serenaded into dreamland by the howling of coyotes during their hunt on the opposite side of the river. It was a wild, chilling sound coming out of the blackened woods under a clear, moonlit sky after a long day of paddling with my young son. Then just before dawn the hooting of an owl awakened us. It's something I will always remember and cherish with my boy. It touched me to the core.

Many people find being alone in the woods at night eerie and intimidating, but I find after watching a beautiful sunset in the mountains and darkness creeping in around me a most relaxing and calming part of the day. The approach of darkness after an adventurous, active and exhausting time in the woods hiking, cutting wood or clearing a trail for hikers signals it's time to hunker down and rest with the closing of another joyous day in nature.

Many evenings I have sat on the banks of a Maine lake, staring at the embers of a waning campfire, in a meditative trance in almost total darkness, when suddenly I am awakened by a cry coming from somewhere out in the darkness of the lake. As my focus now turns from the glowing embers to the lake, I see the light from the fullness of the moon, glistening across the surface of the water towards me. The crying loon is soon answered by another siren, from the darkened end of the lake. This serenade is one of the most beloved sounds of the wild, treasured by so many who have heard it.

Awakened now, I toss another log on the fire and feel my blood pressure, respiration level, heart rate and nervous system in some type of hibernation. I stay up past my bed hour with the fire, the moonlight and that eerie wild and beautiful sound of the loons late into the stillness of the night.

Unplug for a while and take your child to a deserted beach and walk the shoreline. Let them feel the mysteries of nature and immerse in all it has to offer. Pick up shells, skip rocks, play in the sand or go for an exploratory adventure in the woods, climb a little mountain on a crystal clear day, camp out, sleep under the stars, paddle a canoe and sneak up on a beaver at work, or silently paddle a kayak following a loon as it continues to dive and fish, sit on a mountain ledge and talk with your child in the uninterrupted atmosphere of nature. Your son or daughter needs this connection and will thank you for it in the years to come. It is something they will pass on to their own children some day. There is still time to help your children. It could make all the difference in their lives. Nature saved mine.

Epilogue

I'm still married to that beautiful girl. After 44 years, Karen and I feel blessed to have a successful happy marriage. I attribute my personal happiness to my crazy dream, and to a supporting spouse and family who encouraged me even when they did not fully understand my needs.

The General, a widower in 1992, spent more time with us during the last 8 years of his life.

After a week's visit, Karen returned from driving her Dad home saying, "My father was talking about you on the drive."

"Really, what did he say," I asked with curiosity.

"He told me it took him a long time to get to know you, but before he died, he wanted me to know I married a good man, husband, father, and you would have made one helluva Marine."

I couldn't ask for a greater compliment. He witnessed my transformation, thanks to his daughter, and the pioneer thru-hiker, I met so many years ago. A year later he was gone. I will always hold his words close to my heart.

In the years since I hiked the Trail, I have remained part of the Trail's extended community. I decided well in advance of summiting Katahdin that I would give back to this treasure that has been a great focus in my life's journey. The Trail was declared a national park in 1968, and we as a people are so fortunate to have this magical piece of nature extending 2176 miles over the spine of the Appalachians.

I realize I owe a great deal to this path in the woods and to this journey of 33 years that altered and maybe even saved my existence. Catfish returned with me to our home on the lake for a few days after our summit day on September 17 before I dropped him at the Portland Airport to head back home. I knew Karen would immediately fall in love with the respectful, polite, young man from Georgia, and we invited him to return the next summer for a week's vacation on the lake. She wanted all of her friends to meet him.

As soon as dinner was completed he would always hop out of his chair and ask, "Would you like some help with the dishes, Ma'am?"

"Sit down Catfish. You're making me look bad."

We have remained close over the years, and I'm sure it will last forever. Karen and I were honored to attend his wedding, and he and his charming Georgian beauty came to Maine to do all the photography for my son's wedding in 2014.

"Catfish, what's Buzzard saying," she would whisper. She has great trouble with my mixed Boston/Maine dialect, and I love her deep Southern drawl; many times we have had trouble communicating. Hopefully, they will be at the lake with their lovely daughters for a vacation on the lake this summer.

I have also remained close with Freeloader and his wife, "Sled Dog Kristen" (SDK). Their wedding ceremony with Rev. Low, another thru-hiker presiding, was so meaningful to me. Freeloader and I had both hiked many miles with the young Reverend. It's difficult now for Freeloader to get away with a busy job and family, but last year we did a nice winter hike in February in the northern Presidentials staying over night at that life saving cabin, Gray Knob.

I had decided by the time I hit New England on the thru-hike it was time to pay forward what the magic of the Trail had done for me. I volunteered to do trail maintenance and worked on different sections of the Trail in Maine. In 2010 I was asked by the Maine Appalachian Trail Club (MATC) if I would be willing to take over a 2.8 mile section from Black Brook to the summit of Old Blue. I reluctantly took on this piece known to Mainiacs as Ol' Bitch. I have classified steepness as a 1000' vertical gain over one mile. Well, Ol' Bitch has an initial 900' vertical in the first 1/3 of a mile from the brook, and the elevation at the brook is 600' and 3600' on the summit. Mainers don't seem to understand the reasoning for switchbacks like down south. "The fastest way from X to Y is a straight line. Why would you have any curves in the trail?"

It took me some time, but I have now fallen in love with the ruggedness of Ol' Bitch and take care of her with tender loving care. I became familiar with this area of Maine just 4 miles south of the beginning of the all too famous Rangeley Lake Chain. I decided I would search for a piece of land to build that log cabin I've always dreamed about.

"Ya, won't find any land round he-a. It's all paper company land or protected by the state a Maine." A marathoner thru-hiker never gives up, and after searching for 2 years, found my piece just a half a mile from the Trail. I'm now in the process of building "Old Buzzard's Roost" on the banks of Black Brook. The closest wire is 2 miles away; the closest cabin is over a mile, and my abutting neighbor is the protective corridor of the Trail. You can't build any closer to the Trail in Maine than this! I'm sure I'll welcome many a thru-hiker to stay over night once the 24'X24' nest is complete.

I also welcome and feed the hikers each late August on the banks of Black Brook for a 2-day, 1-night gathering. Hankshwa and other hikers help out floating all the food and supplies across the brook to set up in the pines. I brought Old Coach along one year, and this past summer SDK and Freeloader brought their 3 children, ages 4, 2 and 8 months. I was absolutely amazed how the two older children helped out with chores and adjusted to the rugged surroundings.

I have met so many kind and giving people, who help out with this affair, but must mention and give special thanks to Mac Richardson. In 2013, while doing a rugged section hike with the 3 kids he raised himself, he came upon "Old Buzzard's Maniac Magic." We got talking and after introducing him to Hankshwa he said, "What greater gift in life than to be asked by my 3 kids to join them on this hike?" He like me understands.

"This is so wonderful of you to do this. Do you do this every year? I'd like to join you in your kind efforts." Mac also now helps me with trail work and works harder than anyone I've ever met. He has to be the nicest person I have ever come across in my journey.

I started this magic in 2010 with Catfish and peanut butter sandwiches, an assortment of junk food, and soda. As the years past, the magic has grown, and I've tried to include foods more typical of Maine. Hankshwa's friend, "Epic," works on a lobster boat and got us 25 for $100. The word traveled on the Trail that we were going to have some "big magic," and in the 2 days we had almost a hundred mouths to feed. The first 25 hikers got the lobsters. The following other Maine foods were inhaled by these later hungry and appreciative hikers: 48 ears of corn, 3 pounds of butter, 88 hot dogs, 5 boxes of mac and cheese,

6 pounds of potato chips, 2 large cans of baked beans, 5 loaves of bread, 2 large jars of peanut butter, 2 large jars of jelly, 48 cans of soda, a quart of strawberries, and 3 homemade blueberry pies with whipped cream, and assorted fresh garden vegetables compliments of Mac. Now other giving souls want to join us next year. The magic and kindness just keep growing.

I am slowly sectioning back to Springer and hike sections with Otis, Hankshwa and hopefully as time moves on with my grandchildren. My youngest, Brad or "Lil' Buzz," did his first hike with me when he was 4, and on the way down, I thought that when I'm 80 he will be 19. To stand on the summit of that southern terminus with all my grandkids some day is another dream I'm working on. "Lil Buzz" and his older brother, Frankie, are now walking in the woods with Otis and me on weekend mornings and have fallen in love with hiking and nature. Get 'em early and pack the candy. It works every time.

I have been invited to "Trail Days" in Damascus, Virginia to do my Trail Dreams presentation and hope to return each May. This is the biggest gathering of hikers, and every year "the friendliest town on the Appalachian Trail" grows from 900 residents in this little mountain town on the Tennessee border to some 20,000. It's a long ride in the old pickup each spring, but seeing old friends of the Trail, makes it all worth it.

In May of 2016 I met with a representative employed by the Trustees of Reservations of Massachusetts. It seems he and others are now working hard to bring back some of the activities absent from Rocky Woods since 1980. We walked around Chickering Lake on a beautiful sunny day and discussed some of the ideas of how to create the rebirth of this wonderland for children and families. I commend the Trustees in their efforts and hope I can be a part of this important venture.

I look forward to visiting any facility, especially programs for troubled youth, to spread the word of the dream and the power of nature. Anything I can do with Trail Dreams (traildreams.com) to rekindle in America the need to bring our children back to nature will be my mission for the rest of my life. I hope some day to turn that cabin in the woods of rugged Maine into a wilderness therapy camp to help the overwhelming number of suffering young people displaced from the natural world. This now is my greatest hope and dream. I have much work to do.

Karen Marie Antonelli

H.S. Grad. 1968

The General

Karen and me 1972

Turner Pond 2014

Cabin I stayed that first summer in Maine. 1960

203

Boston

L to R: Kevin Gill, Robert Morales, Michael Gomes and Carlos Montrond (4x800 Relay Team).
New State Record, June 9, 2007

Feeding a
mountain jay

Mt. Madison in the Northern Presidential Range

College Graduation day
for Robert Morales

Climbing Mt. Adams December 2000

Burnt Meadow Mountain (my 40 acres)

Our home

Otis at Gray Knob

Trail work with Otis on "Ol' Bitch"

Coach and me 2017

Otis,
my furry friend

At the Quay with Hankshwa and Otis, Mt. Jefferson in the background

Springer Mt.
April 8, 2008

My greatest
piece of gear.

Welcome to Maine

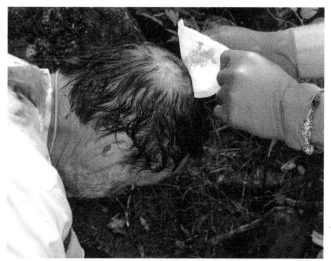

The Fall

Catfish

Freddy the
Freeloader

Fulfilling the Dream September 17, 2008

Hiking with two
of my grandsons

Acknowledgements

There are so many to thank for the fulfillment of a dream I sought for 33 years and for the writing of my story. Many have been mentioned in these pages and many have not. Let me apologize for anyone I may have neglected to mention here. First of all I would like to thank my family for the support and encouragement they have given me throughout.

A special heart felt thanks certainly goes to my wife, Karen, for putting up with me through the times of trouble and never giving up on me. Thank you for always being by my side and helping me "stay on the sidewalk" through all the years. I will always appreciate that you took the time and effort to understand and love me enough to let me out of the house to take this walk in the woods. You were also the best "spell check" a fumbling author could ask for.

This book would never have become a reality if I hadn't crossed paths with Ray "Hamlet" Anderson. He was the first published author to encourage me to write my story, telling me it needed to get out there in these troubled times. "Hamlet" followed me through this journey, mentoring me through the process to completion.

I also want to thank both Cindy Littlefield, a wonderful neighbor and published author, who encouraged me to write my story and Greg Marley of the National Alliance on Mental Health (NAMI) of Maine for the same encouragement and for his guidance.

Judy Hudson, a member of my hiking club, "The Randolph Mountain Club," did a superb job with the final editing and offering her advice, as an established author and editor. She also advised me to take the trip over to Littleton, New Hampshire to consult with Mike Dickerman, another member of the club. Mike took the time to discuss different options of publishing, as he is owner of Bondcliff Publishing. His expertise helped guide me to the publishing and printing of this book. I owe a great deal of thanks to both of them for their help, guidance and support.

I want to give a special thanks to Marci Spink, a long time friend of the family, for all her help with the writing and organization of this book. Her dedication and tireless effort will always be greatly appreciated. A career with the EPA contributed insight and wisdom to this project. Our many phone conversations were most informative and appreciated.

I am also indebted to Mike Keeley, Karen Lock, and Wade Chandler, who acted as readers. I am grateful for all their work and time spent.

Richard DeSorgher, from the Medfield Historical Society, should be mentioned for granting me permission for the use of his article in the town newspaper on Rocky Woods and his kind assistance and information shared.

I'm especially grateful to my daughter, Samantha, for all her work on the design and layout of this book including a beautiful cover design and her assistance throughout. Completing this project with your own daughter makes this project so much more special.

I would also like to thank my old friend, Wes Hollis, for his many conversations to get this story out there to help all those suffering and for his ideas and the direction of this manuscript. Wes was the initial spark motivating me to write and for this I will always be thankful.

Special acknowledgement, also, to my running club, the Marshfield Road Runners, for pushing me through the wind during all those long winter runs. The dream and this book would never have happened without you all.

I will be forever appreciative of all those giving me permission to write their story, especially, Maureen Gaughan, who assisted me in telling Joe's story.

The hike itself became a journey of joy hiking with so many wonderful, high powered, positive individuals, both young and old. I will certainly forget to mention all those I crossed paths with but want to give out a special thanks to Catfish, Freddie the Freeloader, Meat Bag and Doxie, the O.S.U. Boys, Daisy, Space Dots, Wildflower, Rev. Low,

Moccasin, K-Bomb, Stumblefoot, Insomniac and so many others. You made the walk from Georgia to Maine so much more than just a long hike and the fulfillment of my dream.

I owe so much of my life and happiness to this gem in America, they call the Trail. It is maintained with tender loving care by hundreds of volunteers and for this I am thankful. Never take the beauty and magic of this path in the woods for granted.

I want to thank all those students and track athletes who believed in me and inspired me to reach my dreams. I hope in return I was in some small way an inspiration to you and opened your eyes to your own dreams and path to happiness in life.

Finally, I must acknowledge my old hockey coach, Pete Case, who was there when I needed him most. "Coach" always believed in me; to this day he is still in my corner. From early locker room talks so long ago, when he demanded that extra 10%, to his prodding me through the writing of this book, his support has been essential. He will always be my coach, my mentor, and my friend.

ABOUT THE AUTHOR
Brad Cook had a successful career for 35 years in public education as a teacher, health educator, and track coach in the city of Brockton, Massachusetts, as well as in rural and suburban settings. With 3 teaching certifications he taught in elementary, junior high and high school classrooms in a diverse mixture of teaching environments and student populations. He has been an endurance athlete for 40-years and still competes in triathlons. He lives with his wife, Karen, and his dog, Otis, splitting time between Massachusetts and Maine.